THE GODDESS GUIDE

gisèle Scanlon.

Gisèle Scanlon,

a writer, illustrator and
seeker of all things stylish and eclectic,
has exhausted her passport and gathered together
the best of her findings into one unique collection.

THE GODDESS GUIDE

is her gift to you.

From the practical to the frivolous,
the fun to the profound,
the stylish to the surprising...

Sprinkle a little Goddess magic into your life.

HarperCollins*Publishers*

FIRST U.S. EDITION

DESIGN AND ILLUSTRATION BY GISÈLE SCANLON
COVER, TEXT DESIGN, AND PHOTOGRAPHY BY PETER O'DWYER
ROSTRUM PHOTOGRAPHY BY THOMAS BALL

ISBN: 978-0-06-143495-2
ISBN-10: 0-06-143495-7

07 08 09 10 11 IM 10 9 8 7 6 5 4 3 2 1

ACKNOWLEDGMENTS

THANKS TO:

Peter for your brilliance and authenticity. Travelling around the world with you has taught me so much and you always bring home the best of memories on film. Mum, Dad, Babs, Mike, SeànÒg and Granny you have all been such a great inspiration to me, without your wonderful guidance I would never have learned to appreciate the world in this way. Marianne Gunn O'Connor, so much more than just an agent, you're smart and beautiful a true Goddess in every sense of the word and Pat Lynch for your hard work and positivity; Thomas Ball for photographing the pages beautifully, Richard Seabrooke for your typographic genius, Matt and Helena for meals and wheels and Anne and Philip for your hip hide-away in London. A special thank you to Alice Russell who lovingly edited every single last word. Thanks to Maggie for your beautifully crafted words and Gerry for pointing us in all the right directions, Greg and Mark for making me smile and Amanda Ridout, Lynne Drew, Helen Johnstone, Kate Elliott, Nicole Abel, Bartley Shaw, Zoë Clarke and the rest of the stellar team at HarperCollins.

I'd also love to thank D*Face, E*Face & Al, Muteid, Elph, Asbestos, Dave the Chimp, Galo, Chaz, Miss Van, Boris Hoppek, Jon Burgerman, Faile, Calma, Pure Evil, Bo & Microbo, Yann Arthus-Bertrand, Mrs Baker, Frances from Hand & Lock for their embroidery, Jens & Richard, Zach Gold, Rick and Maria, Monica and Kevin, Barry Moore, Philip Treacy, Isabella Blow, Christian Louboutin, Serena Rees and Joseph Corre, Marvin Scott Jarrett, Alice Temperley, Narciso Rodriguez, Dolce & Gabbana, Kathryn and Geordie Greig, David Hockney, Laura Mercier, Emily Cohen, Anika Betz, David Kirsch, Kathy Phillips, Tracey Emin, Martin Parr, Michael Eavis, Cole and Sons, de Gournay, Richard Benson, Catherine and Peregrine St Germans, Heston Blumenthal, Monica Brown, Lisa Stickley, Ralph Steadman, Michael Donovan, Linda Pilkington, Tariq Shaded, Miss Piggy and Kermit the Frog, Debbie and Jim Sewell, Helena Sjöholm, Dr David O'Connell, Dr Andrew Markey, Pat O'Brien, Claire Sawford, Pádraig, Eoin & Elaine, Freddie and Chris, Miss Lecroc and last but not least Brendan Kennelly for his inspirational words that always remind me of home.

XXX

CONTENTS

Introduction (1) **Meet the Goddesses** (2-3)

1. STYLE

2. BEAUTY

3. TRAVEL

4. HOME

The hand embroidered title pages were lovingly created by Hand & Lock, www.hand-embroidery.co.uk.

The Goddess Guide
Gisèle Scanlon
2006

Mixed media work bound in flock
13.5 x 19 cm
(On permanent loan to the nation)

Introduction

Do you know where to buy the best vintage clothing? Have you ever wondered what Tracey Emin collects? Want to know why the soles of Christian Louboutin's beautiful shoes are always crimson red? Going to Paris and need to know where to stay and what perfumes to bring home with you? Perhaps you have a room to decorate and want to put up – and customize – your own wallpaper? Still searching for the best-fitting jeans, the snuggliest duvet, the secret to having perfectly toned arms?

I've always been a collector, whether it's little nuggets of advice, from world-renowned experts in the fashion and beauty industry, or matchboxes, pencils and receipts from hotel rooms – it's all pure gold to me. At the beginning of each new adventure, I set aside a huge chunk of blank pages in my notebook and, as soon as the plane touches down, I'm scribbling… The first entries are always my favourites: What does the air outside the airport smell of? What can I see? What sounds can I hear? Then it's straight into a taxi to meet some local inhabitants – namely designers, artists and hip young things – to unearth the best kept secrets in town.

From having a Hollywood smile makeover in New York, to the hunt for the most delicious steak in Dublin, I've recorded it all in my notebooks – as well as unearthing some great private corners along the way. Who knew that you could climb to the top of the Eiffel Tower, or have a coffee at The Wolseley Restaurant, in London, until midnight every weeknight? That you can have a pair of espadrilles made from scratch for you in Barcelona, if you bring your own fabric? Or that there's a website that will help you find all those retro sweets you so loved as a child?

From Serena Rees and Joseph Corre of Agent Provocateur to Narciso Rodriguez, experts have penned me handwritten notes outlining the passions that are unique to their lives. Learn how to wear a hat with Philip Treacy, how to take a photo with Martin Parr and appreciate wild flowers and plant them with the author of *The Farm*, Richard Benson. Rediscover the joy of reading with British Tatler editor, Geordie Greig, visit the Arctic circle with street artists D*Face, Mysterious Al and Asbestos. Cook up a storm with Heston Blumenthal's popping chocolate cake recipe and learn how to tighten those buns with New York's celebrity trainer, David Kirsch.

Left to my own devices I love nothing more than to dig through the world's decay and decadence, hang with the highbrows as well as the street kids and just listen and learn. I live it, scribble some notes and doodles into my diary, but only enter things that make me tingle with excitement… Here's what has given me the Goddess Vibe so far…

1

Meet the Six Goddesses...

These six Goddesses appear throughout *The Goddess Guide*. I love drawing them on anything I can get my hands on so you will find they pop up all over the place, asking questions about my findings… Perhaps the Home Goddess could help you find the best facial; the Office Goddess a good suit; the Sex Goddess perfume and lingerie; the Urban Goddess a really cool bar. The Earth Goddess will help you cultivate roses and the Luxurious Goddess, well, who wouldn't want to spend a day in her Louboutin shoes?

Each of these Goddesses represents a tiny little part of me. Which one do you think you're most like? To me, Tracey Emin (see pp132), is the ultimate Urban Goddess, whereas Serena Rees (see pp36) is a real Sex Goddess; Alice Temperley (see pp52) leads a true Earth Goddess existence and my best friend Anne is definitely my Office Goddess (with a whole load of Sex Goddess attitude thrown into the mix).

The Earth Goddess in me is always on the look out for little birds and animals. I love them so much that I even need to know their collective nouns. I've included several throughout these pages and only had to invent a couple – can you tell which ones I've invented yet? I'll give you a clue, the first one is below.

Luxurious

Give me luxury every time

I dig cool shops and bars

Earth

I adore birds and animals

Urban

Goddess *n* 1 a female divinity. 2 a woman who is adored or idealized. *Coll. n* a swoon of Goddesses. *(Okay, so I made this one up, but isn't it appropriate?!)*

Definitions used throughout the book taken from **Collins Dictionary and Thesaurus**, © HarperCollins Publishers 2006, reproduced by kind permission of the publishers.

I STYLE

My mum has always been my style icon – a true original when it comes to style. When I was little, she even looked stylish in my doodles: I'd give her a handbag and matching shoes and use a yellow crayon to draw her sun-kissed blonde hair. Every day she would dress my sister and me up as Twiggy and Jean (Jean Shrimpton). My little brother even got to wear special stay-pressed trousers – and this was just to feed the cows on the farm!

There was no uniform in Coolard, the first school I attended, so I was constantly teased about my 'style'. I quickly learned to fight back however, winning friends through my sheer determination and ingenuity. Our end of year school results were based on red stars and Mrs Baker (my favourite teacher of all time) offered books to the pupil who received the most. By December, much to my frustration, there were three of us on a level pegging. So concerned about this was I that I turned to my Dad for advice – his answer: 'Find a job in the school that's so horrible no one will want to do it and then ask the teacher if you can do it in return for some extra stars.' Ingenious! I prepared for the next day's negotiations, my mother, as ever on wardrobe duty, prepared the all important outfit.

The following morning I arrived dressed in red wellies, cord trousers, a mac that practically covered my entire body, and goggles. I got straight down to business and sure enough Mrs Baker soon agreed to let me battle with the toilets out in the yard for an hour every Monday in return for two stars. By first break I'd got her up to three stars, and at dinnertime we finally settled on four. What a result. So, as the other kids recited poetry, I got handy with a mop and a bucket in the loos. At ten, I learned the meaning of dedication and by the summer, needless to say, I easily had the most stars.

By 14 I had started at boarding school. It felt unnatural in every way, as if suddenly I was part of a weird cultish collective, stripped of hairdryers and earrings and mascara. After a year of trying to bleach me of my 'style' they gave up... Well, let me rephrase that: they banished me. (In their defence I think I am the only person in history that has ever been found guilty of attempted nun-inside. My weapon of choice? A pot of strawberry jam.) So, back to state school, short skirts, flat boots, parkas, and experimenting with mullets and The Cure.

Years later and I was writing about fashion for Irish *Tatler* (yikes!) and working at my first London Fashion Week. What I wanted more than anything else in the world was to go to the Alexander McQueen show but tickets were like gold dust so I needed a plan – one like the toilet to stars scheme.

With three hours to go before the show, I overheard some PRs discussing how they were going to transport the cases of champagne to the venue. Of course I immediately offered to lend a hand... and when all the boxes were unloaded and safely delivered I slipped quietly into the toilets, hid in a cubicle, and bided my time... Two hours later I heard the base-line thumping, it was time to creep out and join the show.

Ahhh the echoes and pleasures of not belonging! My heart beat like a runaway train. Girls in a Wonderland landscape, with freakish smiles and wearing razor-sharp tailored suits drenched in snow, paced the runway. A glass box sat centre-stage filled with a swirling blizzard; a wind blew, wolves howled and skaters pirouetted on ice. To this day, it's the best show that I've ever witnessed (I still get goose bumps thinking about it), and it was on that night that I first met Issy – the amazing Isabella Blow. Like my Mum she's one in a million; she doesn't just wear fashion, she embodies her very own style. I can still remember the moment I met her, the music, and the flame-haired twins. It was so edgy and spiky and another great adventure – pity I didn't get to drink some of the champagne.

VIVIENNE WESTWOOD

Claire Wilcox

V&A

CHANEL

AUDREY HEPBURN,
AN ELEGANT SPIRIT

Sean Hepburn Ferrer

Atria

PHILIP TREACY

VANITY FAIR. MARCH 2006

CHEAP CHIC Caterine Milinaire / Carol Troy

Harmony Books

ELLE THE WORLD'S BIGGEST-SELLING FASHION MAGAZINE

KEEP ON ROCKIN' ME BABY

www.nylonmag.com

JAN/FEB 2000

549

WOOD

wouldn't drag in the muddy fields. There was a whole chapter by Zandra Rhodes about gift-wrapping yourself, pages and pages about buying cowboy boots, and the story of a Parisian man called Yves Saint Laurent. Mum used to read the Yves Saint Laurent pages to me omitting the word 'sexy' and replacing it with the word 'stylish' (in the last paragraph the naughty word appeared four times). I hadn't a clue who any of these people were but the book taught me several huge lessons: that though the catwalk was wonderful and compelling, 'style' was about expressing your individuality and celebrating the things about yourself that you liked the most.

In society today the most 'stylish' are honoured in magazines. *Harpers Bazaar, Tatler* and *Vogue* all run Best Dressed Women lists – lists that glorify the power of the stars and their red-carpet wattage and 'style'. Vanity Fair runs the oldest list, first pioneered by Eleanor Lambert in 1940 in America. She created her list to market US fashion to the rest of the world and it soon became the most respected style rating of its time. Eleanor passed away in 2003 at the age of 100 but not before she officially bequeathed the list to the editors of the magazine.

Every season I get the opportunity to see all the latest collections on the catwalk. My own personal favourite style-givers are: Tom Ford, Alber Elbaz at Lanvin, Christian Louboutin, Alexander McQueen, Vivienne Westwood, Chanel, Hermès, Dries Van Noten, Philip Treacy, Narciso Rodriguez, Chloé, Christopher Bailey at Burberry Prorsum, Dolce & Gabbana, Marc Jacobs and Prada. Celebrities everywhere clamour to be dressed by these designers – and many look stunning as a result, however, it's worth remembering how much time, money, hair and make-up, goes into making celebrities look this fabulous. The overall red-carpet moment is a planned event, produced and sustained by a team of experts. For me, it's all about the dress of course, unless you're talking about one of the real style icons of our age, like Audrey Hepburn. Even when she was standing in the garden of La Paisible, her home in Switzerland, picking roses, without a trace of make-up and wearing only a pair of frilly shorts and a t-shirt, Audrey Hepburn embodied 'style'. In fact I was so fascinated by her that I travelled to Los Angeles to meet her son Sean Hepburn Ferrer, to try to get to the bottom of her beautiful, effortless appeal. We talked through his book *Audrey Hepburn, An Elegant Spirit,* and the 300 documents and photographs he'd gathered together to illustrate her lifetime. You need only glance at this book to understand the definition of the word 'Style'. You've gotta hand it to her – she had it in abundance.

PHILIP TREACY

Mum would always spend ages fixing a woolly hat on me when I was small, covering every little opening, so as to stave off the inevitable winter chill on my tractor adventures with my dad to feed the animals on the farm. I have only once experienced this genuine attention to detail since when, some years ago, Philip Treacy fixed a tiny hat on my head in his studio in London. When I told him this at the time, he laughed and explained how, when he was a boy growing up in Ahascragh (a village in the west of Ireland), he 'fashioned hats made from feathers cast off by my mother's hens, chickens and pheasants for my sister's tiny dolls.'

Pointing out a tiny hat with a large curled feather in his studio that day, I asked which doll he had in mind to wear it? 'That one is for Issy,' he explained – he was speaking of course of his muse, the charismatic eccentric, Isabella Blow. In 1989 while working at Tatler with the then fashion editor Michael Roberts (whom Philip Treacy had come to visit), Issy set her sights on a green felt hat that Philip had cut to look like a set of crocodile teeth. Seventeen years later, and Philip and I were discussing all of the hats that he had made for her as he put the final touches to his exhibition in Dublin entitled 'When Isabella met Philip'. There was The Antlers, which he made for her in 1996, The Ship, a replica eighteenth-century sailing ship with full rigging, and The Pheasant (her favourite). She explained to me later that evening: 'You can never really be properly dressed for an occasion without a beautiful hat, and so far, after wearing a Philip Treacy hat nearly every single day since Philip started creating them for me, the pheasant is still the one.'

That evening, surrounded by the excitement and drama of the exhibition, and escorting his neighbour and friend May Belle around the exhibition space by her hand, Philip appeared to be, as ever, the unruffled flower in the manic media storm.

May Belle later explained to me how she had bought Philip his first drawing pad and crayons when he was tiny and how he'd drawn a lady with a hat and a floaty veil for her at her kitchen table in Ahascragh. 'I was amazed', she recalled, 'that such a small boy had drawn a lady with her veil blowing in the wind.'

Philip Treacy has since created hats for Karl Lagerfeld at Chanel, Valentino, Gianni Versace and Alexander McQueen. Having single-handedly changed society's attitude to millinery, I needed to know the secrets of choosing and wearing a really great hat.

When and why should one consider wearing a hat, Philip? *Hats are meant to be for everyone. It's a very potent part of the body to decorate because, when you meet people for the first time, you are not meeting their foot or their hand or their hip, you are meeting their face. The purpose is to enhance the features of the face. It's also a cheaper alternative to cosmetic surgery!*
What shapes suit which head and face shape? *In my opinion there are no specific rules. Try on as many shapes as you have to until you find something you feel comfortable in.*
How should one care for/store a hat? *Hats should be kept away from sunlight preferably, stored on a head to prevent the brim from warping and packed with acid-free tissue paper.*
What if a hat gets bent out of shape? *Take it to the nearest milliner and ask them to try and fix it!*

Favourite smell? Poilane the French baker is on my road and the smell of bread wafting down the street is great. My father was a baker, so it reminds me of him.
Favourite to your sense of touch? My favourite medium to work in is feathers, because it is a natural living and breathing material. I like to use it for it's graphic qualities and I also like to draw with the feathers, they are light and have the appearance of weightlessness.
Favourite flower? The Paphiopedilum Orchid, their beauty inspired my Haute Couture show in 2000.
Favourite sound? Music.
Favourite bird and animal? My two Jack Russells, Harold and Archie.
Favourite book? Pleasure and Privilege by Olivier Berners.
Favourite piece of art? Irving Penn's iconic fashion images.
Favourite possession? My thimble, it goes everywhere with me.
Favourite taste? Mimmo D'Ischia's Risotto – it's legendary!
Favourite colour? Red.
Favourite place? London.

Philip Treacy, 69 Elizabeth Street, London, SW1W 9PJ (tel: +44 20 7730 3992, www.philiptreacy.co.uk). The book **When Philip Met Isabella** is published by Assouline.

CHRISTIAN LOUBOUTIN

Paris-based shoe designer Christian Louboutin's scarlet-heeled creations have won him a cult following. Not only does he design shoes for Roland Mouret, Gaultier Couture, Boudicca and Matthew Williamson but his key styles sell out within days of hitting the shelves in his stores in London, New York and Paris. Even though Sarah Jessica Parker got married in a pair and every second red-carpet star chooses to wear him, Christian hasn't let success go to his head. He's one of the most genuine designers I've ever met (and that's saying something in the world of fashion!).

Strolling casually into his studio on rue Jean-Jacques Rousseau, on a wet Parisian morning, and without any hoo-ha whatsoever, Christian Louboutin offered me breakfast and within five minutes was chatting away about flowers, life and the benefits of his favourite shoes! He confessed that the comfortable moccasins he was wearing were in fact by the British bespoke label John Lobb and that the reason he owns so many pairs is down to 'their comfort and their craftsmanship'. Soon after his morning espresso, we chatted as he started to sketch a green satin stiletto…

What made you want to design shoes? *My shoe fetish started when I visited the now relocated Museum of African and Oceanic Art in Paris and became intrigued by a sign on the wall of a red shoe with a line through it. It meant that stilettos were forbidden for fear of damaging the parquet floor. To me it was like a challenge.*

How did you learn the trade? *At sixteen, I sold my designs to showgirls at the Folies Bergère. And then I went on to work for Charles Jourdan, Chanel, Yves Saint Laurent, Maud Frizon and Roger Vivier. Then I set up my own company in 1991.*

Why are the soles of all your shoes red? *An assistant in the office always used to wear the same colour red lipstick and matching nail polish. One day I asked to borrow it and coated the bottom of a pair of stilettos just to see what it would look like, et voilà! I loved the dramatic red colour against the clean line of the shoe. It was the most beautiful red I'd ever seen. Now it's my hallmark. The first season I used it, one boutique wouldn't buy the red soles from me and only wanted black, so we delivered black – a few weeks later, after customers protested in horror, the store was screaming for the red ones. It's always brought me great luck!*

What are your favourite shoes to design? *My signature styles are the towering three-to-four-inch heels but I also design six-inch heels. I call them my 'bed shoes'. They're so high you can only lie down in them.*

The walls were covered in brown paper

10

eleven

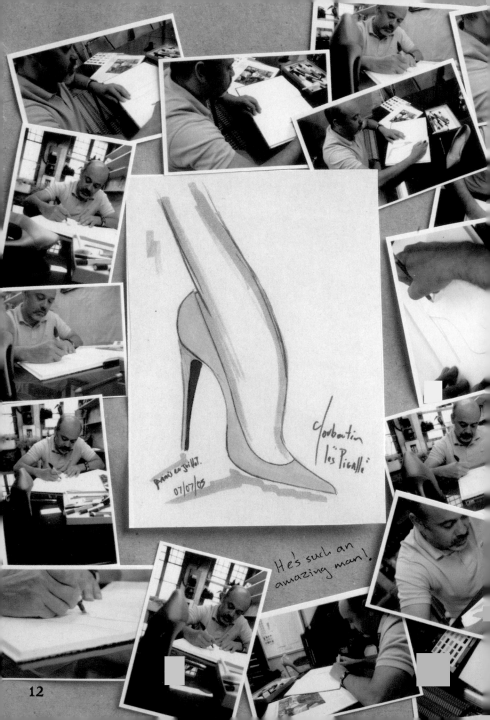

Christian Louboutin
"les Pigalle"

Paris en juillet.
07/07/05

He's such an
amazing man!

12

Do you think heels can help a woman bag some bedroom action then? *Clothes make a woman happy but a good heel can give her confidence and a lot of sex appeal, yes!*

Has anyone ever told you that your shoes have landed them a date? *Yes, one very chic Parisian woman told me that she was followed along the street by a very distinguished gentleman one day. When he caught up with her he asked politely about the beautiful red soles on her very elegant black court shoes. She explained that it was a Christian Louboutin signature design and he complimented her taste and then asked her out to dinner. She told me that she gets huge attention all the time because of the flash of red as she gets in and out of her car in the city. She compares it to ladies years ago dropping their handkerchiefs or wearing hearts on their sleeves to let men know they were available. Maybe it's an animal thing, but the red seems to really attract male attention.*

Have you had any strange customers or requests? *I once had a lady who complained to me by saying, 'But I can't run in your heels, Christian'. I told her that she was crazy and shouldn't run in heels at all. What if she fell over? Silly, no?*

Favourite smell? Bigarade by Frederic Malle.
Favourite sound? Prince.
Favourite taste? Honey on yoghurt.
Favourite texture? Velvet.
Favourite colour? Red.
Favourite bird? Woman – and animal: hippocampus
Favourite flower? Poppies.
Favourite place? The gardens of the Alhambra.
Favourite book? Imperium by Kapuscinski.
Favourite art? Sculpture.
Favourite possession? My company.
If you could have dinner with one person who would it be and what would you ask them?
Marlene Dietrich and I would ask her to cook.

GARDENING BOOKS
Christian's favourite pastime is gardening and at the weekend he loves reading gardening books and growing plants.

Paris
After breakfast he pointed out a few of his favourite addresses in Paris (see Paris section on pp145 for secret addresses for authentic ballet shoes, Parisian ribbons, scent and much, much more).

Hippocamp *n* a mythological sea creature with the forelegs of a horse and the tail of a fish; a sea horse. *Coll. n* a ripple of seahorses. Seahorses are monogamous and mate for life, under a full moon, changing colour and singing while they're doing it.

13

SHOE SHOPPING

My mother has always said that if you have good shoes you've half conquered an outfit. She also says that without the glass slipper, Cinderella would still be scrubbing floors. In any case, I love shopping for new shoes, they have that special smell, don't they? A kind of new box, crinkly paper sort of freshness, and there are so many types to choose from...

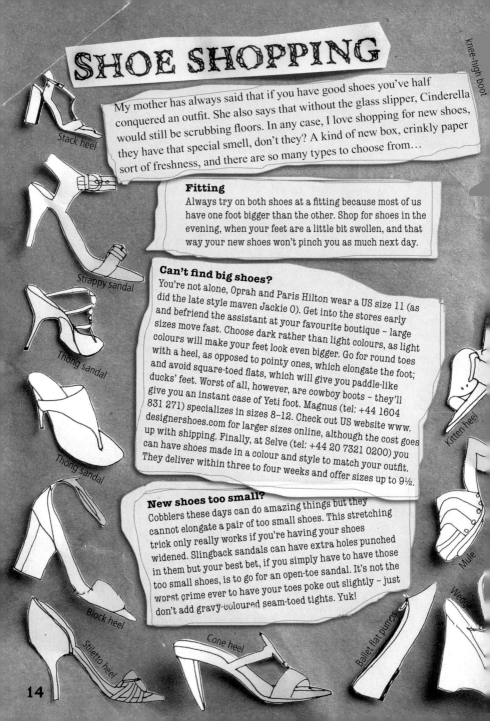

Stack heel

Strappy sandal

Thong sandal

Thong sandal

Block heel

Stiletto heel

Cone heel

Knee-high boot

Kitten heel

Mule

Wedge

Ballet flat pumps

Fitting
Always try on both shoes at a fitting because most of us have one foot bigger than the other. Shop for shoes in the evening, when your feet are a little bit swollen, and that way your new shoes won't pinch you as much next day.

Can't find big shoes?
You're not alone, Oprah and Paris Hilton wear a US size 11 (as did the late style maven Jackie O). Get into the stores early and befriend the assistant at your favourite boutique – large sizes move fast. Choose dark rather than light colours, as light colours will make your feet look even bigger. Go for round toes with a heel, as opposed to pointy ones, which elongate the foot; and avoid square-toed flats, which will give you paddle-like ducks' feet. Worst of all, however, are cowboy boots – they'll give you an instant case of Yeti foot. Magnus (tel: +44 1604 831 271) specializes in sizes 8–12. Check out US website www. designershoes.com for larger sizes online, although the cost goes up with shipping. Finally, at Selve (tel: +44 20 7321 0200) you can have shoes made in a colour and style to match your outfit. They deliver within three to four weeks and offer sizes up to 9½.

New shoes too small?
Cobblers these days can do amazing things but they cannot elongate a pair of too small shoes. This stretching trick only really works if you're having your shoes widened. Slingback sandals can have extra holes punched in them but your best bet, if you simply have to have those too small shoes, is to go for an open-toe sandal. It's not the worst crime ever to have your toes poke out slightly – just don't add gravy-coloured seam-toed tights. Yuk!

14

Rotate

Try not to wear the same pair of shoes two days running – it gives them time to dry out and consequently your feet will be much healthier.

Tenderize new leather

New shoes tend to rub on the heel, so, to soften them up a bit, put the shoe over the arm of a chair, fold a large piece of cardboard in half over the heel and give it a few blows with a hammer. Like tenderizing a steak, your shoes should be softer as a result.

Slippy and sticky soles

If the soles of your shoes are slippy, rub them with a bit of sandpaper. If they're sticky, give them a shot of talcum powder.

Stains – White stilettos

An eraser will remove stains from white leather. Nail varnish remover will get rid of black spots. And finally, you can cover up grass or oil stains with Tippex – remind me why you own white courts again?

Stains – Black shoes

Spruce up black leather by rubbing it with the inside of the rind of an orange.

Stains – Brown shoes

If you've run out of shoe polish, a banana skin acts as a good polish for brown boots or shoes. There's no need to shine them – simply leave them to dry.

Stains – Suede

Bring suede shoes back to life with a good steam over a hot kettle.

Stains – Runners

To get stubborn marks off the white bits on trainers, scrub with an old toothbrush and some toothpaste. If that doesn't work, try Cif – it comes up a treat.

Stains – Patent

Give patent shoes a real gleam with a rub of Vaseline or a spritz of household Pledge.

Shoestrings or laces

If the plastic tips come off the end of your laces, burn the ends with a match to seal them tightly.

Smelly shoes

Place orange peel in your smelly shoes overnight and they'll be citrus fresh next morning.

On a shoestring budget

If you re-heel and re-sole your shoes as soon as you buy them, it'll mean they last far longer. As soles and heels usually come in either black or biscuit, match your sole and heel tips so that they blend in perfectly. Very thin heels always lose the rubber at the end so go for a wider heel if you want longevity.

Non-leather shoes

Stella McCartney makes her shoes from rubber, satin and faux suede. If you're on a tighter budget, you can find beautiful made-to-order non-leather shoes in jewel tones, starting from £89, at Beyond Skin, www.beyondskin.co.uk.

Flat

Ankle strap

Peep-toe stiletto pumps

Pump

Stack heel

Stack heel

Kitten heel ankle boot

Pin heel stiletto

Long boot

Kitten heel pump

Court shoe

Open-toe slingback

Slide

BESPOKE

Jimmy Choo Couture, 18 Conduit Street, London W2, (tel: +44 20 7262 6888). Their hand-made beaded boots are mega expensive but really divine.

John Lobb, 9 St James's Street, London SW1 (tel: +44 20 7930 3664, or 51 rue François 1er, Paris 75008, (tel: +331 4561 0255). This is where Christian Louboutin has the moccasins that he wears made. Frank Sinatra and Jackie O were clients in the past.

Rickard Shah are based in Italy but appointments are held in London and can be booked with Stuart Parvin, 14 Motcomb Street, SW1 (tel: +44 20 7838 9808).

Gina Couture, 189 Sloane Street, London SW1 (tel: +44 20 7235 2932). For a wedding or a special occasion blow the budget and order some hand-made shoes.

Berluti, 43 Conduit Street, London W1 (tel: +44 20 7437 1740). The French know all about style and love Berluti's craftsmanship.

Internet shoe shops
www.brownsfashion.com
(Just like the store – fabulous!)
www.ilovehollywould.com
(Check out the cute ballet pumps)
www.net-a-porter.com
(I love this site and the next-day delivery)
www.scorahpattullo-online.com
(Stella, McQueen, enough said)
www.schuh.co.uk
(Great for Converse and Havaianas)

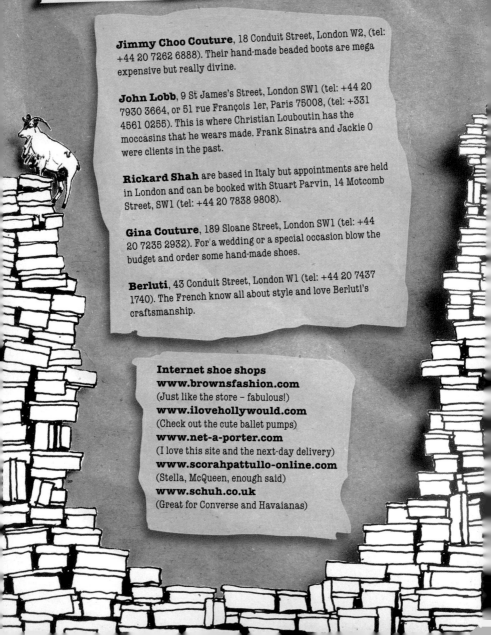

BEST HEEL BARS

London

Mario's Shoe Care, 26a Colville Square, London, W11 (tel: +44 20 7221 5288), is a real hit with the Notting Hill set and treats shoes with great care. Even though it's very popular it still only costs £13.50 for a re-sole or re-heel.

Mayfair Cobblers and Laundry, 4 White Horse Street, London, W1 (tel: +44 20 7491 3426), tends to the customers of Jimmy Choo and Manolo Blahnik. It's also a great place to get your snakeskin sandals, crocodile handbag or vintage luggage fixed as they have over sixty types and colours of leather in stock.

Shoe Department, Liberty, Regent Street, London W1 (tel: +44 20 7734 1234, www.liberty.co.uk).

New York

Shoe Service Plus, 15 West 55th Street, New York (tel: +1 212 262 4823). The mecca of shoe repairs – not only do they customize, dye and fix shoes and handbags, they can change an entire heel type to suit your taste. This place is shoe wonderland!

Arty at Arty's Shoe Service, 243 Eighth Avenue between 22nd and 23rd, New York (tel: +1 212 255 1415). Arty can make your shoes look good as new.

Dublin

Marlowe's, South Great Georges Street, Dublin 2 (tel: +353 1 6796982). This is where I've taken countless pairs of worn-down and broken heels to be lovingly restored to their dangerous glory.

Paris

Altan, 27 rue du Clos, 75020 (tel: +33 1 43 70 98 04). This is Christian Louboutin's shoe and bag surgeon of choice.

Delegate

Get this! This concierge service will pick up your shoes, have them repaired and then return them to you (tel: + 44 207 432 4515, www.kenadia.co.uk).

Ageing espadrilles?

Christian Louboutin's espadrilles sold out around the world within days of hitting the shops. Over time all espadrilles become worn-out and tatty. Christian suggests customising them as they age, with drawings, sequins or ribbons.

HOSIERY

I return to hosiery each September like a migrating swallow to Africa. Even at the tender age of eight my mother was giving me tips on deniers for different occasions. Her most useful nugget I still hear regularly when my legs are like Fozzie bears (full of hairs) – 'a Mafia widow's tights' (high denier black) 'will cover just about anything, Gisèle'. Mmmm anything that is except fat, Mum! But seriously, tights are great aren't they? And there's such a variety to choose from.

Items every Goddess should try

1. Sheer fine deniers
Aristoc Ultra Shine Tights. For everyday office glamour you can't go wrong with these 10 denier, sheer to the waist, high shine, sandal-toed tights.

2. Sheer seamed stockings
Gio Fully Fashioned Seamed Stockings. These stockings from Gio have a high gloss finish and they're made on the original 1950's Reading machines and seams are hand sewn.

3. Black fine deniers
Wolford Individual 10. These 10 denier matt appearance tights are a Wolford bestseller. The lycra technology means these tights stretch in several directions to give a completely even coverage.

4. Fishnets
Jonathan Ashton Stringer Fishnets. Small holes in muted colours, like camel or charcoal, look great with knee-length skirts. Black is sexy but serious when the weave is small. White and red are hideous.

Barn swallow *n* any of various passerine songbirds having long pointed wings, a forked tail, short legs, and a rapid flight. *Coll. n* flight or gulp of swallows. Migrating swallows cover 200 miles a day at speeds of up to 35 mph. They leave for South Africa in September and swoop back into Europe in April – back to the very area where they were born. If I could fly, that's how I'd like to do it, no detours, great views, straight there and straight back. Have you ever seen the air alive with a flight of barn swallows? It's amazing! (see pp194 to coax them to nest at your house).

Are we nearly there yet?

Opaques

My Dad used to tell me that goose pimples were designed by Mama Nature to stop my socks falling down in the cold. Recently however I have found this fact to be fictitious. The technical word for goose pimples is actually horripilations, and my Wolford Velvet De Luxe 50's opaques from www.tightsplease.co.uk are my number one weapon against the little blighters. Unfortunately, they don't make a blind bit of difference when I hear knives and forks scraping across china, listen to Mozart's Requiem, smell heady flowers, see little birds or feel ink soak into beautiful heavy paper. What gives you goose pimples?

Here are my favourite opaques

5. Black opaques
Wolford Velvet De Luxe 50. White and coloured opaque tights can even make model's pins look stocky, so what hope is there for the rest of us? Choose these utterly thinnifying black ones instead.

6. Crochets
Trasparenze 60 Rimbaud tights www.calzetrasparenze.com. Stick to dark colours like plum, olive, brown and black. Crochet, apart from insulating you against winter chills, looks very luxurious.

7. Floral Lace
Emilio Cavallini Floral Lace Tights. Along the same lines as crochet tights these have a lace finish with interwoven florals. Check www.figleaves.com and www.emiliocavallini.com, for more ideas.

8. Prints
Printed tights from www.lookfromlondon.com. Printed hose once you keep the scale small make a solid-coloured skirt or dress come alive. Also try Herringbone (tiny v-shapes), or 'bird's eye' (a tiny diamond design).

All tights, unless otherwise specified, are available at www.mytights.com/www.tightsplease.com/www.victoriassecret.com.

Shopping Tip

Buying the right size tights can make all the difference but because there is no standard sizing Serena Rees, owner of Agent Provocateur, says, "If in doubt, buy the larger size. You'll put less pressure on the fabric." I hear ya, babes! Remember to stretch testers over your hand for a realistic idea of colour and texture (this is especially helpful when buying nude skin shades).

Pregnant?

Aristoc Sheer Maternity Tights provide graduated compression throughout which helps to sooth and support tired legs. They also have an expandable front panel and come in several colours. Spanx® Mama Maternity Tights are very slimming across the hips, thighs and bum. A sheer pregnancy panel ensures your bump is comfortable and supported.

Too tall?

Le Bourget offers fashion tights each season and for fishnets try Jonathan Aston Stringer Tights or Levante's Class tights. Denier 12 go up to 6'2" and 137cm hips – perfect for day and evening wear. Falke's Seidenglatt 15 denier offer a bit more coverage. These also come in 70 denier and both styles go up to 6'2" and 56" hips.

Getting them on

Sheer tights are easily snagged on rough skin and jewels, so keep nails filed, moisturise your hands regularly and remove iceberg diamond finger furniture. If you dampen your hands it helps glide nylons into position.

Tears

In case of emergencies, keep a bottle of clear nail varnish handy: it will stop a ladder from running. Alternatively, if you're stranded in Siberia, a dab of wet soap around the hole will keep it under control for a couple of hours. If you're a fan of sheers, keep a second pair in your bag in case of an accident.

Chubby tummy?

Levante Bodytones Shape Up. These 30 denier tights are fantastic! Nothing wobbles in these: your tummy is tucked safely away and there's even a sculpting band to lift your bottom. Spanx® All The Way Medium Control tights are perfect for banning VPL and achieving a smooth silhouette under a slinky dress.

GODDESS TIP

HAND ON HEART I CAN SAY FROM EXPERIENCE THAT YOU DEFINITELY GET WHAT YOU PAY FOR – EXPENSIVE, GOOD QUALITY TIGHTS LAST MUCH LONGER.

Authentic stockings (Also for the tall)

For that Sex Goddess stocking look Gerbe 10 denier Carnation stockings, with a Cuban heel detail and a very sexy seam, are the best at www.mytights.com. They're 100 per cent nylon (as opposed to silk which bag around the knees) and keep their shape throughout the day. Made in France, they're the ultimate in traditional fully fashioned stockings and are available in 5 sizes so they're also suitable for the extra tall. Le Bouret's Milano Hold-Ups are tall fishnets and Levente's Vanessa have tall stockings at great value.

Slippy shoes?

Falke Step & Stop once placed inside your shoes will keep your feet from sliding all over the place. They are made largely from silicone and can be used over and over again – they feel similar to the silicone band found on hold ups.

Footless tights

Cette Athena footless tights are fabulous. At 70 denier there is no risk of seeing your knickers under your skirt and you can cover lumpy knees! For more colours try Emilio Cavallini 50 Denier Footless Leggings or for an even brighter option Jonahtan Aston Funky Footless Opaque Tights come in fuchsia and pink.

Tights for flip-flops

Falke Henna Toe tights are 15 denier and a powder skin colour. They're perfect for wearing with flip-flops or strappy sandals and have an open toe that's decorated with a pretty floral pattern like a henna tattoo.

Petite with full hips?

Levante Extra Tights 15 denier come in two sizes and in five colours for hips 47"-54" and larger. Aristoc Ultra Tights in extra large are designed for hips 48"-54" and height 5'-5'10". Check the size chart for your height/weight ratio.

Tights for hipsters?

Levanto Flex tights have a unique adjustable waistband which can be positioned on your hips or waist for when you're wearing low cut/hipster trousers or skirts. Also, La Perla Complice 15 Hipster tights are true low-waist tights with a comfortable, uniquely designed 'waistband' resting a good inch below your waist.

Spray on nylons

Stockings are a much better way to stay cool than tights when things heat up in the office during the summer – or you could try Airstocking for size: www.airstockinguk.com or www.hqhair.com (tel: +44 1737700020 for stockists). Created in Japan by Nissin Medico it's essentially a mist in a can. Once sprayed on and left to dry, it looks like you're wearing a pair of nudes. Each can yields 20-25 applications, it comes in three colours and washes off with soap and warm water at the end of the day. Best of all, it won't snag on your desk.

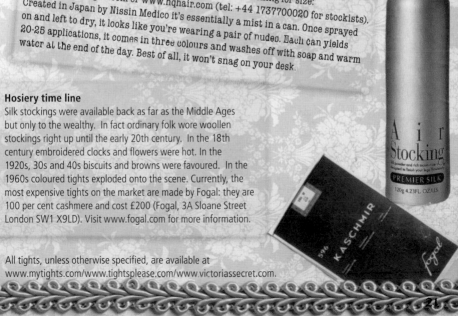

Hosiery time line

Silk stockings were available back as far as the Middle Ages but only to the wealthy. In fact ordinary folk wore woollen stockings right up until the early 20th century. In the 18th century embroidered clocks and flowers were hot. In the 1920s, 30s and 40s biscuits and browns were favoured. In the 1960s coloured tights exploded onto the scene. Currently, the most expensive tights on the market are made by Fogal: they are 100 per cent cashmere and cost £200 (Fogal, 3A Sloane Street London SW1 X9LD). Visit www.fogal.com for more information.

All tights, unless otherwise specified, are available at www.mytights.com/www.tightsplease.com/www.victoriassecret.com.

Can you remember your first handbag? I made mine, at the age of eight, from bits of old brown cardboard and Sellotape. I'd take it on nature walks to collect flowers and little stones and feathers, and then I'd dump its contents (mud and all) onto my bed before refilling it with crayons, sweets and Plasticine. I was very attached to my handbag and didn't feel the same handbag-glow again until 1997, when I bought myself a squidgy, leopard-print Fendi Baguette at New York Fashion Week.

I still love my Fendi Baguette for going out in the evening but it's too small for everyday use so I've graduated to a Fendi Spy. The Spy bag is the most beautiful day bag I've ever owned; it's spacious and lush, it has a compartment (with a built-in mirror) for your lippy, and even has a separate section for me to keep my drawing pencils in. It would need to be pretty special – I worked my ass off to buy it! That's right, even I have to save hard to buy designer. Otherwise I buy thrift store, Westwood, Vuitton and Chanel vintage (see pp69).

Whatever I'm buying the following Goddess Tips have helped me to find gorgeous, reasonably-priced bags that last for ages…

Where can I find a good office bag?

BAGS

BUILDING YOUR
BAG WARDROBE

Occasion

1. Hobo
2. Structured

EVENING
3. Clutch
4. Wristlet

EVERYDAY
5. Structured tote
6. Shopper

Weekend
7. Messenger
8. Backpack

22

Think functional

If you travel with a laptop then you'll need a laptop-friendly bag that isn't an advert for muggers. At www.linandleo.com their laptop bags look nothing like the usual black nylon affairs, and have ample space for your laptop as well as anything else you might need to carry around with you. Check out www.pinklining.co.uk for Charlotte Pearl's really girly, customized 'business class' laptop bags. Or, if you want something more classic, go to www.knomo.com for the leather option.

Leather is best

If you intend hauling books into work invest in a hardwearing leather bag with a distressed vintage look and scratches and scuffs will easily be disguised! Try www.cocoribbon.com or www.melimelo.it for a Meli' Melo', BB Bag or www.belenechandia.com for a Belen Echandia Box Bag; these square-bottomed, strong leather totes are great if you lug a lot of stuff around. Similarly, www.biasia.com, www.activeendeavors.com and www.donnakaran.com offer great leather shoppers and totes. Another great tote is the Piana at www.flotoimports.com.

Top totes
1. Mulberry's "Bayswater"
   www.mulberry.com
2. Marc Jacobs' "Venetia"
   www.marcjacobs.com
3. Mulberry's "Roxanne"
   www.mulberry.com
4. Meli' Melo' shopping bag
   www.melimelo.it

GODDESS TIP

DISGUSTED WITH ALL OF THE FAKES? I AM! (SEE PP73 ON HOW TO SPOT THEM.) IF YOU'RE INTENT ON HAVING A REAL DESIGNER BAG CHECK OUT WWW.BEAFASHIONISTA.CO.UK. FOR A MODEST MONTHLY MEMBERSHIP FEE YOU GET TO TRY OUT DESIGNER BAGS – AS MANY, AND AS OFTEN, AS YOU WANT – SIMPLY SENDING YOUR BAG BACK WHEN YOU'RE BORED AND REQUESTING ANOTHER.

Don't get conned by beauty

Choose a colour that suits your wardrobe and always look at the handles: Are they reinforced where they join the bag with double stitching? Are the straps stitched all the way around underneath the bag for extra support? Likewise, are the zips metal (much better than nylon)? Are all the seams stitched rather than glued? Well, are they? This could be a very costly mistake, girlfriend. Nobody wants to see the entire contents of their makeup bag, yesterday's half-eaten chocolate bar and an empty box of Tampax strewn across the pavement all because they scrimped on the stitching!

Don't be a mug or get mugged

Buy a bag that will keep your possessions safe; one that zips up all the way around with no gaps or openings. If your bag has an open top, take a look at the colour of the lining: your valuables will pulsate like a rob-me beacon if they're set against a pale fabric.

Confuse the competition

For an everyday-bag purchase, shout this question out loud in the store (come on do it with me, girls): 'Will this bag fit all of the belongings currently in my handbag? The lipstick, the purse, the gun?' If you've done this properly you'll then have time to ponder the answer as other shoppers back away from you slowly – leaving you with all the best bags! This works particularly well during the sales.

Shop around

Always buy a bag that you will cherish for years to come, not just a key shape for the season. Keep in mind Urban Outfitters (www.urbanoutfitters.co.uk); Whistles (www.whistles.co.uk); Dune (www.duneshopping.com); Furla (www.furla.it); Jamin Puech (www.jamin-puech.com); Paul & Joe (www.paulandjoe.com); Matthew Williamson (www.matthewwilliamson.com), and Amy Morris bags at www.handbagsandgladrags.co.uk, as well as vintage stores. For the real deal, check out www.mulberry.com, www.billamberg.com, www.tannerkrolle.co.uk, www.hermes.com and www.tods.com.

Buying an evening bag

If you're buying on the high street, a satin or velvet clutch is your best bet. Sequins, embroidery and trimmings can look tatty if you're on a budget so avoid fussy detail; another key sign of quality is not being able to see visible stitching on the outside of the bag.

Fendi Spy bag in velvet

Stella McCartney, Kenneth Cole and Steve Madden offer vegan bags. Synthetic leathers, which are made from PVC, can be embossed with different patterns to make them look like the real deal. Visit www.alternativeoutfitters.com to see a whole range of vegan products or www.mattandnat.com.

25

1. Chanel "2.55 Quilted Classic" Début: February 1955. Coco Chanel designed this envelope shape in quilted black lamb's leather, with a chain handle and a double 'C' clasp, for herself. The name refers to the bag's birthday: February 1955. It has a secret pocket inside the top flap and a cylindrical pocket for your lippie.

2. Gucci "Jackie O" Début: Early 70s. In 2002 Gucci brought out the Jackie O bag again in this Hobo shape.

3. Bottega Veneta "Veneta" Début: 1966. This classic was revamped in 2002 when Thomas Meier joined Bottega Veneta as creative director. Their famous woven leather is called "interciatto".

4. Hermès "Birkin" Début: 1984. Created by Jean-Louis-Dumas Hermès, after spotting Jane Birkin struggling with her hand luggage, on a flight. She explained her perfect bag to him et voilà! Starting at £2000, they're totally handmade. They're beautiful but expensive and the waiting list goes on forever. Try buying vintage.

5. Dior "Lady Dior" Début: September 1995. Presented as a gift to Princess Diana by Madame Chirac during a Royal visit to Paris in 1995. She then made it famous around the world.

6. Fendi "Baguette" Début: Autumn 1997. So-called because it tucks under the arm like a baker's baguette. Created by Silvia Venturini Fendi, each design is said to have its own personality. The fact that designs change every six months have made them worth their weight in gold.

7. Prada "Bowling" bag. Début: Autumn 1999. This came in leather and canvas, and in two sizes, medium and small. A super day-bag.

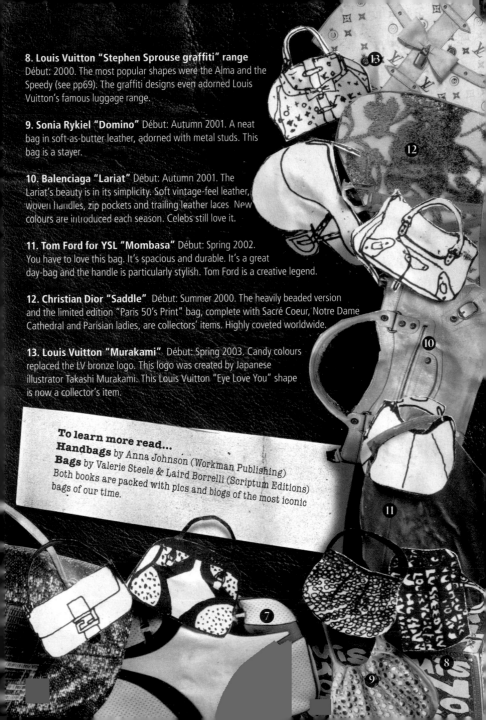

8. Louis Vuitton "Stephen Sprouse graffiti" range
Début: 2000. The most popular shapes were the Alma and the
Speedy (see pp69). The graffiti designs even adorned Louis
Vuitton's famous luggage range.

9. Sonia Rykiel "Domino" Début: Autumn 2001. A neat
bag in soft-as-butter leather, adorned with metal studs. This
bag is a stayer.

10. Balenciaga "Lariat" Début: Autumn 2001. The
Lariat's beauty is in its simplicity. Soft vintage-feel leather,
woven handles, zip pockets and trailing leather laces. New
colours are introduced each season. Celebs still love it.

11. Tom Ford for YSL "Mombasa" Début: Spring 2002.
You have to love this bag. It's spacious and durable. It's a great
day-bag and the handle is particularly stylish. Tom Ford is a creative legend.

12. Christian Dior "Saddle" Début: Summer 2000. The heavily beaded version
and the limited edition "Paris 50's Print" bag, complete with Sacré Coeur, Notre Dame
Cathedral and Parisian ladies, are collectors' items. Highly coveted worldwide.

13. Louis Vuitton "Murakami" Début: Spring 2003. Candy colours
replaced the LV bronze logo. This logo was created by Japanese
illustrator Takashi Murakami. This Louis Vuitton "Eye Love You" shape
is now a collector's item.

To learn more read…
Handbags by Anna Johnson (Workman Publishing)
Bags by Valerie Steele & Laird Borrelli (Scriptum Editions)
Both books are packed with pics and biogs of the most iconic
bags of our time.

Rainy day

Preserve your leather and use a canvas bag on a rainy day. Line it with a discreet plastic liner and valuables should stay dry.

New bag

As soon as you buy your leather bag Scotchgard it. Also continue to feed the leather with a specialised conditioner, such as Hide Care by Connolly (tel: +44 20 7439 2510) or Mulberry's leather nourisher (tel: +44 20 7299 1635, www.mulberry.com), on a regular basis. Allow 24 hours for the cream to sink in and then buff.

Wet bag

Will it ever be the same again? Don't be tempted to dry it with a hairdryer or place it near a radiator. Instead stuff it with tissue paper and place it in a dark, warm, aerated cupboard.

Marks

Shine up your leather handbag and get rid of marks with a liberal spray of pledge. It works a treat.

Pen marks

Got biro on you bag? Squirt on a little Elnette hairspray and wipe it away.

Grubby

For dark leather apply leather cleaner from www.leathermagic.com sparingly. Only place a little on your bag with a very clean white (preferably cotton) cloth – old panties do the job. Extremely expensive light-coloured leather bags should always be placed in the hands of the professionals for cleaning.

Grease

Been eating greasy food and ruined your bag? Lighter fluid will get it out in a flash.

Marked suede

Little stains on suede will come off easily if rubbed with a hard rubber in a circular motion. Dunkelman & Son (tel: +44 1536 760 760, www.dunkelman.com) stocks a great range of products to help nourish and revive your suede including brushes with brass bristles, and Dasco Suede & Nubuck cleaner. (Use a brass brush only on heavy suede.)

Delicate Suede

To brighten up delicate suede use a crepe suede brush, or one made of horsehair, to effectively remove dust and raise the nap. Cover lightly in talcum powder and then brush or vacuum for a new lease of life.

Giorgio Armani lizard-skin shopper

Chloé "Silverado" python

Luella Bartley python

Fendi lizard-skin "Vanity" bag

Since 1973, the Convention on International Trade in Endangered Species has protected all endangered plants and animals on the planet. All design houses featured comply fully with these industry guidelines.

Alligator

n a large crocodilian of the southern US, having powerful jaws but different from the crocodiles in having a shorter, broader snout; a smaller but similar species also occurs in China. *Coll. n* a congregation of alligators. The alligator lacks the same salt-filtering system as the crocodile so it can only live in fresh water.

Ostrich

n a fast-running flightless African bird that is the largest living bird with stout two-toed feet and dark feathers, except on the naked head, neck, and legs. *Coll. n* a wobble/flock of ostrichs. An ostriches eye is bigger then its brain. It lays the biggest egg of all birds.

Gucci Ostrich bag

Alexander McQueen "Novak" in shiny crocodile, so-called after cool-as-ice Hitchcock heroine Kim Novak.

Crocodile

n a large tropical reptile having a broad head, tapering snout, massive jaws, and a thick outer covering. *Coll. n* a bask/float of crocodiles. A crocodile cannot stick its tongue out. Females lay between 20 and 60 eggs and babies hatch in 90 days. They swallow stones so that they can dive deeper. Have you ever cried crocodile tears? It's a term used to describe insincere crying and comes from the belief that crocodiles wept over their prey to attract further victims.

Python

n any of a family of large non-venomous snakes of Africa, S Asia and Australia. They can reach a length of more then 20 feet and kill their prey by constriction. *Coll. n* a knot of pythons. Pythons have very poor sight and locate their prey with the scent-sensory organs on their constantly flicking forked tongues. Their jaws can be stretched to swallow animals larger than their heads. Unlike boas, pythons are egg layers.

Lizard

n any of a group of reptiles typically having an elongated body, four limbs, and a long tail: includes the geckos, iguanas, chameleons, monitors and slowworms. *Coll. n* a lounge of lizards. A lizard can break off its tail to distract a predator. The lizard then escapes and can re-grow the tail later. Most female lizards lay soft-shelled eggs.

Vintage alligator bag

Before I get too misty-eyed about the contents of my own handbag, it's worth explaining exactly how I came to have it painted. Nathalie Lecroc (or Miss Lecroc), has been painting these handbag portraits for €90 (£62) at her kitchen table in her rose-scented apartment on the rue St Denis in Paris since 1998. She had given me specific instructions before my visit that nothing was to be put into or taken out of my everyday bag until she had painted it (she'll know if you cheat!). Emptying my bag of all of its secrets, we first gave each item a name (this bit took about an hour), and then she started to sketch. She analysed as she drew…

It's your lifeline, non? Do you always carry your passport in your bag?
I do.
And you have no electronic diary?
No way!
This is good – a written diary is more creative… And the pressed orchid?
It's from Oscar Wilde's room at L'Hôtel.
And the love letters?
From an admirer.
And the photo negative?
It holds a special secret.
There's no cheap tat here! (Phew!)

Miss Lecroc
183, rue Saint Denis
75002 Paris
tél./fax : + 33 (0)1 45 08 13 87
e-mail : pypaul@club-internet.fr
Sur Rendez-Vous

Miss Lecroc, have you ever painted your own bag?
*My bag, sketch No 0000, contains an address book,
coin purse, silk tassels, sealing wax, a fan and an
angel wallet tied together with a tape measure.
I found it empty and abandoned in a bin in a posh
Parisian postcode!*

Who has been your most unusual client?
*Anne de Peufeilhoux, a doctor turned actress, kept
firecrackers in her bag which she randomly set off;
or a Brazilian who vanished mysteriously after his
bag was painted (it contained the only existing draft
of his boyfriend's novel). John Froger, a performing
street artist who lives near Nantes, exchanges one item
with everyone he meets so his bag was full of other
people's things.*

Any surprises? *An adoring Northern Irish husband had
a bag painted as a surprise for his wife for Christmas.
He photographed her bag and its contents over a
period of nights and had the watercolour posted to the
school where he worked so she wouldn't suspect.*

Most amusing bag? *(No 71) A bag containing a dirty
uniform belonging to a friend who works for a hotel.
This bag is very common in Paris, you get it with
almost everything you buy.*

What have you learnt overall? *Asian ladies are secretive,
Americans, extra tidy; the French mix labels in a very
chic way and the British are the most original and
creative. In general your mode of keeping information
says a lot about your personality: Artists, writers,
actresses and dreamers always use paper and ink.*

I left with an original signed, stamped and numbered
portrait (No 284), and Miss Lecroc kept a colour scan
of it for her forthcoming book. Currently at bag number
640 she will publish 1001 bag portraits in 2008.

Lingerie

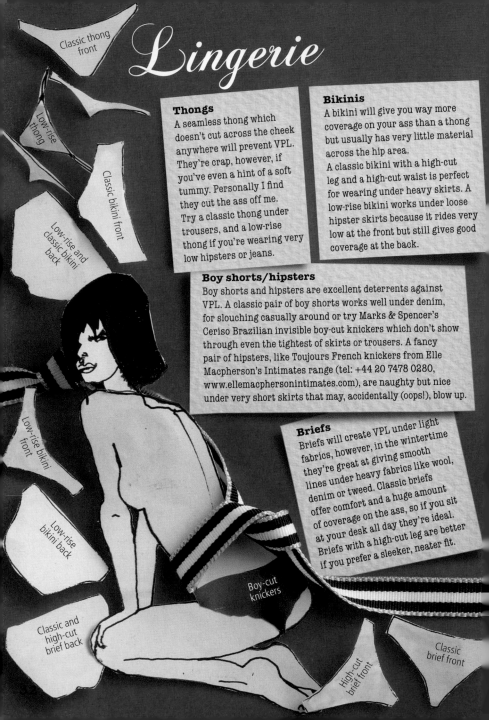

Thongs

A seamless thong which doesn't cut across the cheek anywhere will prevent VPL. They're crap, however, if you've even a hint of a soft tummy. Personally I find they cut the ass off me. Try a classic thong under trousers, and a low-rise thong if you're wearing very low hipsters or jeans.

Bikinis

A bikini will give you way more coverage on your ass than a thong but usually has very little material across the hip area.

A classic bikini with a high-cut leg and a high-cut waist is perfect for wearing under heavy skirts. A low-rise bikini works under loose hipster skirts because it rides very low at the front but still gives good coverage at the back.

Boy shorts/hipsters

Boy shorts and hipsters are excellent deterrents against VPL. A classic pair of boy shorts works well under denim, for slouching casually around or try Marks & Spencer's Ceriso Brazilian invisible boy-cut knickers which don't show through even the tightest of skirts or trousers. A fancy pair of hipsters, like Toujours French knickers from Elle Macpherson's Intimates range (tel: +44 20 7478 0280, www.ellemacphersonintimates.com), are naughty but nice under very short skirts that may, accidentally (oops!), blow up.

Briefs

Briefs will create VPL under light fabrics, however, in the wintertime they're great at giving smooth lines under heavy fabrics like wool, denim or tweed. Classic briefs offer comfort and a huge amount of coverage on the ass, so if you sit at your desk all day they're ideal. Briefs with a high-cut leg are better if you prefer a sleeker, neater fit.

Classic thong front

Low-rise thong

Classic bikini front

Low-rise and classic bikini back

Low-rise bikini front

Low-rise bikini back

Classic and high-cut brief back

Boy-cut knickers

High-cut brief front

Classic brief front

Frilly pants

The US tennis player Gertrude Moran was the first woman to wear frilly knickers on centre court in Wimbledon in 1949. It earned her the name Gorgeous Gussie and caused uproar. Although far less controversial, I've started to wear mine around the house while writing and doing the housework. They keep me cool while hoovering, don't ride up, stay put when I'm bending over to do the dusting and they make my thighs look bearable when reflected in shiny surfaces because of the huge frill which runs around the top of the leg. I got them from Buttress and Snatch (tel: +44 20 7502 3139, www.buttressandsnatch.co.uk). The line includes frilly hand-made knickers in every material from gingham and polka dot to satin worthy of an Oscar-winning role in Moulin Rouge. Also check out Myla (tel: +44 8707 455 003, www.myla.com). For more big frilly pants try Glamorous Amorous (tel: +44 870 609 1878, www.glamorousamorous.com), for labels such as Damaris; and Frankly Darling (tel: +44 20 77347957, www.franklydarling.com).

GODDESS TIP

FOR MY MARILYN-ON-THE-SUBWAY-GRATING MOMENT OR A NIGHT DANCING ON BAR TABLES I'VE GOT TO HAVE MY AGENT PROVOCATEUR KNICKERS ON – THEY REALLY PACK THE SEXIEST PUNCH OF ALL. I BUY THEIR SENSUAL SILK WITH FRILLS IN THE WINTER AND THEIR COTTON BOY SHORTS FOR THE SUMMER. I LIKE TO PRETEND I'M POP-STAR PERFECT IN THEM, SKIPPING AROUND THE HOUSE OR CHILLING OUT IN A HOTEL ROOM. (FOR ADVICE ON FITTING AND CARING FOR YOUR LINGERIE, SEE TIPS FROM SERENA REES OF AGENT PROVOCATEUR ON PP37.)

For PC pants

Peopletree (tel: +44 845 450 4595, www.peopletree.co.uk), offer 100 per cent organic, certified Fairtrade cotton briefs, thongs, vests and camis. And not only do their thongs prevent VPL under tight trousers, they also offer breathability – a godsend if you're prone to thrush or any other little infections.

What shapes do you really need ?

Bras

Are you a breast or a thigh woman? Lacking long legs, I prefer my boobs. They're 100 per cent my own, but I won't be averse to getting them lifted, if they start hitting my knees. Anyway, they're good for now and I love them. If you're into your boobs, *The History of the Breast* by Marilyn Yalom makes fascinating reading. One piece from the book has always stayed safely in my mind – Yalom says of breasts, 'Babies see food. Men see sex. Doctors see disease. Business people see dollar signs. And, finally, women have seen in them pleasure, power, sustenance, fear, or failure to measure up.' Funnily enough, women are quite literally not measuring up at all and until recently I hadn't even measured up myself. Eventually when I did, I learned that several factors can change the size of the breast, namely hormonal changes, the pill, weight gain and different diets. Do you know your size? Why not have yourself measured this week and try some of these bras to see which suits you best?

No-wire bra

Contour bra

Weekend bra

Convertible bra

No-wire bra – For travelling
With no underwire, seamless cups, wide shoulder straps and a below-the-bust-line band, it's pure comfort! After breaking it in for a few weeks, there's nothing better to prevent discomfort on a long-haul flight. Wireless means you won't set off the airport security gates either! Try the Verde Veronica exotic flower bra (tel: +44 870 609 1878, www.glamorousamorous.com), or the Bra-llelujah bra from www.spanx.com.

Contour bra – For T-shirts
Great for wearing under a T-shirt or a Diane von Furstenberg slip dress, its skinny straps, flexible underwires and soft, seamless, spongy cups give boobs a very smooth finish. Try the Chantelle T-shirt bra, (tel: +44 870 4999 002, www.figleaves.com).

Weekend bra – For lounging
With underwires, seamless stretch cups and skinny straps, this style will be the lightest bra in your drawer. Calvin Klein's weekend bras, from www.cku.com (cheap as chips in the US), come in a gazillion colours and are really light. Perfect for weekend lounging or if for some artistic reason you decide to hold court from your bed. Also check out www.barelythere.com.

Convertible bra – For dilemmas
A convertible has straps with clips which can be positioned to give five different variations, namely halter, criss-crossed, over one shoulder, over both shoulders or strapless. Marks & Spencer's five-way nude padded convertible bra (tel: +44 845 302 1234, www.marksandspencer.com), is a must-have for your lingerie drawer.

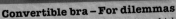

Low-back basque – For low-back dresses

If you're a D cup or larger, a low-back strapless basque from Rigby & Peller (tel: +44 020 7491 220, www.rigbyandpeller.com), or Maidenform (tel: +44 800-373037, www.maidenform.com), offers more support than a normal backless bra because the ribcage at the front takes the weight of the breasts. This is not to be confused, however, with a bra which will save you if your Goddess dress is cut so low you can see the top of your bum. For this you'll need backless support (see pp64).

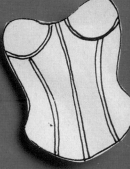

Low-back basque

Plunge bra – For V-necks

This enlarges and sculpts the overall bust by pushing the breasts together. Try a Wonderbra (tel +44 870 4999 002, www.figleaves.com), and wear it to the office under a V-neck cashmere cardigan or sweater for a beautiful sexy shape.

Minimizing bra – Shrink a size

Minimizers are designed to reduce your bust by one full cup size. Marks & Spencer do a whole range, as do Maidenform (tel: +44 800-373037, www.maidenform.co.uk). Look for wide straps and cups that distribute the breasts equally.

Minimizing bra

Balconette bra – For round-necks

Cups are underwired, padded and cut low and, as they mould around the breasts, they expose the upper part, giving breasts a lifted-up effect. Straps are thin and wide, revealing the maximum amount of décolletage. Try a balconette from Myla (tel: +44 870 745 5003, www.mylalingerie.co.uk), and ensure when you're putting it on that the underwires lie flat against your chest.

For the ultimate sports bra for your gym kit, see pp116.

Huge boobs

Marks & Spencer's Truly You underwired padded plunge bra is part of a range that goes from DD–G created especially for women with generous curves.

Balconette bra

Plunge bra

GODDESS TIP

REMEMBER TO CHECK YOUR BOOBS REGULARLY FOR LUMPS AND IRREGULARITIES. ONE IN NINE WOMEN WILL BE AFFECTED BY BREAST CANCER IN THEIR LIFETIME. IF IN ANY DOUBT, GO SEE YOUR DOCTOR.

Agent Provocateur

For me there's just one name when it comes to dancing-on-the-table, flashing-your-panties type lingerie and that's the sexy, high-voltage, Agent Provocateur. A combination of the magnificent talent of Joseph Corre (Vivienne Westwood's son) and his sexy wife, Serena Rees, Agent Provocateur is the leader in the lingerie revolution. In fact Serena Rees is 100 per cent a Sex Goddess: smart, beautiful, with deep brown eyes that hide secrets of nights in the desert, hammams in mysterious locations and parties in Vegas, she's exotic and slinky – in a word, pure Sex.

When I hung out with Serena and Joe, it was obvious from the start how sexy and powerful they are as a couple. The air around them crackles with sexual energy, they have movie star quality – that frisson, that buzz – and it runs right through the Agent Provocateur collections like electricity. With shops in Tokyo, Vegas and LA, I asked them what they'd learned about lingerie in the past eleven years.

What is your first memory of lingerie, Joe? *My first memory of lingerie was the items that my mother had for sale in her shop here in London. I was very young but it meant that I was comfortable from a very early age with all types. As a teenager, however, the bra bamboozled me and I grappled with the difference between a front and back fastening on many dates.*

And Serena? *I remember going out with my girlfriends to buy my first ever bra and looking for something really special, only to be disappointed for up to fifteen years at the lack of imagination in design. I couldn't find anything that I wanted so I decided to create my own.*

What makes the perfect bra then, Joe? *The perfect bra is sexy. There are lots of different ideas of sexy, and the perfect bra has to suit the individual. Some bras are quite frivolous, but if a woman wants to wear a crop-top bra, go right ahead.*

Should you keep anything in mind when shopping for the perfect bra, Serena? *Get fitted and remember that the bra is the first layer next to the skin, so it should be comfortable. It should do the job in terms of support but also make you feel sensual.*

What's the biggest lesson you've learned about lingerie, Joe? *I think it's terribly sad when women wear those minimizer bras because it means that they're not enjoying their femininity.*

Why do bra cups wrinkle sometimes, Serena? *This usually happens if a bra is just too big. Go down one bra size and not a cup size and it should be fine.*

Why do boobs pour out over cups, Joe? *Breasts spilling out over the top and at the sides of a bra means you need a larger cup size.*

Is there any need to try on panties, Serena? *No store will take panties back if you go home and then decide they are the wrong size. Slip them on over your own before buying them.*

Why do knickers sometimes cut into hips, Joe? *If this is happening it's either because you've bought them too small or you've bought the wrong shape for your body. You need to look for a style that's cut deeper on the sides. Also if you're curvy, buy fabric with a lot of give and stretch.*

How do you minimize VPL? *Look for seamless knickers which won't cut into your bulkiest area. Choose lightweight fabrics fashioned into a thong which cuts way above the cheek or shorts which drop beneath.*

Have you both got a golden rule? *When bra-buying, go for the best quality you can afford and treat it with respect. Hand-wash with baby shampoo and dry press in a towel or over the shower rail in the bathroom. And enjoy your lingerie, let it poke out under outfits – a hint of cleavage and a ribboned strap is sexy.*

Agent Provocateur, 6 Broadwick Street, Soho, London (tel: +44 20 7439 0229, www.agentprovocateur.com). For other locations see website.

GODDESS TIP
AGENT PROVOCATEUR'S SIGNATURE FRAGRANCE IS PERFECT FOR YOUR DRESSING TABLE OR FOR SCENTING YOUR LINGERIE (BURY A SPARE BOTTLE AMONG YOUR SMALLS!).

Agent Provocateur

Dear Gisele –

Herewith my tips :
1. Remember lingerie shopping is great fun + good for your health!
2. Always try on bras for perfect fit, don't be shy to ask for help.
3. Always hand wash your delicate scanties.
4. Remember don't keep your AP lingerie for special occasions only, wear it everyday – you never know what might happen!

love Serena + Joe xxx.

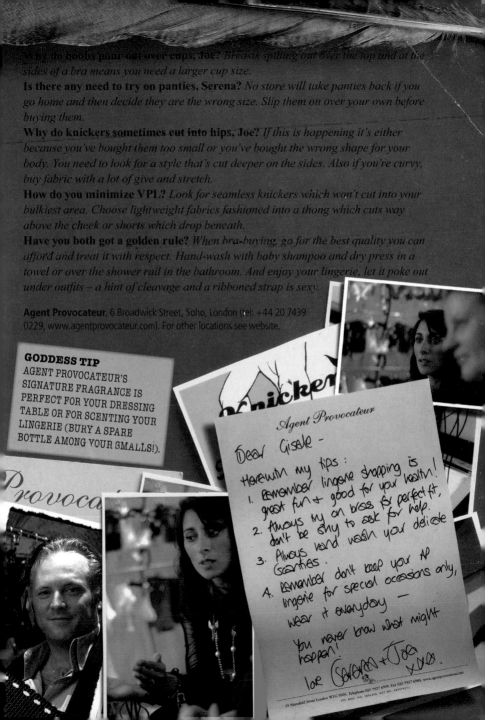

Bling

As a child, I adored watching Marilyn Monroe play the diamond-hungry Lorelei Lee in Gentlemen Prefer Blondes. So it's hardly surprising my idea of good jewellery is always set to a little background voice in my head humming the movie's signature tune – 'Diamond's are a Girl's Best Friend'. For me, a superior piece of jewellery has almost always got to be handmade or vintage. Here are my hottest hunting grounds and the six smartest ways I've learned to buy bling…

Charity shops
Check local charity shops regularly. One day you could be lucky enough to find some interesting goodies. There are 750 Oxfam shops in Britain (tel: +44 845 3000 311, www.oxfam.org.uk) and 75 in Ireland (tel: +353 1 6727662, www.oxfamireland.org).

The internet and thrift online
www.madaboutjewellery.com seizes on seasonal trends and points out what items have been featured in which magazines. Also try www.agatha.fr, www.angelahale.co.uk and www.ebay.com. See vintage pp71 for a host of thrift and vintage websites.

Commission your own piece
The current trend in contemporary jewellery is to have a piece commissioned. The most helpful and affordable service comes from Rumour (tel: +44 20 7575 3031, www.jewellery-maker.com) where prices start at £300 and, once agreed on design, only take ten working days for delivery. EC One in Notting Hill (tel: +44 20 743 8811, www.econe.co.uk) are also worth considering for engagement jewellery. Chopard (tel: +44 20 7409 3140, www.chopard.com), Sotheby's (tel: +44 20 7293 6430, www.sothebysdiamonds.com), Mappin & Webb (tel: +44 207 478 8700, www.mappin-and-webb.co.uk) and William Asprey (tel: +44 20 7493 8385, www.williamandson.com) also fashions diamonds and stones – the sort luxurious dreams are made of.

Auctions
Auctions are another interesting way to find jewellery pieces. What's more, it doesn't have to cost you a fortune: Bonhams, New Bond Street (tel: +44 20 7447 7447) and Bonhams, Montpelier Street (tel: +44 20 7393 3900, www.bonhams.com), held an auction in their Montpelier Street branch and every item went for under £2000. Pieces are always on display a few days before auction so check the website of each auction house for details. For fine jewellery auctions try Christies, King Street (tel: +44 20 7581 7611, www.christies.com) and for twentieth century and contemporary items try Sotheby's Bond Street (tel: +44 20 7293 6409, www.sothebys.com).

Antique shops, markets and indoor vintage fairs
Scour antique shops and markets for one-off vintage finds. Get yourself to the Friday market at Bermondsey, Portobello market on Saturdays or Camden market on Wednesdays and Saturdays (see pp71), or trawl indoor vintage jewellery fairs (see pp70).

Eco jewellery
Mining enough gold for an average sized wedding band produces approximately twenty tons of waste. Furthermore, cyanide from the process can contaminate the local water supply. Buy vintage jewellery instead and look at it as recycling! Or, try John Hardy who has an eco-friendly policy (tel: +1 212 219 4288, www.johnhardy.com).

Goddess Jewellery Tips
Put your jewellery on last - cosmetics, hairspray and perfume can be corrosive.
Wipe jewellery with a soft cloth when you take it off at night – perspiration and germs can also cause jewellery to dull.
Store your jewellery separately in pouches or compartments and keep them from touching or scratching. If using an antique jewellery box with no compartments, cut the cups from an egg carton and line them with velvet to store jewellery pieces.
Bring shine back to your gold by soaking it in an eggcup of gin. Leave for a few minutes then rinse with warm water.
Don't soak sterling silver for too long in detergent and warm water – some oxidized finishes will change.
Put aside old soft toothbrushes and mascara wands for cleaning stubborn dirt stains.
Caution: some materials are vulnerable to damage from ammonia or any hot solution. Take care with malachite, mother of pearl, jet, pearls, peridot and turquoise.

GODDESS TIP
IF YOU LOOSE THE BACK OF YOUR EARRING IN THE OFFICE USE A SMALL PIECE OF RUBBER FROM A PENCIL TOP AS A TEMPORARY BACK UNTIL YOU GET HOME.

Guy tips
Buying the iceberg
(Boys) buying the correct iceberg is something you'll only do once (hopefully) and anyone selling you the stone is only too aware of this. Arm yourself with the basic facts (below) which are really only the tip of a giant iceberg (ahem sorry!) and then read the diamond information on www.jewellery-maker.com (great site to order from) or the comprehensive tutorial on www.howtobuyadiamond.gia.edu from the Gemological Institute of America before you part with 10 per cent of your annual salary (what most men are expected to invest in an engagement ring). Bonus points are given for having it made to order and/or inscribed.

The four Cs
Cut: This is often confused with the shape of the diamond. In fact this term refers to the stone's facets (craftsmanship determines this).

Colour: This is the amount of brown or yellow tint in a 'colourless stone'. The whiter the stone the better the diamond!

Clarity: This is the quality used to evaluate the internal imperfections and external flaws of a diamond. The grading works like this: it goes from the rarest, FL (flawless when magnified ten times), all the way down to I1, I2, I3… (inclusions or flaws that affect the diamond's brilliance).

Carat: This term refers to the diamond's overall weight. A carat is 1/5 of a gram and is also worth 100 points. For a more accurate reading of your diamond ask your jeweller for the point size of your stone. Remember this single fact: Carat weight alone is no indication of a diamond's value or beauty.

COATS

Do you remember your most favourite coat ever? I do and in fact I have two. The first, my parents bought me when I was eight on our annual Christmas shopping trip to Dublin; a grey wool princess coat with suede grey moccasin boots to match. The second, I bought six years ago at Paris Fashion Week; a Miu Miu goatskin tailored coat which has aged really well. This particular coat has been on some great trips and means so much to me because it has lasted so long. Nowadays, this is the first thing I keep in mind when shopping for a new coat along with these other little tips:

Forget trends
Forget the catwalk. Think years, not just seasons ahead and choose what suits your figure not that of a supermodel.

Pay the price
Rethink your price barriers. Pay more if you can afford it and remember a truly great coat won't date.

Check linings
Analyse garments inside and out. Strong, substantial linings are essential. The lining should be sewn well and sit comfortably against the coat. If the lining is too baggy around the bottom then it will start to show below the hem – too tight and it will tear at underarm pressure points.

Buy good fabric
Good fabric is crucial so always look at the label. All garments, whether Calvin Klein originals or market stall knock-offs, stick to the basic principle that total cost is based on the cloth and the time it takes to make each item. Pick pure wool rather than synthetic with cashmere content, or expect your fabric to crease easily and wear out quickly. You should never skimp on fabric.

Buy a generous fit
Complete the full outfit in your mind. Be aware of what you'll be wearing underneath and any extra weight you may have gained over the winter months.

So does the colour of the coat that you've fallen in love with suit your complexion?

Blonde
Pale yellows, pinks and greens are instantly draining. Instead try browns, berry red, plum or shades ranging from navy to black, and use a coloured scarf or some jewellery to lift that look even further.

Redhead/Brunette
Redheads and brunettes have warmer complexions which make it easier to shop for. Rich tweeds, sumptuous velvets and exotic prints in luxurious shades of green, chocolate, blackberry, royal blue or black will look great.

Care for it well

Look after it. The average
life span of a coat is three
years, but this can be
extended to five if you get
it cleaned properly. Put
it away at the end of the
season and repair it when
required.

Petite

If you're small in size, don't be tempted to buy a tall person's coat in the hope a few minor alterations will make it suit, it just won't work and the proportions will turn out all wrong.. To create the illusion of height, wear knee-high boots and tights under a just below-the-knee or knee-length coat to elongate the legs.

Tall

If you're tall you can easily carry off a military style or belted trench (belts break up the body beautifully). Alternatively if you feel that you're in and out of the car all the time and can't cope with the whole length issue stick to the military theme but choose a jacket instead. Always check the arm length though – if your wrists are too exposed your coat or jacket is too small!

Full-figured

Those with fuller figures should avoid excess volume; seek out thin tweeds and avoid sheepskins, pale colours, horizontal stripes and excess detailing. Do choose a coat which doesn't look as if it's pulled taut over your chest and forget belted coats with large pockets on the hips opting for tailored styles instead. Coats of mid-calf or above the knee length worn with boots will help create a slimmed-down silhouette.

Pear-shaped

Belted coats on the waist work well for a pear-shaped figure though do run a mile from padding, especially around the bum, or you could end up looking like the Michelen Man.

Slim

If you're lucky enough to be naturally slim, I have no pity, everything suits you. Everything that is except a big coat begging the question, did you borrow your coat from someone with boobs? For perfection, look for belted styles or military cuts which will hug your slim figure and give your waist perfect definition.

STYLES

Belted

Instead of threading it through the loops, try casually knotting the belt. Threading it tightly will accentuate an hourglass shape and is great if you're tall and trying to create a more shapely body or, you're pear-shaped and want to hide a huge ass.

Three-quarter length with bracelet sleeves

Pair a polo neck, leather elbow-length gloves, skinny jeans and knee-high leather boots to instantly update this old style of coat.

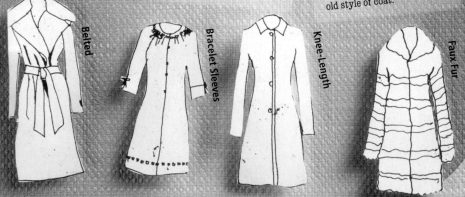

Belted   Bracelet Sleeves   Knee-Length   Faux Fur

Princess

The most forgiving of all coat shapes, if you're petite or worried about a shelf-like ass, the princess shape is perfectly flared from the waist out. Its romantic, ladylike shape works equally well worn open, teamed with jeans slouchy boots and a scarf, during the day, as it does closed with courts and nylons in the evening.

Military

Disguising a thick waist and hiding big hips, the military style gives great structure to shoulders and can be worn open with the belt tied round the back if you're carrying a lot of weight on your tummy. Floor sweeping versions are best suited to tall gals while the shorter lengths are flattering to petites.

GODDESS TIP

TAKE EXTRA CARE WHEN CHOOSING A COAT FOR THE SUMMER BECAUSE LIGHTER FABRICS WILL REVEAL ANY LUMPS AND BUMPS.

Faux Fur

A faux fur coat can easily look like the real thing without all the issues. Edward An designer, Lori Schlachter-Batt, uses fake fur – for more information on individual items log onto www.shopcitygirl.com It is also well publicised that Stella McCartney does not work with animal skins.

Knee-length

Particularly good for petites, just add boots to this knee-length coat and let four inches of skirt show to create a lengthened silhouette.

Tweed

Tweed has been woven and finished in the UK for centuries. British tweed became popular in the 1890s when fashioned for women and in Paris in the 1920s when Coco Chanel first started using it. Although it wasn't until the 1950s and 60s that she introduced her famous bouclé tweed suit and made her mark with what will forever be known as the Chanel bouclé jacket.

Tweed Types

Bouclé

Check

Herringbone

Houndstooth

Luigi Boggio Italian tweed

Oatmeal tweed

Silk tweed

Tartan

Fleck

Princess

Military

Tweed

DENIM

I'm gonna have to come clean with you here about denim. I love it! I love it because it has that I'm-too-hot-to-get-dressed-up attitude. But, sadly, denim does not love me back, and it isn't every day that my jeans fit me at all. In fact, if I'm having an off-day they won't go past my chubby little bottom. It's my own fault, I suppose, for choosing skinny jeans as my favourite shape... In my case it took me two whole years to find 'the ones'. I tried loads of others on before them in shops around the globe, but without success – because the fit of each style is so entirely different. I was wondering whether to blame the jeans-makers or my Maker for the kinks. Eventually, though, after all of my traipsing, fittings and perspiration I found them. Here's a rundown of what I learned along the way.

Washes

The colour of your denim is called 'the wash'. It's called the wash because jeans are made in indigo and are then 'washed' to either the darkest inky navy or the palest stonewash blue. Washes and finishes include chalky rinse, streaky rinse and sandblasted, and manufacturers use everything from pumice stones and sandpaper to hand-distress them, and clothes pegs and over-dyed tint to give the denim different character and a mix of shades. All of this takes time of course, and the longer the jeans have to be worked on by hand, and the higher the quality of the wash that they go through, all tells in the end price. Labour-intensive jeans means more money, so expect to pay big bucks for hand-treated denim.

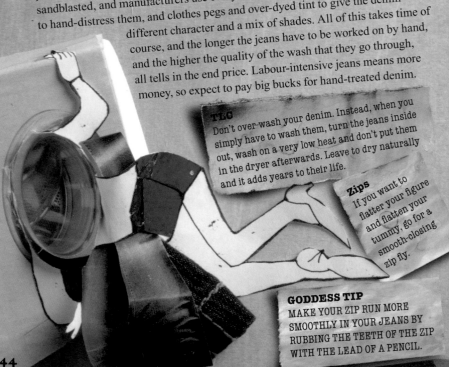

TLC
Don't over-wash your denim. Instead, when you simply have to wash them, turn the jeans inside out, wash on a very low heat and don't put them in the dryer afterwards. Leave to dry naturally and it adds years to their life.

Zips
If you want to flatter your figure and flatten your tummy, go for a smooth-closing zip fly.

GODDESS TIP
MAKE YOUR ZIP RUN MORE SMOOTHLY IN YOUR JEANS BY RUBBING THE TEETH OF THE ZIP WITH THE LEAD OF A PENCIL.

Types of denim

Denim comes with 'give' that runs anywhere from super-stretch, stretch, and stretch with a little Lycra, all the way down to rigid. Contrary to what you might think, if you're on the chubby side, super-stretch spells big trouble. The stretch will allow your bulgy bits to bulge and the denim will cling like cling-film to two cheese sandwiches. This is not a good look, girlfriend, and leads to uneven and lumpy leg terrain. Choose a stiff, rigid denim to disguise this, and try denim with two per cent Lycra if you're lucky enough to have an ass of glass and legs like steel poles.

Expert help online

Before you hit the shops, check out www.shopbop.com, where designer denim labels (7 for All Mankind, Earnest Sewn) are all halfprice, as are T-shirts from C&C California. The site also has a 'look book' of seasonal trends and a guide to buying denim which suggests the best shapes for your body. It's brilliant! Check out the shapes, head to the shops, try them on and then go home and buy them on this site at discount. Simple! It's even got the coveted Sass & Bide skinny jeans in ink blue, black or white! Mmmmmmm, heaven!

Denim with conscience

A lot of denim companies couldn't give a flying fuck where their jeans are made, or by whom. And not to get all political on you or anything, but it's about time they did. Thankfully there are some companies who do deliver above-board product and Rag and Bone and Edun are two. For Rag and Bone everything is made in North and South Carolina, Kentucky, and New York. For Edun, Bono, and his wife Ali Hewson and the designer Rogan, have produced jeans from good organic cotton, that are made in family-run factories in South America and Africa with fair-labour practices. They even have Rainer Maria Rilke poems stitched inside.

Vintage

Even though high waists are popular among waifs, the waist on vintage jeans usually sits way higher than on today's fits and can look a bit, well, odd. A good tailor can alter this for you with ease. Thighs, bum, a flared leg and position of button and height of zip can also be changed by a good tailor. Some tailors can even turn your favourite pair of jeans into a pair of maternity jeans and return them back into their original state afterwards. Isn't that like magic? Denim Doctors in Los Angeles – a store that specialises in authentic recycled and refitted jeans – offers this service. They are Hollywood's denim fix. Speaking of which, I met up with one of the movie industry's movers and shakers, the delectable movie director and editor of NYLON magazine Marvin Scott Jarrett (see pp48). He publishes a special denim issue of NYLON every year and owns over 300 pairs of denims himself.

GODDESS TIP

A VERY DARK WASH IS THE MOST FLATTERING AND SLIMMING WASH OF ALL. IF YOU PREFER YOUR JEANS TO HAVE A LIGHT DENIM CONTRAST THEN TRY AND HAVE THE LIGHTER BIT RUNNING ALONG THE FRONT OF YOUR THIGHS. IF THE OUTSIDE AND INSIDE OF YOUR THIGHS ARE A SHADE DARKER THAN THE FRONT OF THE JEAN IT CREATES THE ILLUSION OF LONGER, SLIMMER LEGS.

Faded

Dark wash

Worn-in

Distressed

True Blue

Fitting

There's no magic formula for finding the right fit, I'm afraid. You just have to keep trying on pairs until you find the right one for your shape. However, you should keep in mind your height and which part of your body you want to flatter, and for this you have to keep the rise of the jeans and the type of leg in mind.

Getting slimmer thighs

Boot-cut jeans are amazing at balancing out a chunky thigh area. Also, when trying them on look for a hand-distressed premium pair with fading down the front of the thigh area and a darker wash on either side of the thigh. Dark shading on both the inside and outside of the leg will elongate it – try 7 For All Mankind.

Looking taller

If you'd like to appear taller then there are several tricks that you can use when choosing jeans to give the illusion of height. For example, by choosing a dark colour you automatically slim the leg and this instantly makes you look tall. If you're buying dark jeans but with a boot-cut leg then try to buy them in the perfect length. If you shorten a boot-cut leg it looses its boot-cut flare and will make you look short and stocky. For additional height iron a crease down the front of your dark jeans and team with heels for a few extra inches – try True Religion.

Medium rise

Medium rise means the waistband sits a couple of inches below the belly button. For women within a medium height range who have a pear shape, the medium rise is more flattering on your bum than any other rise. Bootlegs in dark denim also help flatter – try Top Shop.

Low rise to super-low rise

Low rise means that the waistband is way more than a couple of inches below your belly button and it shows off a flat tummy beautifully. However, if you're any bit chubby you'll end up with muffin tummy pouring out over this low waistband. Likewise with super-low rise. However, if you've a short, androgynous body and you choose a straight leg shape with super-low rise you can give yourself both height and a little feminine shape – try Earl.

Looking taller

Low rise to super-low rise

Slimmer thighs

Medium rise

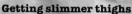

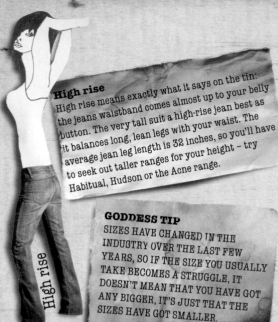

High rise

High rise means exactly what it says on the tin: the jeans waistband comes almost up to your belly button. The very tall suit a high-rise jean best as it balances long, lean legs with your waist. The average jean leg length is 32 inches, so you'll have to seek out taller ranges for your height – try Habitual, Hudson or the Acne range.

High rise

GODDESS TIP

SIZES HAVE CHANGED IN THE INDUSTRY OVER THE LAST FEW YEARS, SO IF THE SIZE YOU USUALLY TAKE BECOMES A STRUGGLE, IT DOESN'T MEAN THAT YOU HAVE GOT ANY BIGGER, IT'S JUST THAT THE SIZES HAVE GOT SMALLER.

Denim Wardrobe

Okay, so you've followed a few of the tips here and found the perfect pair of denims. They are so perfect, in fact, that you even want to wear them to bed. Newsflash, girlfriend: one single pair of jeans does not a complete wardrobe make. One pair will not cover all of life's surprises and eventualities. Different occasions call for different finishes or styles so shop accordingly. Dark, clean denim with a flared leg is most slimming and best suited to night-time adventures – red-hot dates, clubs with the gals – while your slouchy wide-legged loose flop-around-the-house jeans? They are best kept to nurse the hangover the next morning.

The bottom line
Big ass

Fact: the size and positioning of the pockets on a pair of jeans dictates exactly how big or small your ass is going to look. For example, large pockets situated low on the rear (beginning halfway down your cheek and running onto the top of your thing) give the illusion of confining your ass to the pocket area. The pocket also gives the illusion that it's perking up what's right above the thigh and makes your ass look smaller in the process.

Small ass

If you've a small ass you can have small pockets. If you've a big ass it'll wobble around small pockets like blancmange. Think about it: small pockets cover a small ass, but when it comes to a big ass they don't. Simple as.

Flat ass

A flat ass will only be flattened by plain, straight, flat pockets. Pockets that are positioned so that they are leaning slightly towards the hip give a little curve to the ass. Curved like this and covered with intricate embroidery and you're on to a winner.

Different jeans widths to choose from to add to your wardrobe

Wide leg: Perfect for relaxing.

Flared: Slimming, great with heels and flattering on bums. Can it get any better?

Boot-cut: Add high-heeled boots for daywear and stilettos for evening. A boot-cut leg balances out heavy thighs beautifully and is flattering and a great choice for everyday wear.

Skinny: The choice of the super-waif and wasp-waisted – wear under knee-high boots or with flat ballet pumps if you're slim or very tall.

MARVIN SCOTT JARRETT

I will never forget my first meeting with *the* Marvin Scott Jarrett at New York's Soho Grand Hotel. I climbed the Batman-like stairs with excitement that morning at the very prospect of meeting the visionary behind the cult music magazines *Blah, Blah, Blah, Huh, Ray Gun* and *Bikini*. These magazines have won more than one hundred design awards and have been featured in both the Rock and Roll Hall of Fame and the Design Museum, London. For me it was like meeting a Rolling Stone.

By invitation, I dropped in on a fashion shoot for monthly New York based magazine *NYLON* with rock n' roll photographer Mick Rock. I slipped unnoticed into the penthouse suite as Rock snapped Jessica Miller. And, within minutes, Marvin Scott Jarrett, the Editor of *NYLON*, and I, were talking denim – and the vintage belt he had slung around his waist.

Over the years I have got to know Marvin quite well; one of the movie industry's movers and shakers, the last time we spoke he had just returned from the Sundance Film Festival at Park City, Utah. There he premiered 'Fast Future Generation', a documentary shadowing The Good Charlottes' lead singer Joel Madden on the band's tour of Japan. I couldn't help wondering, was denim still his preferred choice for trips, work, parties and his documentary's premiere?

Firstly Marvin, I need to ask honestly, is denim your second skin? *I wear denim for every single occasion. Seriously, whether it's going into the NYLON office in the mornings or going to dinner at night, denim jeans are my suit.*

How many pairs of jeans do you own then? *I've lost count. It's gotta be around 300 pairs or more. I can never get rid of any of them – every pair is special, unique and I suppose, in a way irreplaceable. How crazy is that?*

You're really asking the wrong kitten, Marvin. I don't own 300 pairs of jeans or anything like it. Impressive! Do you wear a different pair everyday then? *I have five or six pairs on the go at any one time but I don't go a week without getting a new pair.*

So you're a collector then? *Yes and no. I collect jeans but I don't treat them like special objects like serious collectors do. I wear mine because they're there to be enjoyed.*

What's your favourite wash? *Changes by the week, by the day or the occasion. Like I was at Teddies last night and I wore a pair of black Tsubi jeans because dark is good for the evening.*

Do you have a quintessential rule for jeans buying? *Yes, it has to be five pocket that's what it's all about.*

Favourite smell and perfume? *The beach and I don't wear scent.*
Favourite sound? *Waves breaking on sand.*
Favourite taste? *Sweet things like cookies and sweets.*
Favourite thing to touch: sand, stone, water or silk? *Water.*
Favourite colour? *Blue.*
Favourite bird or animal? *Swans (at a distance) and puppies (I just got one).*
Favourite flower? *Roses.*
Favourite place? *Wherever I am at that moment.*
Favourite book? *Illusions by Richard Bach.*
Favourite street or contemporary artist? *Andy Warhol, Jean Michel Basquiat, Futura, Kaws.*
Favourite possession? *My creativity.*
If you could have dinner with anyone in the world who would it be and what would you ask them? *Jesus and Einstein. We'd all discuss E=mc² and then one could wash up and the other could dry.*

Look out for NYLON's next denim issue at www.nylonmag.com.

Marvin's Label Tip-offs for 2007
• **Nudie Jeans** (www.nudiejeans.com): a unisex label from Sweden.
• **45rpm** (www.45rpm.jp/denim) a hot Japanese label.
• **Ernest Sewn** (see New York): Scott Morrison's label.
• **Tsubi** (www.tsubi.co.uk): an Australian label for girls and boys.
• **Diesel** (www.diesel.com): a consistently good fit.
• **Miss Sixty** (www.misssixty.com): versatile.

NYLON

394 west broadway
2nd floor
new york, ny 10012
t 212 226 6454 f 212 226 7738
www.nylonmag.com

Hi Gisele,

Sorry this took so long to write but you probably know I've been traveling a bunch.

Was in Sydney hanging out with the Tsubi guys. (one of my favorite denim brands.)

R.E. my first denim memory was getting 3 new pair of Levis 501's for 7th Grade. Used to wear them with surf shirts and sneakers growing up in Florida.

I have always been an anti-authority type person, and I think denim has always had that rebellious DNA to it.
It also stands for individuality and identity.

100 people could wear the exact same pair of jeans, but the way the person wears them i.e. the things they mix with them says a lot about the person.

I have about 5 or 6 hundred pair of jeans now. I just wish there were more days in the year so I could wear them all.

Marvin

ALICE TEMPERLEY

Designer, Alice Temperley, is the ultimate Earth Goddess; she designs the most beautiful, dresses – and the first time I wore one I received loads of compliments. Her vivid use of embroidery and eclectic colours, with clean, fluid lines, helped me look and feel as light and gorgeous as a Degas ballerina. I was dressing-up to spend a magical few days in a big, white tipi from Hearthworks in Glastonbury (see pp274), having been told that I was very lucky Alice Temperley hadn't needed it for her summer party, a few hours away in Somerset. I'd never met Alice but from that moment I had a feeling that, like so many things in my life, one day, because of the dress and the tipi, our paths would cross. Her name cropped up again when Michael Eavis, the man behind Glastonbury festival, told me all about her parents' big, painted cider bus which keeps revelers at the festival going every year with the best cider in the country. I wanted to learn more about her dresses, her love of tipis, and of dressing up for fun on the family farm in Somerset, every summer – and finally, we got to talk…

I love the farm I grew up on Alice and return to it like a migrating bird whenever I get the chance. Do you feel that your rural upbringing has shaped your life? Do you miss it? *Yes I miss it terribly and am doing everything possible to move back to the countryside. I miss the feeling of space, grass, animals, peace and quiet and can't wait for the day that I can spend half of my time back there.*

Do you remember any one piece of clothing from your childhood? *Yes, from the age of three, I was attached to a little fur collar that belonged to my grandmother, and used to insist on wearing it with everything.*

Why did you decide to work in fashion? *Weirdly it was something that happened very quickly. I studied textiles at Central Saint Martins and the Royal College of Art and sold the clothes that I made to support myself through college. Then I made my first wholesale collection and the rest happened very quickly to the point that I am still in shock that I am in the fashion industry.*

There are unwritten rules in fashion about colour; blue and black, for example, are not supposed to be seen together. Do you pay any attention to this? *No, I love wearing navy and black together and have just done a print with blue and green in it. I don't play by the rules…*

Where do you look for inspiration when planning your collections and your home? *My nickname is Magpie because I'm always collecting, collecting, collecting pieces. There is never anything specific – my answer would I guess be from life.*

Why do you like tipis so much? Do yours ever leak in the rain, like mine did that very wet weekend, last summer? Was I doing something wrong?! *I love tipis and have one set up in the country as my summer house. And yes it has rained – almost drowning me once – but the rain-catcher wasn't attached properly; once attached*

properly it is the best home in the world because you could be anywhere.
You love dressing-up, what's the best thing you've ever dressed-up as? *I have a thing about headdresses – my biggest one was a four-foot-high showgirl headdress.*
For everyday dressing, what makes a well-dressed Goddess, in your opinion? *Anything natural, uncontrived, comfortable.*

Favourite smell? Frangipani and Vanilla.
Favourite sound? Trickling rivers for relaxing, Ska music for dancing.
Favourite taste? Vanilla ice cream doused in Kingston Black Aperitif (a blend of Cider Brandy and the juice of one of the finest and rarest of vintage cider apples).
Favourite to your sense of touch? Highest count linen and piles of soft feather duvets.
Favourite colour? Green.
Favourite bird and animal? Hummingbirds and big black bears.
Favourite flower? Sweet pea.
Favourite place? Kenya.
Favourite book? The Catcher in the Rye by J.D. Salinger.
Favourite piece of art? 1920's advertising lithographs.
Favourite possession? Just about to be a big black thunderbird.
If you could have dinner with one person who would it be and what would you ask them? God. Could I have lots of children and could I live forever.

Hummingbird *n* a very small American bird having a brilliant iridescent plumage, long slender bill, and wings specialized for very powerful vibrating flight. *Coll. n* A shimmer of hummingbirds. The smallest bird in the world is generally agreed to be the male Bee hummingbird from Cuba which weighs a mere 1.6 grams or 0.056 ounces.

Alice in her fur collar

Cashmere

Cashmere

My favourite wool of all is cashmere. The word 'cashmere' comes from Kashmiri, the Tibetan name for the Kashmere goat. It comes in different grades, and you usually get what you pay for as the more expensive the item, the longer it will last – and with reduced bobbling. Did you know that it takes four goats to make a single sweater?

Ply

This refers to the number of strands twisted together to achieve a certain thickness. The higher the ply, the more weighty the feel of the material, and the more expensive the garment. Most cashmere comes in one-ply, but two-ply (two strands of yarn twisted together before knitting) is also common.

Caring for cashmere

Before wearing, wrap the garment in a brown paper bag and put it in the freezer for 24 hours as this minimizes pilling. Some cashmere fans swear by hand washing, while others prefer dry-cleaning; experts suggest alternating between the two and either way it is always worth checking the care label of the garment to see what the designer recommends. To hand wash, use lukewarm water and a cashmere shampoo from Brora (see next page). Tocca's Laundry Delicate or Tocca's Delicate Shampoo, available at Pout's flagship store at 32, Shelton Street, Covent Garden, London WC2H 9JE (tel: +44 20 7379 0379 www.pout.co.uk), or a bottle of Woolite should also be part of everyone's cashmere laundry kit. To dry your item, roll it into a sausage shape in a towel. Pat it gently dry, making sure never to wring it, and then take it out of the towel before leaving to dry on a flat surface. Brora's defuzzing comb is also great for getting off bobbles.

Moth *n* any of numerous insects that typically have stout bodies with antennae of various shapes. *Coll. n* a swarm of moths. Almost all moths lay their wings out flat when resting as opposed to butterflies which hold them up over their backs. Moths don't fly towards light, instead they try to fly to the blackest spot which is directly behind it.

Moth holes?

The Cashmere Clinic, 11 Beauchamp Place, London SW3 1NQ (tel: +44 207 5849 806), specializes in invisible mending of moth damage.

Moths

To prevent moths from taking your wardrobe hostage, invest in natural clove, peppermint and sandalwood moth sachets at Cox & Cox (tel: +44 870 442 4787, www.coxandcox.co.uk), or buy lavender balls from The White Company (tel: +44 870 900 9555, www.thewhitecompany.com). A cheaper alternative would be to scatter dried orange peel, horse chestnuts, shredded newspaper or bay leaves near to, but not touching, your garments as moths apparently hate these smells. Remove any old carpet you may have lurking at the back of your wardrobe as moths love to breed in it, and take moth-infested clothes to the dry-cleaners, informing staff so they can remove any larvae. Then thoroughly clean your wardrobe using moth-killing products or have it professionally seen to.

Other popular wools

Angora
From the white Angora rabbit, this is super-soft and flecked with shorter hairs. Often mixed with wool or acrylic this is a great choice for evening knitwear.

Lamb's wool
Shorn from baby sheep, lamb's wool is a particularly comfy, and less scratchy, wool to wear.

Merino
From the backs of sheep bred in Australia and New Zealand, merino wool is very soft because of the climate. It has a smooth surface with little shagginess so is particularly smart for office-wear.

Mohair
From the Angora goat, mohair can grow as long as 10 inches. It has a shaggy look and the hairs have a distinctive sheen.

Knitted prints
For printed cashmere try **Ann Louise Roswald** (tel: +44 207 250 1583, www.annlouiseroswald.com), and also have a look at her beautiful printed coats which are great for weddings.

Beautiful alpaca and musk ox
Christina Oxenberg, available from Browns, London (tel: +44 20 7514 0016), and Barneys and Bloomingdales in New York, makes shawls, scarves, gloves, headbands and hats made from the musk ox, Suri Alpaca, and the Guanaco, of Patagonia.

Light mohair scarf
Jo Gordon (tel: +44 20 7235 5000, www.jogordon.com): for handmade, delicate lace, scarves.

GODDESS TIP
ALWAYS FOLD HEAVY WOOLENS AND HANG FINE GAUGE CASHMERE SWEATERS ON PADDED HANGERS.

Super luxury cashmere shawls
Loro Piana, 153 New Bond Street (tel: +44 2074999300, www.loropiana.com): the Rolls Royce of the cashmere world, Lora Piana's Vicuña shawls have saved the Vicuña from extinction in the Peruvian highlands.

Slinky knitwear
Alex Gore Brown (tel: +44 20 7419 1200, www.alexgorebrown.com): think sexy, slinky separates and dresses, and even knitted swimwear. Alex has also designed pieces for Matthew Williamson and Alexander McQueen.

Blankets
Ballantyne, 153a New Bond Street (tel: +44 20 7493 4718, www.ballantyne-cashmere.co.uk): gorgeous blankets.

Bespoke cashmere
Ballantyne offers a bespoke service that allows you to compose your own jumper by choosing the colours of the diamonds on the front. Alternatively, **Belinda Robertson**, 4 West Halkin Street, London, SW1X 8JA (tel: +44 20 7235 0519, www.belindarobertson.com), offers ready-to-wear plus a bespoke service featuring over 120 different colours. She also offers alterations to body and sleeve lengths for tall or petite customers.

Classic cashmere
Brora, 344 Kings Road, London (tel: +44 20 7352 3697, www.brora.co.uk): the first place you should look for good quality, classic cashmere. They also run a mending service. **Pringle**, 141-142, Sloane Street, London (tel: +44 207 881 3060, www.pringlescotland.com): amazing wooly camis – their 'Pringle Red' label is particularly hip. **Marks & Spencer** (tel: +44 845 302 1234, www.marksandspencer.com): offers a great range of affordable wools and cashmere separates.

Sleek, understated knitwear
Caz, 177 Draycott Avenue, London, SW3 3AJ (tel: +44 20 7589 1920): created by a former Gucci knitwear specialist, this company will 'redress' your cashmere if it's looking a bit shabby and tired – perfect for those Luxurious Goddesses out there.

Everyone wants to wear Narciso Rodriguez. His exquisite clothes combine classic style with a hint of sex whilst paying full homage to the female form. And he has the accolades to prove it: in 1998 he was awarded Best New Designer at the Vogue/VH1 fashion awards and in 2003 Sarah Jessica Parker, well-known for breathing life into his stunning designs, won a Muse award at the same ceremony. To this day, when she needs a dress, chances are SJP calls on the man who came running out to greet me at the front desk of his Irving Street offices in New York, 'Come in. Come in! I can't wait to show you everything'. Relaxed and charming, he was soon sitting on the floor of his studio, comfortably chatting away in the lotus position, as he flicked through his sketch book.

'See those sketches? I did these by the pool... I always do shoes when I'm relaxed and on vacation.' Did he dream up his fragrances by the pool? (I'd been in Manhattan all week and rumour had it that Narciso had hit upon the fragrance world's next big thing: musk oil!) 'When I embarked on the fragrance project,' he explained, 'I gave my perfumers a small vial of the Egyptian musk oil that I myself had been a fan of for 23 years. From that, perfumer Francis Kurkdjian, along with Christine Nagel of Quest International, created an eau de toilette and a perfumed oil.'

Narciso had been wearing the same musk since he was a teenager and had always dreamed of finding a way to evolve it. One year and 862 prototypes later and he had. The result, a sultry, musk-based oil, lightened by notes of orange-blossom, a laboratory-made amberlyn and an oil derived from an Indian grass called vetiver.

He penned me a personal note explaining his first encounter with musk and placed a bottle of the perfumed oil in my hand. 'From me to you, use it sparingly,' he smiled. He watched, as I popped open the bottle and dabbed a little of the oil on the back of my left hand. I was hooked. Put simply, this oil is heaven!

GODDESS TIP
I FIND THAT AFTER A FEW MINUTES OF WEARING THIS OIL, ITS DEEP, SENSUOUS, NOTES SWIRL HEADILY AROUND ME. THIS SCENT ALSO CLINGS TO CASHMERE AND WOOL SO IF YOU WEAR IT REGULARLY ITS DARK SECRETS WILL TUMBLE OUT WHENEVER YOU OPEN YOUR WARDROBE. IT'S MY TRUE WINTER MUST-HAVE.

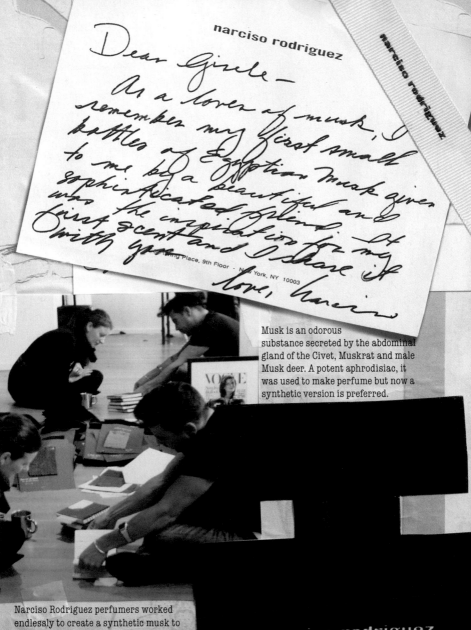

narciso rodriguez

Dear Gisele —

As a lover of musk, I remember my first small bottles of Egyptian musk given to me by a beautiful and sophisticated friend. It was the inspiration for my first scent and I share it with you.

love, narciso

...Place, 9th Floor - New York, NY 10003

narciso rodriguez

Musk is an odorous substance secreted by the abdominal gland of the Civet, Muskrat and male Musk deer. A potent aphrodisiac, it was used to make perfume but now a synthetic version is preferred.

Narciso Rodriguez perfumers worked endlessly to create a synthetic musk to form the basis of his oil and perfume. Their musk is every bit as heady as the naturally occurring kind.

narciso rodriguez

musc
for her

57

Narciso's Goddess Tips

After a few hours of talking I learned that Narciso Rodriguez believes that a Goddess should be first and foremost extremely sensitive towards practicality. He claims that 'whether you have to look sexy to impress a guy or luxurious to appear more alluring, keep in mind that what you're wearing should always remain functional. Buy styles that will last. Avoid anything that seems entirely over-the-top and be comfortable.'

So what should I be investing in for daywear? *1. Low-waisted cotton pants; you can dress them up or down. 2. A chiffon, airy, silk top – very feminine over trousers. 3. A tailored skirt. 4. A figure hugging shirt. 5. A tailored pants suit. Dress it up with the sexy figure hugging shirt. 6. A coat, a pair of leather boots and a leather bag.*

And for the evening? *A black dress – teamed with high courts for luxury, and sandals for sex. A velvet pant suit with high shoes and a daring piece of jewellery. Keep all of your overtly sexy pieces for wild parties, not classy affairs.*

Any fast tracks to sartorial success? *A good bra. A well fitting bra is an instant way to a more proportioned figure. Have one in black, one in white and one in a nude colour as a basic fashion foundation.*

What's New York City glamour all about then? *The clothes don't count without the confidence. It's a package. When a woman feels secure she can light up a whole room. That's sexy!*

I can't sleep the night if I don't have enough of this in the house for the morning.

Narciso is kind humble and warm. He understands the real essence of a Goddess.

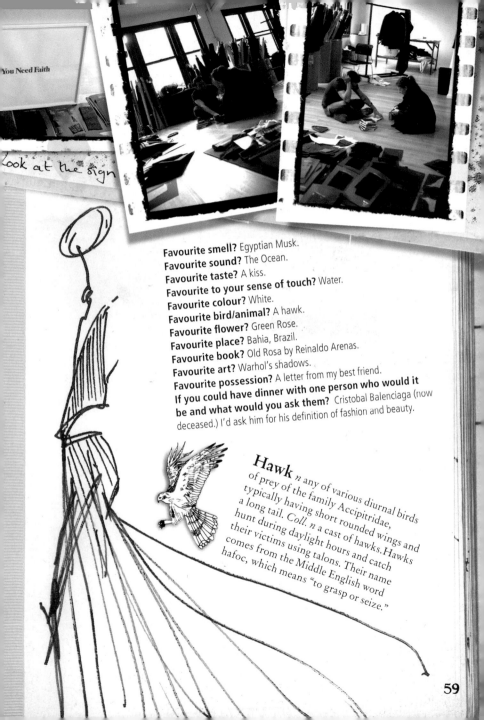

You Need Faith

Look at the sign

Favourite smell? Egyptian Musk.
Favourite sound? The Ocean.
Favourite taste? A kiss.
Favourite to your sense of touch? Water.
Favourite colour? White.
Favourite bird/animal? A hawk.
Favourite flower? Green Rose.
Favourite place? Bahia, Brazil.
Favourite book? Old Rosa by Reinaldo Arenas.
Favourite art? Warhol's shadows.
Favourite possession? A letter from my best friend.
If you could have dinner with one person who would it
be and what would you ask them? Cristobal Balenciaga (now
deceased.) I'd ask him for his definition of fashion and beauty.

Hawk *n* any of various diurnal birds of prey of the family Accipitridae, typically having short rounded wings and a long tail. *Coll. n* a cast of hawks. Hawks hunt during daylight hours and catch their victims using talons. Their name comes from the Middle English word hafoc, which means "to grasp or seize."

SUITS

In an industry where you're judged on how 'smart' or polished you look it's imperative that you wear a well-tailored suit.

BUYING A SUIT

Lining
The most important thing to check is the lining. If it's pulled too tight, your jacket will pucker; too loose and it'll make you look bulky and add unnecessary pounds.

Fabric
Wool is by far the best fabric to invest in. Check the label for wool that is mixed with 3 or 4 per cent elastin as this allows a little give.

FITTING

Sleeves
Check the sleeve length last when you're trying on a jacket. On well-made jackets the buttonholes on the sleeves are sewn together, so that your tailor can adjust the sleeves if they're too long – a relatively easy job. If the sleeves are perfect (just touching the wrist bone), then slit the buttonholes carefully yourself and tie the buttons.

Vents
The vents, which are splits at the bottom of the back of the jacket, should lie flat against the backside. If they are spreading and straining, it means the jacket is just too small.

Trousers
Trouser hems should be left slightly longer at the back than the front to allow for the slope of your heels. Bring the shoes you intend to wear with your trousers to the alterations shop so that they measure you just right. Alternatively, have a friend pin the hems for you and take them up yourself.

I want to look really slim and tall

Shoulders
The shoulders must fit. If you're carrying weight on your upper arms, don't squeeze into a size that hugs the arms tightly and is restrictive around the shoulders. Instead, make sure the shoulders are comfortable (not tight) as you can always have the sleeve width altered if it's too wide.

SUIT YOUR SHAPE

Busty

Shirts

When was the last time you were fitted for a bra (see pp34)? Dark tops instantly disguise a large bust so swap the white shirt for a darker colour. Avoid polo necks and T-shirts except those with boat or scoop necks, which draw attention to the collarbones. A V-neck sweater (not dipping into your cleavage) will also camouflage the girls.

Jackets

Choose single-breasted with slim lapels and buy in a dark colour with a bright thin pinstripe and bright lining. Add a dark shirt underneath and the suit stripe will give the illusion of height while the dark shirt inside will make your bust look thinner.

Dresses

Try a wrap dress. It'll accentuate your waist and, by placing a beautiful brooch on the collarbone area, you can draw attention away from your boobs.

If you're short

Wearing one colour top to bottom will make you look taller and more streamlined. If you wear different colours on top and bottom, it cuts your body in half.

Skirts

Choose knee-length, or just above the knee if you've got good knees. Mid-calf skirts are a no-no – they'll shorten your legs and swamp you.

Trousers

If worn a tiny bit too long so that they graze the office carpet, they'll make your legs appear much longer.

Very tall

Suits

Try and mix colours to break up your tall proportions. Only wearing one colour will further emphasize your height. Opt for a blouse or shirt that has a three-quarter length sleeve and load your beautiful long arms with expensive bracelets and a chunky watch.

Trousers

Ensure that shorter styles of trousers don't make you look like your clothes have shrunk in the wash.

Skirts

A-line skirts ending just below the knee look great.

Jackets

Always make sure sleeves are long enough. Three-quarter length on a jacket can look as if it's too small.

Pear-shaped

Jackets

Choose a jacket or a knee-length coat with good tailoring around the waist. Wear a fitted top inside it which just skims the top of your hips and this will instantly slim you from the front, while a long coat will camouflage a big behind and large hips.

Trousers

Avoid straight-leg or tapered trousers as they make your hips look even bigger. Opt for boot-cut or a slight flared leg instead.

Skirts

A-line skirt shapes are your best friend, as they nip in your waist while slimming down your hips.

Where to look

When it comes to tailoring, the more you spend the better the result.

Stella McCartney, Alexander McQueen and **Chloé** cut a mean pair of trousers.

New York design duo **Proenza Schouler** at Harvey Nichols does a great pinstripe trouser.

Alexander McQueen cuts the best jackets – however, they look best on thin girls.

All department stores and most high street outlets feature affordable tailoring.

DOLCE & GABBANA

There should be a picture of Dolce & Gabbana printed next to the word 'sexy' in the dictionary. They are inspired by three things: life, a woman's curves and Goddesses Anna Magnani, Sophia Loren and Madonna.

Domenico Dolce, left, and Stefano Gabbana, right.

Photo: Mariano Vivanco

I love my Dolce & Gabbana dress and tights. Don't they look fab?

They tell me that they first met while sitting opposite each other in a design studio in the early Eighties and that they launched their own label in 1985. Since then they've gained a worldwide reputation for creating gutsy, voluptuous clothes, and my own Dolce & Gabbana pieces are no exception: one of their signature corset dresses – a heavily boned number, that hooks up like a bra all the way up your back – and a black lace dress and deep purple slip that ties at the back of the neck with a leather strap. Both are serious entrance enhancers and have garnered me huge compliments at parties over the last few years.

I've seen first hand why the entertainment community turn to Dolce & Gabbana for wow-factor so I wondered what their take on red carpet dressing was.

Does black-tie mean black dress? *No, if invited to a black-tie event, you can really wear any colour. Rich, red carpet colours like burgundy, emerald green or royal blue, in satin or velvet, are beautiful and sequins and lace work well at any time. The main thing is that you wear whichever dress you choose with confidence!*

You dress so many A-listers. What should all women keep in mind when dressing up? *Women and men should always interpret clothes according to their style, be ironic and self-confident and let clothes take a supporting role to their personality. A dress should never look like its overpowering the wearer.*

What's the story with showing some cleavage? *Choose a beautiful dress and carry it with confidence. We have always been faithful to our roots and to our inspiration: we are Mediterranean, we love sensual ironic fashion and that always includes cleavage.*

What if you lack the curves or confidence to wear a very sexy dress? *There are many ways to be sexy – a masculine suit worn with a Swarovski top or a corset, for example. Pieces with Swarovski always work as they catch the light and draw attention to your face. What matters most is your confidence.*

(Dolce & Gabbana, June 2006)

How do I care for my beautiful Dolce & Gabbana dress?
Apply products (hairspray, make-up, perfume) before getting dressed and allow time for them to dry, as products ruin silk, satin, lace and velvet. To fix a wrinkle suspend the item, away from a wall, in a steamy bathroom for a few minutes. Remember to remove it promptly though as excess condensation can cause some materials to dull. Never use a hot iron and be wary of big, clawed rings or pendants as they snag material easily.

I like nothing more than lounging around at home or relaxing in a hotel room in my civvies. When an occasion arises however, it does take a bit of planning and effort to get that Goddess look right. Backless dresses, tummy hugging skirts and stray boobies have all caused me bother at one time or another; these little Goddess tips sort me out every single time.

How to go backless...

If you're wearing a backless dress or top, there are several different options for supporting your bust, depending on its size. For smaller busts, Hollywood Fashion tape from www.austique.co.uk or Reveal & Hold double-sided tape by Myla (tel: +44 870 745 5003, www.myla.co.uk), sticks to both fabric and skin without harming either. Start by applying it sparingly around the sides of your boobs, slowly taping your top all the way up your body to secure it. The tape comes as part of a kit which also contains bra extenders, four pairs of nipple covers, a pair of cleavage enhancers and a self-adhesive backless and strapless bra. Valisere's Arinna nude satin body (tel: +44 1793 720232, www.valisere.com), is also another good strapless-look option for small boobs, with straps that convert to allow it to be used as a halterneck, a crossback, or there's a clear strap alternative for the backless look. If you're an A or B cup, then Magicup press-on by Braza at Rigby & Peller (tel: +44 20 7491 220, www.rigbyandpeller.com), provides medium support. Or try Fashion Forms' divine NuBra Ultralite adhesive backless bra with front clasp available from the US (tel: +1 888 530 2727, www.lingeriesolutions.com). You position the cups in place and clip them together; it lasts for about 100 washes.

Alternatively, if you're a D Cup or over, have a good dressmaker sew an underwire bra into the front of your dress or look for a dress with a corseted front and tons of boning. Do not let your boobs loose in silk or chiffon if they're anything over a B cup. Promise?

VBS (visible bra straps)

Ban unsightly bra straps with OnGossamer's Satin Zip-It-Up Racerback bra, available at www.galapagosboutique.com. This underwire bra is amazing and offers full support while allowing you to zip the straps together at the back so that they disappear under a tank or vest with either a T, U or V-back.

If you own a bra you're happy with, and wish to go strapless, add a set of comfy detachable straps from www.femalefirst.co.uk. Otherwise, the 'sticky' seams of the Halo Lace Convertible Strapless bra from Wacoal (tel: +44 20 7629 9161), and at Harrods, will ensure you remain successfully strapless, without bulging out of your bra cups. Spanx® strapless cami, available at www.mytights.com, is excellent at holding in your boobs and sucking in your tummy. And if your dress is silk, jersey or bias-cut, it'll spotlight the tiniest dimples so slip on a Cosabella Bella Shaper from www.freshpair.com, which slims the body from the ribcage down.

Breathe in!

If your tummy's a little bloated in your trousers try Floxees nude control thong (tel: +44 870 4999 002, www.figleaves.com). Otherwise, go the whole hog and get Spanx black Power Panties at Rigby & Peller (see pp64). A tight pencil skirt calls for a stomach, hip and thigh-slimmer. Spanx® Hide & Sleek half slip from www.figleaves.co.uk is a must. For trousers, Magic Knickers (tel: +44 20 7371 0276, www.practicalprincess.net), will lift south-spreading buttocks with their strategic support panels. Up top choose a balconette bra if you're wearing a scoop neck, and a wonder-bra or plunge bra if you're wearing a V-neck sweater (see pp35). Under a miniskirt a pair of Calvin Klein lycra-fortified boy shorts from www.cku.com will minimize bulges around the stomach and lift your ass.

Hide those nips

If you're small-breasted, buy Nippits' nipple concealment strips at www.galapagosboutique.com or cut your own from strips of skin-coloured plaster bandage to hide your nipples. For something a little more modest, pick up a vest in a nude colour from Bodas (tel: +44 20 7229 4464, www.bodas.co.uk), or if you're large-breasted Bodas also make a mesh bra in a shade which blends right into the skin.

Bolder holders

The Miracle Frontless body from Ultimo (tel: +44 845 130 3232, www.ultimo.com), is a great investment as the straps can be worn five different ways. It's good for light to medium hold, but for bigger boobs the diamanté front bra from Splendour (tel: +44 20 8964 7820, www.splendour.com), is better.

GODDESS TIP

STAND IN FRONT OF THE MIRROR AND ENSURE THAT YOUR OUTFIT PROVIDES THE NECESSARY COVERAGE. CHECK UNDER THE ARMS (SIDE CLEAVAGE IS A GODDESS'S ENEMY). FOR AN OCCASION, HAVE A TAN DONE A FEW DAYS BEFORE AND POLISH OFF YOUR SKIN TONE WITH YOUR FAVOURITE TRANSFER-RESISTANT FOUNDATION.

TINY COVER-UPS

I've ruined many a shawl by accidentally dipping them into and drinks and sauces at parties. Finally, I've realised that there are a lot of advantages to wearing small wraps and capes; they keep me warm without requiring adjusting, and they leave my hands free so that I can get my groove on. Capetastic!

I want a tailored cover-up!

Bolero
The bolero is the most tailored of all the little cover-ups – it's like a tiny cardigan really. Buy in sequined fabric for the festive season or in velvet or cashmere for the rest of the year.

I'm looking for a glitzy show-stopper!

Capelet
If you invest in a loose, sequined capelet it will lift your outfit as dramatically as a large piece of sparkly, expensive jewellery. Slip a sequined capelet over a bias-cut evening dress for that glitzy bash.

What will show off my great boobs?

Shrug
Shrugs have sleeves for you to thread your arms through and fasten at the collar thereby revealing the chest area. Consider fur, faux fur or naturally moulted marabou feather shrugs at www.wonderfulwraps.com for formal events.

Marabou *n* a bird which is the largest of the stork family genus Leptoptilos which scavenges for carrion and has a soft white down on its underside. *Coll. n* a mustering of storks. Although thought to be quite ugly, with their long dangly pink neck pouch, the down on the underside of these birds was once used to make and trim many vintage shrugs and stoles. The storks which bring babies on postcards are a different species entirely. The story of the baby-bringing stork is thought to have originated in Holland in the 1800's. It was said that if a stork built its nest on your house, you were more likely to be blessed with children – and so the tradition began.

Stole

Stoles are the best value of all little cover-ups as they're so versatile and can be worn with/over anything: from jeans and a long sleeved top to a halterneck dress (remember a necklace will disappear under a stole so you can save the price of it and buy some chandelier earrings and a bag instead).

Eco Evening Shawls

If you're considering buying a shawl then the most beautiful are from Argentinian model turned designer Cecilia De Bucourt www.ceciliadebucourt.com. Way back her signature colourful silk shawl was bought in Barney's New York for $200 by Jessica Simpson and worn on Newlyweds on MTV. The pop star created an economic mini-boom in Florencio Verela, just outside Buenos Aires where local ladies crochet and hand dye the shawls for the Cecilia De Bucourt label. You can still order one on the website or by calling New York on (tel: +1 212-564 9738) and while you're at it try to bag one of her limited edition Eskimo scarves.

Eco Day wear shawls

For day wear shawls with a conscience People Tree's mail order catalogue and website (tel: +44 20 7739 0660, www.peopletree.co.uk) offers a dusky pink shawl handknitted in Nepal. The small communities who produce the website's alpaca jumpers, embroidered bags and pretty jewellery use traditional skills and methods and all receive a fair wage.

Four ways to wear a silver sequined waistcoat

The silver sequin waistcoat is the ultimate party accessory. During the day, wear with a t-shirt and skinny jeans or a pencil skirt and a chiffon camisole. For evening, team it with a boho dress and boots for dinner or a dress and pin stilettos for an ultra-trash glam look.

Remember, keep accessories to a minimum with a sequined waistcoat as it's sparkly enough already without adding extra wattage.

VINTAGE

The case of the illusive luggage!

Vintage clothing and luggage has soul and trying to guess a piece's past makes the chase all the more exciting. I've been hunting for the right Louis Vuitton vintage wardrobe trunk for years. Unfortunately my champagne taste buds cannot be satisfied on a lemonade budget...

The auction (ouch!)

The first Louis Vuitton trunk I wanted belonged to Katharine Hepburn and was up for auction at Sotheby's in New York on 10 May 2004. I flew out from Dublin to bid for it specially (lot 36). Among my favourite items also on offer was a telegram dated 12 May 1907 announcing her arrival into the world to her great uncle (lot 1) and her Smythson address books, with entries including Laurence Olivier and Vivien Leigh (lot 254, which went for $9,000). My trunk eventually sold for $4,500. Outbid, I set my sights on a wooden painting board (lot 247) which she used as a desk while she sketched and painted. It was made out of the top of a wooden airmail box from a movie studio with a handwritten return address, and also affixed to it was an address label from the wardrobe department at Lowe's Inc Metro-Goldwyn-Mayer Pictures with Miss Hepburn's address typed in. How I would have loved to have had this as part of my doodle kit, to do my sketches and embroidery and crafts on. Anyway, it wasn't to be: it sold for way more than I could afford and I consoled myself with a cocktail on the way home. It is so easy to get caught up in a bidding frenzy. I set a budget and didn't budge. I know I lost out on all the items that I wanted, but I got a real sense of Katharine Hepburn's style and taste by sitting in on the two auction days in New York. Anyway, if you buy something very expensive you have to insure it for ten per cent of its value. In fact some of the world's most expensive paintings, silver-wear and diamonds lie in vaults because they are too expensive to have in the house.

What to look for

If you're into bags and luggage – I am, and how – invest in vintage crocodile, ostrich, alligator and lizard framed 1950s styles from Linda Bee at Grays Antique Market (see pp70). Otherwise keep your eyes peeled for designers like Hermes, Chanel, Dior, Gucci and Louis Vuitton. The Louis Vuitton 'Speedy' 1959 shape was created in 1930, the monogram in 1886. The coated canvas which launched in 1959 made it a classic. Also look for Vuitton luggage. the Hermès Birkin, like the Kelly bag that came before it, acquired its name from a film star. These are also highly collectable if in good condition. The padded Chanel 2.55 Quilted Classic débuted in February 1955, it will always be valuable and a good vintage find can be stunning (see "It bags" pp26).

Dear Santa,

I know I already own a few (ahem) designer bags, but could you please see if the elves are planning on delivering that hand-crafted vintage Louis Vuitton wardrobe trunk I asked for a few years back? Oh and please could you remember, the darker and bigger, the better – at airports it'll make me look thinner. Thanks

Hugs + kisses

Speedy Bag

Flea markets

Prices are low, which means you'll have to compete with dealers. Haggle to knock the price down and try and get a ten per cent discount. Sometimes on a slow day bargains can be had at the end.

GODDESS TIP

CHARITY SHOPS IN THE POSHEST AREAS IN EACH CITY CAN HOLD REALLY GREAT VINTAGE FINDS.

MARKETS
VINTAGE
G-SPOTS

Indoor vintage shops and markets
I favour second hand Vuitton trunks over new ones.
Try: Appleby, 95 Westbourne Park Villas, London, W2 5ED (tel: +44 20 7229 7772) and Bentleys, 204 Walton Street, London SW3 2JL (tel: +44 20 7584 7770, www.bentleyslondon.com).

Chanel, Gucci and Dior handbags, 1930-1970s clothing and couture and Gucci shades circa 1965. Try: One of a Kind, 253 Portobello Road, London W11 (tel: +44 20 7792 5284). The vast wall of Polaroids in the store bears testimony to the fact that stars make a beeline for this vintage treasure-trove in their hundreds.

1930-1980s, including Pucci, Ossie Clark, Jean Muir, Biba and classic Westwood. Try: Rellik, 8 Golborne Road, London W10 5NW (tel: +44 20 8962 0089), and Steinberg & Tolkien, 193 Kings Road, SW3 5ED (tel:+44 020 7376 3660).

1930-1970s clothing and jewellery. Try: Virginia, 98 Portland Road, London W11 4LQ (tel: +44 20 7727 9908).

Antiques, vintage clothing, costume jewellery 1880-1980s, cameos and Victorian jet. Try: Alfies Antique Market, 13-25 Church St, London, NW8 (tel: + 44 20 7723 6066, www.alfiesantiques.com). Tin Tin Collectables, for amazing vintaget finds, Unit G38 (tel: +44 20 7258 1305, www.tintincollectables.net).

Georgian jewels, Schiaparelli, and fashion from 1940-1960s, bags, antiques and books. Try: Grays Antique Market, 58 Davies St and 1-7 Davies Mews, London, W1 (tel: +44 20 7493 9344, www.graysantiques.com), see Beverly R's for jewellery and Linda Bee (tel: +44 20 7629 5921) for bags. And just around the corner…

Vintage clothing, Art Deco and Edwardian paste and Victorian jet jewellery and handbags. Try: Butler & Wilson (www.butlerandwilson.co.uk), 20 South Molton Street, London, W1 (tel: +44 20 7409 2955) and 189 Fulham Rd, London, SW3 (tel: +44 20 7352 3045).

The Royal Borough of Kensington
and Chelsea
PORTOBELLO
70 ROAD

Outdoor vintage markets

The markets at Bermondsey (Fridays), Portobello (Saturdays), and Camden Passage (Wednesdays and Saturdays) are the best for one-off vintage pieces.

Victoriana and the odd one-of-a-kind finds

Dealers and those in the know visit Bermondsey market most Fridays so get there early before they do and there will be more stock to choose from. This is the best market in London for finding really beautiful pieces for you to squirrel away for that special occasion. Bermondsey Market, Bermondsey Sq, SE1 (tel: +44 20 7525 6000). Visit: Friday, 4 a.m.-2 p.m.

Cameos, costume 1900-1980s, British designer and filigree jewellery, lace, cutlery, clothing.

Try: Portobello Road Market, Portobello Road, W11 (tel: +44 20 7341 5277 or go to www.portobelloroad.co.uk). Visit: Saturday, 5 a.m.-4 p.m. (summer till 8 p.m.).

Antiques and an Aladdin's cave of jewels and vintage clothing.

Try: Camden Passage and Pierrepont Arcade, London, N1 (tel: +44 20 7359 0190). Visit: Wednesday and Saturday, 7.30 a.m.-4 p.m.

Vintage online

As well as eBay, check out these specialist vintage sites that offer superb-quality vintage goods. Most auction houses also allow you to place a bid for a lot on the internet. In this case, I always prefer to examine the lot carefully first.

www.corsetsandcrinolines.com
www.dandelion-vintage.com
www.fireflyvintage.com
www.heyviv.com
www.poshgirlvintage.com
www.rustyzipper.com
www.thecostumestore.co.uk
www.vintagebag.com
www.vintagetrends.com
www.beyondretro.com

Wasp *n* a social insect, having a black and yellow body and an ovipositor specialized for stinging and two pairs of membranous wings. *Coll. n* a nest of wasps. Only female wasps have a sting. If you get stung, remove the sting carefully and apply white vinegar, or pickle juice to the affected area. If a wasp-waisted dress won't fit you, it's because vintage sizes are really tiny.

GODDESS TIP
NEVER BUY ANYTHING WITH SWEAT MARKS ON IT, OR THAT HAS RIPPED SEAMS OR ANY SPOTS OF MILDEW, AS NO CLEANER CAN EVER FIX THESE. ALSO, IF A SWEATER OR DRESS HAS A LOT OF MOTH HOLES IN IT, BE CAREFUL NOT TO INTRODUCE IT INTO YOUR HOUSE OR YOUR WARDROBE UNTIL YOU'VE SENT IT TO THE DRYCLEANER'S FIRST. HIDDEN LARVAE COULD INFEST YOUR WHOLE WARDROBE, AND IT TAKES LOADS OF TIME AND MONEY TO GET THEM OUT.

Schiaparelli

VIRGINIA
ANTIQUES
Portland Road
W11

Click Chic

Buying online

The thing I love about shopping online? I can do it in bed (just like reading), and you can't get more luxurious than sitting in bed with a nice cup of tea and a few hours on www.net-a-porter.com. My daily addictions are www.eyestorm.com to have a look at nice art and www.pineidershop.com for paper. (I created the original pages for my book using their Vaticano cotton range. It's said to be the smoothest writing paper in the world and if it's good enough for the Pope, well, then it's good enough for *The Goddess Guide*.)

If I decide to buy designer clothing, I'll check the fit in the shops first. Then I visit an internet café to see if I can find the item at a better price or in a rarer colour and sometimes I compare the price on www.kelkoo.co.uk. When I finally decide to make my purchase, I head for home, have a bath, potter around a bit, make some tea and only then am I ready to buy. I've made fewer mistakes this way, weighing up the pros and cons of a piece of clothing while soaking in the bath or cooking. Sometimes I end up just consoling myself with a top from www.topshop.co.uk, a book from www.amazon.com or a new pen for my doodles from www.euroffice.co.uk.

If you're totally in love with a piece from an American site but they refuse to ship to your country, don't worry: www.americangoodies.com will act as an intermediary service. They receive your goods then forward them on to you – it can be expensive, however.

Should I buy a fake?

I've just two words when it comes to fake handbags and luggage: badly made. Personally, I think it's a much better investment to buy vintage from thrift stores and charity shops. If you think a bag might be fake, log on to www.mypoupette.com. This online community of devoted Louis Vuitton buyers and sellers shares information and personal stories about buying new, vintage, thrift and the nasty fakes.

How to spot a fake

Online

Do your research: Study your item closely on the brand's official website and know its characteristics. Fakers skimp on leather, labour and often get proportions wrong (is a bag too tall, too deep or too long?). The most telling sign of all is uneven handles (one slightly above the other) or handles that are just too big for the body of the bag. Also look at the logos – a sure sign of a fake Louis Vuitton bag is if the logos run into the stitching at the sides.

Proof of purchase: Ask to pay using Paypal online and judge the reaction...

In the stores

Location, location, location: If the 'store' is based somewhere like Canal Street, New York and has a corrugated shutter as a door, chances are ten out of ten times you're looking at fakes. If the store is more boutiquey, though...

Stitching: Check that the stitching on the outside and in the lining is even, not frayed, and that stitches aren't lumped over each other and messy.

Leather: Smell it – if it smells a bit 'strong' it could be made from substandard leather. Squeeze it to see that it's soft.

Logos, zips and labels: Are the logos exactly like the brand's official website? Does the label have the correct spelling and is it stitched on, not glued? Zips should run smoothly and not be stiff and sticky.

Trust your Goddess instinct: If your gut is telling you that there's something not quite right, walk away.

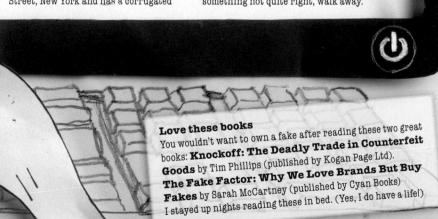

Love these books
You wouldn't want to own a fake after reading these two great books: **Knockoff: The Deadly Trade in Counterfeit Goods** by Tim Phillips (published by Kogan Page Ltd). **The Fake Factor: Why We Love Brands But Buy Fakes** by Sarah McCartney (published by Cyan Books) I stayed up nights reading these in bed. (Yes, I do have a life!)

For months Irish banks had laughed at my feeble requests for a 'building work' loan; apparently my teeth did not qualify in the 'home improvements of a sound, stable kind' category. There had to be a quick (legal) way to raise the amount of money ($38,000) I needed; the answer lay hidden in my wardrobe at home...

Having worked in fashion for years I'd compiled a wardrobe of pretty cool designer items. So, convinced that this really was the only way to pay for my new teeth, I pitched the idea to some friends. They were pretty shocked and looked at me in horror as if to say, 'Are you really so desperate you'd actually sell your own clothes?' In truth, I had no other option, were they going to give me 40 grand?

I decided to stick to a strict selling schedule and gave myself a month with ebay. I shot each item on beautiful hangers paying particular attention to labels and any other distinguishing features which might ensure they stood out from the crowd. Next, I trawled magazines for celebrity pictures so I could quote which issues the items had appeared in – and on whom. I wrote a clear, one hundred word description of every piece, including all American, European and UK sizes. I also checked for similar items on ebay so that mine wouldn't be going up against anything too similar.

There were the Louis Vuitton check-print shoes and Chloé coats and dresses, as worn by Madonna, by the score; Gucci boots, a Jean Paul Gaultier top, and my magical bottom-shrinking, leg-lengthening jeans by Helmut Lang: 'Come on, baby, I told myself, biting my nails to ribbons, you can do it! Your teeth are all wonky, you just need to let go!'

The first day I'd eighty new emails with questions, ranging from 'What is the size for this boot in US sizing?', to 'Did Britney Spears really wear your dress?'. The strangest came from Idaho: 'Does this mean I can sponsor one of your new teeth?'; and the most honest, from Milan: 'Would your stretchy Jean Paul Gaultier top suit me? I'm a really fit gay guy?'. My response seemed to be the answer he was looking for: 'Fits all sizes. Looks great on me. Was borrowed on several nights by my best gay buddy and always got him hot male action. You really need to have this, so bid high and bid now!'

As items were sold, I started having nightmares about losing my identity, of having huge, horsey teeth and no stylish clothes. I changed outfits about six times a day, trying everything on before it left me. Eventually I parted company with my stylish hoard though I did manage to hold onto a few favourites; my Fendi bags, my Miu Miu coat and my (priceless) Christian Louboutin shoes.

Some of the items I sold: Gucci brown leather trousers ($730) to a 19-year-old LA rich kid; Gucci bondage boots ($500) to a doctor in New York; Chloé cream dress ($640) to a paralegal in Texas; Gucci purple dress (€460) to a husband for his wife in Hamburg; Chloé jacket with metal bat detail ($2,800) to a lady in Michigan who collects bat ephemera (riiiight!); Marni wool dress ($730) to a club promoter in New York; Dries Van Noten shawl (€460) to an artist in Rome; Dries Van Noten cotton dress ($200) to a stylist in Florence and a Diane von Furstenberg wrap dress (£255) to a teacher in Leeds.

And the one I didn't… a Hobo Gucci handbag to a drag Queen in Barcelona named Romey – and to this day I've never been paid. Bitch!

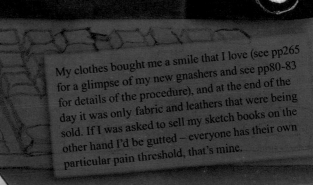

My clothes bought me a smile that I love (see pp265 for a glimpse of my new gnashers and see pp80-83 for details of the procedure), and at the end of the day it was only fabric and leathers that were being sold. If I was asked to sell my sketch books on the other hand I'd be gutted – everyone has their own particular pain threshold, that's mine.

Kathryn Greig Bags

Kathryn Greig's brilliant new handbag range shows her passion and artistic brilliance simultaneously at play. It was quite appropriate therefore that we first met, quite by accident, while I was shopping for an antique paint box at Linda Bee's store at Grays Antiques Market in Mayfair. Having left Tracey Emin's studio the day before, totally inspired by her work and her set-up, I'd promised myself something to store my watercolours and inks in at home and the Winsor & Newton box sitting in Linda Bee's window was perfect. I asked Kathryn Greig (at the time a fellow shopper and complete stranger), for a second opinion on a further purchase – a crocodile clutch in chocolate brown. She was so utterly charming and charismatic that, within ten minutes, not only had she persuaded me to take her advice and purchase the vintage handbag but I was pouring over the drawings and plans for her own collection of handbags, due to launch this year.

She explained to me how her bags would be fashioned from the hair of horses' tails – a material more traditionally associated with upholstery and mattresses. The hair is sourced from horses in Siberia and Mongolia used for agricultural purposes, whose tales would be docked anyway so as not to get tangled in the farm equipment. This method of traditional farming is still widely practiced in these countries and Kathryn emphasized that the horses do not suffer in any way – their tails grow back and in any case are not really needed to swish away insects or keep cool, due to the coldness of the climate where they come from.

The horsehair is dressed and woven by ladies who come in from the fields to prepare it, before being shipped to Florence where Kathryn works with second and third generation handbag manufacturers. The results are stunning! Created using a colour palette that runs from the deepest violet to the most sumptuous silver, it is only a matter of time before the beautifully crafted 'Spring Roll', inspired by her move as a young teenager from a small town in Texas to China, will be the 'It' evening bag for those who respect artisan craftsmanship and artistic passion.

Can you remember your first ever handbag, Kathryn? *A bag purchased with my own pocket money as a little girl at Disneyland. The bag had an image of Mickey and Minnie Mouse holding hands. The bag I was most proud of was my first Gucci, bought in Hong Kong at sixteen; only to learn later that it was a fake.*

You say you drew your colour inspiration from the paintings by David Hockney. Could you explain a little about that? *I often wish when looking at one of his paintings that his colours would suddenly begin to run down off the canvas so that I could quickly sponge them up and use them again as dyes for my horsehair fabrics.*

How long did it take you to find these Mongolian horses? *A year's search for the Mongolian horses and then journeys back and forth to China and Italy where I found the right manufacturers willing to work with this rare fabric.*

What do you feel that your bags have that's different to others? *The use of horsehair fabric is rare as is my desire to dye the fabrics in colours that have never been attempted before. I would like to bring the use of horsehair to a new generation and audience who may be unfamiliar with such a beautiful and useful fabric.*

How would one care for horsehair? *Horsehair is very durable. Just lightly brush the fabric with a soft bristled brush or use a slightly damp cloth to clean the surface.*

Favourite smell? Peat fires and magnolias.
Favourite sound? My children playing 'Twinkle Twinkle Little Star' during their Suzuki Violin Lessons.
Favourite taste? Spicy Chinese Food.
Favourite to your sense of touch? The soft nape of the neck of my three young children, twins Octavia and Monica, and son Jasper.
Favourite colour? All shades of green.
Favourite bird? Dove.
Favourite flower? Peonies.
Favourite place? Winter in Kenya, summer in Scotland, spring in Texas for the Blue Bonnets and fall on the Grand Canal in Venice and nothing beats Christmas shopping in NYC.
Favourite book? Kazuo Ishiguro's The Remains of the Day, Alice in Wonderland and Out of Africa are all books that provide strong visual images and a sense of place. Also big art and interior design coffee table books.
If you could have dinner with anybody who would it be and what would you ask them? I much prefer dinner parties. My dream dinner party guests would be Peggy Guggenheim, Samuel Beckett, Rosencrantz and Guildenstern, 50 Cent, my husband Geordie Greig, Lucian Fraud and Bill and Melinda Gates and I would just let the wine and conversation flow.

For details of collection see www.kathryngreig.co.uk

Portrait of Kathryn and Geordie Greig, by David Hockney.

2 BEAUTY

A hint of Chanel No. 5, the sweet, soapy-scented dust as she dips her white powder puff into the peach coloured face powder, piled high in the ageing black Max Factor box. Escaped particles dance about in the shafts of light streaming through the tiny window frames. She looked like a Princess to me, my Mum, her milky-white ponytail perfected by a spritz of saccharine Elnett. This image of my mother and my memory of her make-up has held a special place inside me for decades. I'd sit on her bed, drawing and yapping away, while she carefully groomed and preened. Ever since I can remember I've tried to emulate her delicate femininity, her dainty way with powder and paint, but as a child I felt unnatural, and even more so as a teenager – the outdoor elements mocking my experiments with mascara, lipstick and blush. Instead Vaseline became my make-up staple; after all what more could a little Goddess need to keep lips and hands from cracking, while riding out her spirited Palomino gelding.

As a teenager, I also wished my hair was more like my mothers – straight and a brilliant white like the tail on my sister's pony, Snowball. I dreamed of having it attached to my own head but by that age my hair had turned a yucky mousey colour which I toyed with the idea of changing daily. The choices were limited: my parents deemed 14 year olds too young for permanent hair dye so it was either brunette from a box or illegal peroxide blonde – like the pictures of Annie Lennox and Blondie that hung on my bedroom wall. Friends helpfully suggested loo cleaner, pure peroxide or 'Sun In' but they also warned me of the hassle of roots. No, brunette seemed the safer option. I hatched a plan to 'borrow' a packet of brunette dye from my Granny Noonie's shop in Tralee –where we'd go to visit for a few weeks each summer. My mind was secretly made up: by September – and my return to school – I'd be a ravishing brunette.

It was a hot July morning and with the dye smuggled successfully out from behind the shop counter, I went with confidence (and a picture of Madonna, from *Just 17* magazine), into my grandmother's cream bathroom. I read the instructions on the packet, then wet my hair and drowned it, and the walls, in dark brown dye; the bathroom looked like somebody had exploded in there – why had none of my friends warned me? After a quick scrubbing of the walls I towel-dried my new hair and positioned myself in front of the mirror. It looked like a huge fuzzy rabbit, with mange, had decided to hibernate behind my earlobes. I was gutted and prayed to Granny's statues of Jesus and Mary at the top of the stairs for forgiveness; I asked for a miracle and promised, if one came, that I'd never break another Commandment again. However, the evidence against me was overwhelming and as punishment, my parents insisted I return to school the following September with my disgusting hair.

Ever since that first, horrible experience, I've studied beauty like a Professor of Science and have learned which products are hopeless and, thankfully, which do exactly what they say on the tin. DDF, Dermalogica, Sisleÿa, Skinceuticals and SKII, work mini miracles for me every day and are stalwarts in my beauty kit; and likewise nothing equals Crème de la Mer Concentrate for any type of scar or patch of eczema (a fact that I accidentally stumbled upon when dry skin on my chest healed almost immediately when I rubbed the cream down beyond my neck). Aside from myself, other objective testers on my team include my sister and mother. I shower them with the most expensive of products sent to me by cosmetic and skincare companies for testing. As a result Mum has a varied collection of Yves Saint Laurent eye compacts, a penchant for expensive fragrance and lipstick, and swears by Sisleÿa's Global anti-ageing cream. I post her padded packages, tied with ribbon and stuffed full of goodies, and she phones to tell me that, 'the loot has arrived, I'll get back to you soon with the results!' I love that I can treat Mum to creams that she never dared invest in years ago, spending her money instead on my brother, my sister and me (she did however always buy good quality perfume, old habits die hard). I regale her with tales of meeting perfume noses, having facials and trying out massages, and rang her before my first ever Botox® session. Dad surveyed my smooth forehead a few weeks later and asked why I'd felt the need to inject poison into my face to alter my expression. Mum replied, 'For professional reasons – it's all about undercover research, just like that session she had with the guy in New York who keeps all of those supermodels thin.'

Before my trip to New York I was petrified at the prospect of having my teeth veneered. 'Come on,' I told myself, biting my lip to pieces, 'you can do this!' I did and I can honestly say that it changed my life forever. I've kept notebooks crammed with information on all of the products and procedures I've tested and have opened these up to you to give you the very best advice. Overall, I've learned that beauty is about being healthy: always test new products on the inside of your elbow, always check your breasts once a month, brush your teeth twice a day and never leave the house without an SPF 15. And as for seeing beauty in other people: my mother and those I love will always look beautiful to me, with or without expensive products.

TEETH

I've always wanted nice white even teeth – the kind you see on movie stars when the camera goes in real close. Unfortunately, smuggling Time bars and gobstoppers to bed as a child prevented this and as I grew older my teeth got progressively worse until finally they were gappy, brown and small. I knew I wanted to do something about it; I'd watch as Sarah Michelle Gellar smiled at all of the vampires in Buffy the Vampire Slayer – those whiter-than-white perfect teeth zapping the bad monsters away. It was plain and simple, I wanted Buffy's smile! After months of searching and researching I eventually tracked down Gellar's dentists in New York City – Marc Lowenberg, DDS & Gregg Lituchy, DDS, PC. I phoned them with my request...

'Could you give me Buffy the Vampire Slayer's smile please?'
'Do you want the good news or the bad news first?' asked Gregg Lituchy.
'Get the bad out of the way,' I pleaded.
'Sarah Michelle Gellar's teeth are all her own, and to get a look similar from veneers would cost you in the region of $38,000.'
'And the good?'
'I can give you those exact same teeth but it will take two days and a stay in New York of a week. Have you got the time?'

Dr Lituchy cleared his calendar, and I raised the budget. Within eight weeks, safely tucked up in economy, I was winging my way to New York. From the moment I arrived, it was obvious that I was swimming in celeb-land – their office walls groaned under the weight of framed magazine covers autographed with personal notes of thanks and praise from half of Hollywood. As I stared at the movie-star pics, Gregg Lituchy stared at my gaping jaws. 'Your front teeth are too short. They'll be better when whiter. It won't be that difficult, don't worry, you'll look great,' he assured me. He would build my teeth up with veneers so that it would also give me a fuller mouth. It was Monday afternoon. By the following Monday I would have them. (Eeek!)

With masseur Michael Cameron massaging my feet as I reclined in the chair and watched TV, Lituchy filled my mouth with pink glob and gave me Novocain. My own teeth were prepared and filed so that the veneers would take.

Lituchy had the lightest touch I've ever experienced – patient after patient refer to him as 'an artist', and he is. So is his ceramicist/oral designer Jason Kim, who works in his own small lab called Oral Design in New York City, crafting porcelain powder into crowns and veneers.

My hero!
Gregg helped
me blossom
into a butterfly.

81

The next day Gregg arranged for me to visit Jason while he crafted my upper and bottom teeth. Jason would hand-make each individual tooth. First he mixed porcelain powder (in 'supermodel white', the whitest colour – as instructed by Lituchy) with distilled water. With a brush that looked almost exactly like my very thin Shu Uemura eyeliner brush, he 'painted' a veneer in layers onto a piece of platinum foil, which took an hour or so, and baked it in an oven for two minutes at 1,800 degrees Fahrenheit.

'These teeth will absorb and then reflect light because the powder I'm using gives them a brain,' Jason explained. 'They'll be amazing in front of cameras, but won't look fake. An artistic tooth is not a perfect tooth. Marc and Gregg hate fake and so do I. Thick teeth that look the color of correction fluid (Tippex) look ridiculous. I want something that looks beautiful, healthy, but real, even if it's not perfect.'

Five days later I returned to have the look installed. It took four hours – and I had to get shot up with Novocain the same as on the first day. Lituchy began by setting down the veneers. He prepared each tooth, individually and poured the bonding onto them and applied each veneer separately. A few hours later and he'd finished. It was my birthday and I couldn't have wished for more. It was a dream come true, to blossom like a little butterfly.

Marc G. Lowenberg, DDS & Gregg Lituchy, DDS, PC,
230 Central Park South, New York, NY 10019 (tel: +1 212 586 2890, www.lowenbergandlituchy.com).

Care tips from Drs Lowenberg and Lituchy
Brush twice a day, floss at least once a day (twice or more if you can). Visit your dentist twice a year for a check-up and a clean. You should increase your visits if you drink cola, coffee, tea or red wine, these are all stainers. Oh and if you like candy, just clean your teeth every 24 hours to counteract the sugar build-up – it takes 24 hours for sugar to do any harm.

Dr Lituchy's perfect dental kit
A tongue-scraper (to keep breath fresh), the Prevents Improve toothbrush or if you are an electric fan, Sonicare electric toothbrush, Reach Whitening floss, Arm & Hammer Advance White toothpaste and Crest Whitestrips*. (*Note: Veneers need to be cleaned professionally every six months and thereafter brushed and flossed as normal.)

Stainers in order of strength
The worst is tea, the next is red wine and then coffee and cigarettes.

L-27

Jetlag: The Anne Sémonin treatment from Paris (see pp92) is also available in New York – exclusively at Yasmine Djerradine Spa, 30 East 60th Street (tel: +1 212 588 1771) – their spa menus can be seen on www.spa-addicts.com.

Conditioning jaded hair: Salon Ishi, 70 East 55th Street, between Madison and Park Avenues (tel: +1 212 888 4744). Mineral water from Okayama, Japan, is applied with a foundation sponge, then a halo-like air purifier is affixed to your head for eight minutes, all for $125 plus blow-dry. Mr Ishi is a hair-conditioning genius.

Blow-dry, manicure and pedicure (60 minutes for everything): Josephine's Beauty Retreat, 200 East 62nd Street (tel: +1 212 223 7157, www.dayspahairsalon.com).

Cut and blow-dry: Bumble & Bumble, 8th Floor, 415 West 13th Street (tel: +1 212 521 6500, www.bumbleandbumble.com). I love this salon!

Colour/cut: John Frieda, 797 Madison Avenue (tel: +1 212 879 1000, www.johnfrieda.com).

Cut, colour and blow-dry: Eiji Salon, 601 Madison Avenue (tel: +1 212 838 3454, www.eiji-newyork.com).

Wow deep hair-conditioning treatment and blow-dry: Miano Viel, 16 East 52nd Street (tel: +1 212 980 3222, www.mianoviel.com).

Waxing: J. Sisters, 35 West 57th Street (tel: +1 212 750 2485, www.jsisters.com).

Podiatrist: Dr Suzanne M. Levine and Everett M. Lautin MD, Institute Beauté, 885 Park Avenue (tel: +1 212 535 0229, www.institutebeaute.com) – best podiatrist in the business.

Tracie Martyn Firming Serum is fantastic. This purple gel firms the face, takes years off my complexion, and used on its own or after her salon tightening facial (Brad Pitt even has these facials) gives younger, tighter skin. Tracie Martyn Amla Purifying Cleanser is a clarifying concentrate that deeply cleanses and gently exfoliates the skin. It reduces redness and fine lines. Both also available at Harrods, London, but if in New York please visit this amazing guru.

Firming facial and bum lift: Tracie Martyn, 59 Fifth Avenue, Suite 1 (tel: +1 212 206 9333 or go to www.traciemartyn.com). Treatments start at $220 an hour – models and a long list of famous faces swear by her results. She's the best. For product info call +1 212 206 7315.

Deep cleansing facial: Mario Badescu, 320 East 52nd Street (tel: +1 212 758 1065, www.mariobadescu.com) uses all natural ingredients. Mario Badescu Drying Lotion (this product dries up blemishes overnight), Mario Badescu Lip Wax for under lipstick, and also Mario Badescu Moisture Magnet are all available mail order on +1 212 223 3728 or visit the website. The facial and products, are also available in London at HQ hair and beauty store, 2 New Burlington Street, W1 (tel: +1 871 220 4141, www.hqhair.com) and Harvey Nichols (tel: +44 20 7235 5000).

Dr Perricone's Vitamin C Ester Eye Area Therapy and Dr Perricone's ALA Eye Area Therapy clear up dark circles under your eyes. His ALA Face Firming Activator is legendary and his lip plump is used by all of the usual suspects. Visit his flagship store at 791 Madison Avenue (tel: +1 866 791 7911) or in the UK, tel: +44 20 7329 2000, www.nvperriconemd.co.uk), buy his products at Harvey Nichols or have his facial at Liberty.

Dermatologist: Frederick Brandt, 317 East 34th Street, Sixth Floor (tel: +1 212 889 7096, www.drbrandtskincare.com). Dubbed the Baron of Botox®, his celeb clients are many. He spends one week a month in his Manhattan office and his products are good, especially his microdermabrasion cream.

Dermatologist: Dr Patricia Wexler, 145 East 32nd Street, Seventh Floor (tel: +1 212 684 2626, www.patriciawexlermd.com). Wexler is one of the famous names in Manhattan for Botox and fillers, and she also performs liposuction while patients stand to see how the skin falls back into place. Order her Spot Damage Lightening Serum, De-puff Eye Gel or No-injection Lip Plumper, only available from her website, or book an appointment with the famous dermatologist herself.

Personal trainer: David Kirsch, Madison Square Club, 210 Fifth Avenue (tel: +1 212 683 1836, www.theultimatenewyorkbodyplan.com) – responsible for the tight bodies of Heidi Klum, Liv Tyler, Linda Evangelista and Sophie Dahl. He gave me the best legs and butt in New York City in four weeks flat (see pp114).

Make-up tips from a pro: Laura Mercier and her team are constantly appearing around the US and Europe. Her make-up technicians at Saks and Bergdorf Goodman are superbly trained. Visit www.lauramercier.com for further details.

Laura Mercier Purifying Oil Rich removes impurities and excess oil from pores and effectively rinses away even the most stubborn make-up, revealing fresh, supple skin. Also available at Space NK (tel: +44 20 8740 2085).

Chemist: Ricky's, 590 Broadway between Prince & Spring streets (tel: +1 212 226 5552, www.rickys-nyc.com) – you haven't seen colour and hair products until you've been to Ricky's.

Brows: Paulo Siqueira, 40 Park Avenue, Suite 11D (tel: +1 212 779 9270, www.paulosiqueira.com). Paulo was the first brow designer to pluck Gisele's (supermodel) brows. Naomi swears by him. He's fab!

Dermatologist: Dr Dennis Gross, MD Skincare, 444 Madison Ave, 8th Floor (tel: +1 888 830 7546, www.mdskincare.com). I never travel without his Pure™ Intense Moisture Cream, which removes metals from foreign waters from my skin (see pp122).

Facial surgery: Dr Alan Matarasso, 1009 Park Avenue (tel: +1 212 249 7500).

Lasers and injectables: Dr Howard Sobel, 960A Park Ave (tel: +1 212 288 0060, www.drsobel.com). A cosmetic surgeon and dermatologist who is popular for his Botox®, Sculptra and Polaris laser – a radio-frequency treatment that reduces wrinkles and tightens skin – and his outstanding DDF products.

Bodywork: Dr Gerald Pitman, 170 East 73rd Street (tel: +1 212 517 2600, www.drpitman.com).

Dr Howard Sobel's Luminous Moisture Shelter SPF 15 from his DDF range is legendary. You can buy it at Harvey Nichols, London (tel: +44 20 7235 5000).

Chemist: Bigelow Chemists, 414 Sixth Avenue (tel: +1 212 533 2700, www.bigelowchemist.com). Browse the vintage-style shelves and know that Mark Twain used to collect his prescriptions here. Bring home the Rosebud salve.

Massage: The Spa at the Equinox, 140 East 63rd Street (tel: +1 212 750 4671, www.equinoxfitness.com). Book the Neuromuscular Therapy (really great de-stressing deep massage with oils and heat) – see if you can get Heloisa Demelo as your masseuse.

Dr Brandt microdermabrasion in a jar contains magnesium oxide crystals that polish away dead skin cells leaving skin radiant and beautiful. The Dr Brandt crease release, which smoothes out wrinkles, is favoured by many celebrities. All are available in the UK at Space NK (tel: +44 20 8740 2085).

Laser expert: Dr Karyn Grossman, 154 East 85th St, New York (tel. +1 212 879 9504, www.grossmandermatology.com) is especially good with lasers including the Fraxel laser which improves stretchmarks.

Oils and creams: Kiehl's New York Flagship Store, 109 Third Avenue and 13th Street (tel: +1 212 677 3171, www.kiehls.com) opened at this address in 1851 as a tiny pharmacy selling the most beautiful oils and creams. Have a mud coffee at their coffee bar and mull over the many choices. Look at the beautiful pear tree outside the door, which I helped plant a few years ago. Kiehl's Abyssine Cream contains a survivor molecule that allows micro-organisms to thrive in 900-degree hydrothermal vents two miles below the ocean's surface. There's always a waiting list. Also, Kiehl's Centella Recovery Skin Salve helps skin recover from stress or laser treatments and Kiehl's Powerful Strength Line-reducing Concentrate helps with crow's feet and facial fine lines. Some of Kiehl's perfume oils, for example the Original Musk oil, are only available in the US. For UK shoppers try Kiehl's, 29 Monmouth Street, WC2 (tel: +44 20 7240 2411).

Fake Lashes: Shu Uemura Tokyo SoHo beauty boutique, 121 Greene Street, SoHo NYC, 10014 between Prince and Houston St. (tel: +1 212.979.5500, www.shuuemura.com). Celebs order these by the hundreds and I always have a pair of their 24 carat gold eye-lash curlers on hand.

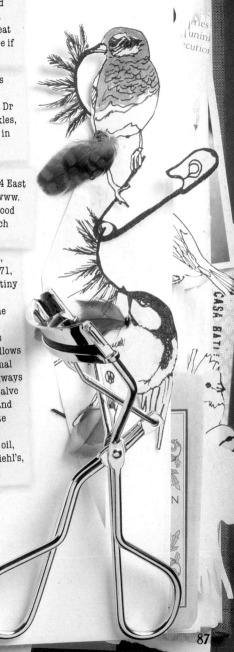

Jet lag: Jurlique's Total Restoration Treatment at the Dorchester Hotel, Park Lane, W1 (tel: +44 20 7495 7335, www.dorchesterhotel.com). Flight Reviver, full body massage (face and scalp, too), using English peppermint, rosemary and eucalyptus oils.

Cut: Real Hairdressing, 6-8 Cale Street, Chelsea (tel: +44 20 7589 0877, www.realhair.co.uk). Try to book director Belle Cannan for a cut that'll transform you.

Blow-dry: Bloww, Regent Square, 4 Regent Place, W1B 5EA (tel: +44 20 7292 0300, www.bloww.co.uk).

Blow-dry: Sizzers, North End Road, Hammersmith (tel: +44 20 7603 3287). Quick and no hassle £20 blow-dry.

Colour: Jo Hansford, 19 Mount Street, Mayfair (tel: +44 20 7495 7774, www.johansford.com). Jo was the first female hairdresser to launch retail haircare products. A fab range for colour-treated hair.

Colour: John Frieda, 4 Aldford Street, Mayfair (+44 20 7491 0840, www.johnfrieda.com).

Blow-dry and relaxation: Sejour, 3-5 Bray Place, SW3 (tel: +44 20 7589 1100).

Jet leg: Agua, The Sanderson, Berners Street, W1 (tel: +44 20 7300 1414, www.sandersonlondon.com).

Manicurist: Sophie Robson at the Berkeley Hotel, Wilton Place, SW1 (tel: +44 20 7235 6000, www.the-berkeley.com), is an expert at the half-moon manicure. Also, if you love the DDF range of products you'll love the brand's new manicure and pedicure treatment here.

Hair extensions or wow deep treatments: Daniel Hersheson, Harvey Nichols, 109-125 Knightsbridge (tel: +44 20 7201 8797) and 48 Conduit Street, W1 (tel: +44 20 7434 1747, www.danielhersheson.com). Hair is sourced after an appointment so that it can be ordered to match your hair type. Detachable hair extensions here are £400. His straightening irons are the best; the salon sells over 300 pairs a week!

Honey and Milk Ayurvedic body treatment: Agua, The Sanderson, Berners Street, W1 (tel: +44 20 7300 1414, www.sandersonlondon.com).

Aromatherapy and pregnancy massage: Aromatherapy Associates (tel: +44 20 8569 7030; www.aromatherapyassociates.com). The treatments are available at Agua, The Sanderson, Berners Street, W1 (tel: +44 20 7300 1414, www.sandersonlondon.com) and several other spas. Their Bath and Shower Oils are so relaxing, they're a must.

Manicure and pedicure: NYNC (New York Nail Company), 118 Westbourne Grove (tel: +44 20 7229 4321, www.newyorknailcompany. com). There are four other branches in London.

Manicurist: Leighton Denny at Urban Retreat at Harrods, 87-135 Brompton Road, Knightsbridge (tel: +44 20 7893 8333, www.urbanretreat.co.uk), does the best acrylic nails in London. If you ask nicely he'll even come round to your house.

Manicurist/pedicure: Iris Chapple at The Nail Studio, 3 Spanish Place, W1 (tel: +44 20 7486 6001). She can transform gnarly fingers and toes into things of great beauty with her super-thorough treatments.

Home visits: Unlisted London (tel: +44 870 2255 007, www. unlistedlondon.com) is well known and trusted for the wide range of stylists, hairdressers and masseurs who will make home visits seven days a week.

Waxing and make-up lessons: Beauty Lounge, 3 Percy Street, W1 (tel: +44 20 7436 8686, www.beautyandthedirt.co.uk).

Waxing. Otylia Roberts, 142 Wigmore Street, W1 (tel: +44 20 7486 5537, www. otyliaroberts.co.uk). Her Brazilians are the best and they start at £40.

Balinese massage ritual: Calmia, 52-54 Marylebone High Street, W1 (tel: +44 845 009 2450, www.calmia.com). The Coconut and Vanilla Tropical Body Polish is a must. Also great for yoga wear.

Indian head massage: E'spa Oriental head massage at The Spa at the Mandarin Oriental, 66 Knightsbridge (tel: +44 20 7838 9888, www.mandarinoriental.com).

Deep tissue massage, pregnancy massage and best plumping facial: Elemis Day-spa, 2-3 Lancashire Court (tel: +44 20 7499 4995, www.elemis.com) or the Urban Retreat spa at Harrods, Knightsbridge (+44 20 7893 8333, www.urbanretreat-harrods.co.uk). Best in London.

Pregnancy massage: Isabella Weber at Beautopia (tel: +44 20 7402 5570) gives the best.

Colour: Louise Galvin, at Daniel Galvin hair salon, 58-60 George Street, W1 (tel: +44 20 7486 9661, www.daniel-galvin.co.uk). Louise Galvin's cleansing products are super! Also see www.louisegalvin.com. Louise Galvin Sacred Locks hair cleanser, conditioner and masque are detergent and preservative-free so won't strip away your pricy blonde highlights, but will leave your dyed hair soft, conditioned and shiny. Galvin's top piece of advice to me? Deep condition coloured hair but don't comb the product in immediately. Leave it in your hair to take effect, half rinse it out, comb through and only then rinse fully. It works!

LOUISE GALVIN
Sacred Locks
HAIR CLEANSER

Eyelashes: Martyn Maxey, 18 Grosvenor Street, London W1 (tel: +44 20 7629 6161, www.martynmaxey.co.uk). Individually bonded eyelashes that last for up to three months.

Eyelashes: Shu Uemura Tokyo Lash Bar, Harvey Nichols, 109-125 Knightsbridge (tel: +44 20 7235 5000, www.harveynichols.com), for amazing lashes, tools, make-up and the best brushes.

Body waxing: Strip, 112 Talbot Road, Notting Hill (tel: +44 20 7727 2754, www.2strip.com). Try to book Judit Sinka.

Eyebrow waxing and Mascara: Shavata Singh brow studio, Urban Retreat, Fifth Floor, Harrods, Knightsbridge (tel: +44 20 7893 8333, www.urbanretreat-harrods.co.uk or check out www.shavata.co.uk).

Facial and healing: Anastasia Achilleos, Earl Douglas, Motcombe Street, SW3 (tel: +44 79 3933 1889), has a huge celebrity following and she'll also make home visits.

Deep-cleansing facial: Eve Lom, 2 Spanish Place, W1 (tel: +44 20 7935 9988; www.evelom.co.uk). Legendary!

Customized facial: Una Brennan, 41 Moor House Road, Notting Hill (tel: +44 79 5216 8678 or +44 20 7313 9835). She uses dermatological brand SkinCeuticals, creates her own organic peels from fresh ingredients and makes amazing seaweed masks. She's also excellent at treating pregnancy hyperpigmentation.

Body waxing or bio laser hair removal: Body & Soul, 98 Cochrane Street, St John's Wood (tel: +44 20 7722 8086, www.bodyandsoul-health.co.uk). Izabella Osvath is super at defuzzing.

Facial: Bharti Vyas, 24 Chiltern Street, W1 (tel: +44 20 7935 5312 and +44 20 7486 7167).

Luxurious facial: Amanda Lacey (tel: +44 20 7351 4443, www.amandalacey.com). Known for her luxurious intimate bespoke facials, at her clinic she uses the most expensive and purest of oils.

Facial and massage: DDF Facial, The Berkeley Health Club and Spa, Wilton Place, Knightsbridge (tel: +44 20 7235 6000, www.the-berkeley.co.uk). Skin is analysed, problems targeted and resolved using this range from the US.

Facial and acne specialist: Julie Ward, Martyn Maxey Salon (+44 20 7629 6161; www.martynmaxey.co.uk), prefers to use medically researched products and is excellent at clearing up breakouts.

Anti-wrinkle facial: Sarah Chapman (tel: +44 70 5009 7796) – her facials are renowned for banishing wrinkles.

Hydrating facial: Odile Makhoul, The Paris Beauty Institute, 32 Thurloe Place, South Kensington (tel: +44 20 7581 0085).

Tan airbrushing: Susie Lung Beauty Salon, 50 Manchester Street, W1M 5PB (tel: +44 7957 771503). Susie Lung is 'tanner to the stars'.

Facial/eyebrows/eyelashes: Vaishaly Patel, 51 Paddington Street, W1 (tel: +44 20 7224 6088). Lymphatic drainage, microdermabrasion and perfect eyebrows.

Fake tanning: Jean Paul Mist-On Tanning at Heidi Klein, 174 Westbourne Grove, Notting Hill (tel: +44 20 7243 5665). A 60-second spray tan, done in a flash.

Reflexology: Angela Telford at the Third Space (tel: +44 20 7439 7332, www.thethirdspace.com/medicine).

Yoga: The Life Centre, 15 Edge Street (tel: +44 20 7221 4602; www.thelifecentre.com), offers an extensive yoga programme including good pregnancy yoga.

Body work: Laurence Kirwan, 56 Harley Street, W1 (tel: +44 20 7935 8844; www.drkirwan.com).

Make-up tips from a pro: Pout, 32 Shelton Street, Covent Garden (tel: +44 20 7379 0379; www.pout.co.uk). See pp98 for the works.

Non-invasive surgery: Dr Andrew Markey, consultant dermatologist, The Lister Hospital, Chelsea Bridge Road, SW3 (tel: +44 20 7730 1219). He's been my dermatologist and he's magic!

Non-invasive surgery: Dr Nick Lowe, Cranley Clinic, 3 Harcourt House, 19a Cavendish Square, W1 (tel: +44 20 7499 3223).

Facial surgery: Barry Jones, 14a Upper Wimpole Street, W1G 6LR (tel: +44 20 7935 1938, www.barrymjones.co.uk).

One-stop beauty emporium: HQ Hair & Beautystore, 2 New Burlington Street, W1 (tel: +44 871 220 4141, www.hqhair.com) for all those cult products and hard-to-find international bestsellers.

Calmia's Karmic Incense at Calmia, 53-54 Marylebone High Street, W1 (tel: +44 845 009 2450). The Coconut and Vanilla Tropical Body Polish is a must.

Amanda Lacey: I discovered Amanda Lacey a while ago and her products are just amazing! She tailor makes her facials to suit me. The Amanda Lacey Cleansing Pomade is a rich blend of calendula oil, palm wax and camphor and is so good at recharging skin that it sells out fast. The Amanda Lacey Oils of Provence facial oil is loaded with eucalyptus, lavender, bois de rose and sage and is particularly good for dry/sensitive skin. The Amanda Lacey Persian Rose Water toner is alcohol-free and her Pink Cream is the perfect moisturizer for hydrating and feeding the skin, helping it to cope with daily skin stress. All at Harvey Nichols or mail order (tel: +44 20 7351 4443; www.amandalacey.com). Why not try her starter kit?

Vaishaly Patel's Vaishaly Day Moisturiser shields skin brilliantly. Based on sun-blocking zinc oxide, rather than chemical sunscreens, it nourishes skin with vitamin E and an anti-irritation blend of arnica, ginkgo and calendula. Available from her clinic (tel: +44 20 7224 6088) and Harvey Nichols nationwide (mail order tel: +44 20 7235 5000).

Chemist: The Organic Pharmacy, 396 King's Road, Chelsea (tel: +44 20 7351 2232, www.theorganicpharmacy.com).

SkinCeuticals CE Ferulic stimulates collagen production and SkinCeuticals Hydrating B5 Gel contains B complex vitamins and hyaluronic acid, the body's natural hydrator. These two products are simply fantastic and I use two or three drops of the latter to soften my face before moisturizing. Available in the UK (tel: +44 20 8997 8541, www.skinceuticals.com or www.hqhair.com).

Pout Bustier is a luxurious soufflé cream that enhances the bust area. The subtle shimmer intensifies the appearance of your natural curves, making your cleavage look fuller and feel irresistible (See pp98).

CASA BATLLO

Jetlag: Anne Sémonin, 108 rue du Faubourg (tel: +33 1 42 66 24 22). Here you can get a 45 minute jetlag treatment that revives and heals a well-travelled soul.

Massage: La Maison Guerlain, 68 Avenue des Champs Elysées (tel: +33 1 45 62 52 57, www.guerlain.com).

De-bloat legs/Indian head massage/eye treatments: Talika Spa at The Pershing Hall Hotel, 49 rue Pierre Charron (tel: +33 1 58 36 58 03, www.pershinghall.com).

Facial and skin perfecting: Joëlle Ciocco, 8 place de la Madeleine (tel: +33 1 42 60 58 80, www.joelle-ciocco.com). Parisians whisper this facialist's name – she's a magician with skin.

Hair Colour: Christophe Robin, 7 rue du Mont Thabor (tel: +33 1 42 60 99 15, www.colorist.net).

Blow-dry: Carita Montaigne, 3 rue du Boccador (tel: +33 1 47 23 76 79).

Deep-cleansing facial: Odile LeCoin (tel: +33 1 45 04 91 85, www.odilelecoin.com) – the best facialist in Paris.

Christophe Robin Lemon Cream Cleanser. This shampoo is hair-friendly and kind to colour. For mail order call +33 1 40 20 92 12, www.colorist.net. Available in the UK at Daniel Hersheson (see pp88).

Hammam: Nuxe Spa, 32 rue Montorgueil (tel: +33 1 55 80 71 40, www.nuxe.com). Have a hammam and indulge in their gorgeous body products.

Hair conditioning: Leonor Greyl Salon, 10-15 rue Tronchet (tel: +33 1 42 65 32 26, www.leonorgreyl.com). Models whisper this hair salon's address – her nourishing treatments have been legendary since 1968.

Massage: Madame Serrano, rue Brezin (tel: +33 1 45 40 85 71). Book the aroma-luxe message and ask for her way ahead of time.

Lifting facial: Carita, 11 rue du Faubourg, Saint Honoré (tel: +33 1 44 94 11 11, www.maisondebeautecarita.com). Also available in London at Spa Illuminata, 63 South Audley Street, W1 (tel: +44 20 7499 7777) or call +44 20 7402 9474 for Carita treatments and products in London and +353 1 822 2711 for salons and products in Dublin.

Hydrating facial: Anne Sémonin hydrating facial at Hôtel le Bristol, 112 rue du Faubourg Saint Honoré (tel: +33 1 53 43 43 00, www.lebristolparis.com) – see also jetlag treatment above.

Bodywork: Dr Bernard Mole, 15 Avenue de Tourville (tel: +33 1 45 51 85 85, www.chir-esthetique.com).

Hair cut: Salon Dessange, 39 Avenue Franklin Roosevelt (tel: +33 1 43 59 31 31, www.jacques-dessange.com).

Facial surgery: Dr Bernard Cornette de Saint Cyr, 15 rue Spontini (tel: +33 1 47 04 25 02, www.cornettedesaintcyr.com). He's particularly good at hiding facelift scars in the hairline.

COLORIST
Christophe Robin

crème lavante au citron

SOIN LAVANT TRAITANT POUR CHEVEUX COLORES
CLEANSING CARE WITH LEMON FOR COLORED HAIR

7 rue du Mont Thabor
PARIS

Natural treatments: Yonka, rue de Sèvres (tel: +33 1 45 44 39 79, www.yonka.com). For UK stockists call +44 20 7518 8370 and for Dublin call +353 1 832 1412.

Moisturising body treatment: Darphin, Place Vendôme, 356 rue Saint-Honoré (tel: +33 1 47 03 17 77) and Spa Institut Darphin Beaute, 97 rue du Bac (tel: +33 1 45 48 30 30, www.darphin.fr). Find Darphin in the UK at 73–75 Grosvenor Street, London W1K 3BQ (tel: +44 870 034 6700). Products also at Space NK.

Lipglosses, signature treatment and beautiful aromatic tea: Institute Lancôme, 29 rue du Faubourg Saint Honoré (tel: +33 1 42 65 30 74, www.lancome.co.uk). Massages are the name of the game here and if you are a Juicy Tube fan you'll think you've found lip gloss heaven.

Natural facial and massage: Institute Decleor – Printemps Nation, Espace Beauté – Rdc – 21-25, cours de Vincennes, 75020 (tel: +33 1 43 48 27 85, www.decleor.com or call +33 1 72 76 73 73). Also available in London at Spa Illuminata, 63 South Audley Street, W1 (tel: +44 20 7499 7777), and call +353 1 822 2711 for salons in Dublin.

Anything from **Sisley Paris.** I simply love this range (tel: +44 20 7491 2722, www.sisleya.com).

Non-invasive surgery: Dr Nelly Gauthier, 9 rue de Marignan (tel:+33 1 53 75 04 60) – by targeting lips, lower face and neck she's the best line-filler in France.

Make-up tips from a pro: Terry de Gunzburg, 64 rue Pierre Charron (tel: +33 1 47 48 79 62, www.byterry.com) gives make-up application seminars at her boutique. She worked at Yves Saint Laurent for 14 years and was the lady who invented Yves Saint Laurent's Touche Eclat.

Facial for Sensitive skin: Institut Payot, 10 rue de Castiglione (tel: +33 1 42 60 32 87).

Hammam: Hammam Med Centre, 43-45 rue Petit, 19th (tel: +33 1 42 02 31 05, www.hammammed.com). Have the Rose de Nuit treatment and be wrapped in rose petals and Argan oil from Marrakech. Amazing!

Intense Eye Kohl: Stephane Marais is one of France's best-known make-up artists and her products are available at 217 rue Faubourg, St Honoré, Paris, or Space NK (tel: +44 20 8740 2085).

Annick Goutal Crème Splendide from Annick Goutal, 14 Rue de Castiglione (tel: +33 1 42 60 52 82) (see also her scents, pp237). Based on roses, this nourishing moisturiser is super-hydrating and smells so gorgeous you'll want to wear it all of the time. You can also order it mail order on +44 870 837 7377 or find it at Liberty (tel: +44 20 7734 1234).

And I always buy macaroons too!

I love this product to bits

DrSebagh

Carita La Cure Parfaite: 11 rue du Faubourg, St. Honoré, Paris (tel: +33 1 44 94 11 11, www.carita.fr) is a rejuvenating treatment which contains sweet almond proteins, a pigmentation corrector and beta carotene. Also add Carita La Crème Parfait to your basket, an excellent cream for your body when you feel really puffy at that special time of the month. Call +44 20 7313 8780 for your nearest Carita spa, or you can get them at Spa Illuminata, 63 South Audley Street, London W1 (tel: +44 20 7499 7777).

Darphin Aromatic Purifying Balm at Darphin, Place Vendôme 356, rue St Honoré, Paris (tel: +33 1 47 03 17 77, www.darphin.fr) a pre-flight must-have – it nourishes and hydrates without clogging pores. This range was developed by the Paris dermatologist Dr Pierre Darphin. Call +44 1730 232 566 for UK stockists.

Decleor Aromessence Neroli oil: (tel: +33 1 72 76 73 73, www.decleor.fr) is a must-have for your home facial kit. One kilo of orange blossom goes into each gram. It's perfect for putting on under moisturiser or face creams as it grabs the cream and brings it deeper into the face tissue. You can buy Decleor at Spa Illuminata, 63 South Audley Street, London W1 (tel: +44 20 7499 7777), or call +353 1 8222711 for salons in Dublin.

Non-invasive surgery: Dr Jean Louis Sebagh, 64 rue de Longchamp (tel: +33 1 47 04 65 75) customises anti-aging routines for skin (good fillers and Botox®). He also holds appointments in London at Cosmetic Doctor at Work, 25 Wimpole Street (tel: +44 20 7637 0548, www.drsebagh. com). Dr Jean Louis Sebagh For Your Eyes Only is a product that I simply love. The two-product system comes with a dark-circle-reducing vitamin C powder, which I mix with a cream, and it reduces my dark circles in mere seconds – allowing me to party hard and still look great at 10 a.m. the following day. Other amazing fixer-uppers by Dr Jean Louis Sebagh include his Dr Sebagh Crème Vital (moisturises and prevents premature ageing), Dr Sebagh Serum Repair (nourishes, repairs and plumps the skin while you sleep) and Dr Sebagh Vitamin C powder (which turns into a cream on contact with the skin, combats free radicals and fights against the signs of ageing). All are available in the UK at Space NK (tel: +44 20 8740 2085).

Anti-age facial and Guinot Energising Lifting Mask from the Guinot Salon, Institut Guinot: 4 rue de la Paix (tel: +33 1 42 86 08 30, www.guinot.com) or 17 Albemarle Street, London (tel: +44 20 7491 9971) and in Dublin call 0818 719 303 to find a salon in your area. Buy the Energising Lifting Mask for home use (see pp112 for more).

Massage/jetlag/traditional Chinese medicine: Emily B. Miggin, 23 Upper Mount Street, Dublin 2 (tel: +353 1 678 8762, www.ebmclinic.com), specializes in acupuncture, cupping, hot stone therapy, deep tissue massage, sports massage and Shiatsu, and at the peril of never being able to get an appointment with her again I'm releasing this number.

Fake tanning: St Tropez at Papillon Beauty and Skincare, 129 Upper Leeson Street, Dublin 4, (tel: +353 1 660 4222). Book ahead to guarantee your slot with the best St Tropez-ers in Dublin

Facials and cellulite: Anne Rossi Health and Beauty Clinic, 15 Howth Road, Sutton, Dublin (tel: +353 87 662 0453).

Laser specialists: Silk, Skincare Ireland Laser Clinic, 4–5 Chatham Street, Dublin 2 (tel: +353 1 635 1686). This clinic can offer consultations with Dr Mataxatoc who pioneered the natural face lift. They are also really great at zapping hair with lasers.

Glycolic peels, microdermabrasion and rosacea: Anne McDevitt, 13 Wicklow Street, Dublin 2 (tel: +353 1 677 7962, www.annemcdevitt.com). Using Dr Daniello products, the clinic can tackle almost any skin problem. Dr Maurizio Viel, the skin wizard, also administers Botox® here and takes consultations for his Harley Street clinic.

Dermatologist: Dr Rosemary Coleman, Blackrock Clinic, Dublin (tel: +353 1 283 2222, www.blackrock-clinic.ie), is one of the country's most renowned skin specialists.

Facial: Nuala Woulfe Beauty Salon Ltd, 4c Glasthule Road, Sandycove, County Dublin (+353 1 230 0244). For a facial with serious pampering.

Botox®, fillers and lasers: Dr Kate Coleman-Moriarty, Blackrock Clinic, Dublin (tel: +353 1 283 2222; www.blackrock-clinic.ie). For those lines under your eyes that Botox® can't fix, she does CO_2 laser resurfacing.

Body work: The Beacon, the Well, Sandyford Industrial Estate, Dublin 18 (tel: +353 1 213 6220, www.beacon). A consultant-led surgical, dermatology and laser clinic offering everything from breast augmentation to toning, tightening, rejuvenating and hair removal by laser (including carboxytherapy for cellulite).

Spots, acne and amazing results for Irish skin: The SkinCeuticals range (tel: +44 20 8997 8541, www.skinceuticals.co.uk) is scientifically brilliant! The CE Ferulic applied under sunscreen prevents skin damage and stimulates repair. Their Serum 10 applied after sun exposure protects against and repairs sun damage and SkinCeuticals Primacy, a vitamin C serum, is also amazing; it promotes production of collagen, a natural fixer-upper. All these products are available in Dublin from Sanctum, 4 Scarlet Row, Essex Street West, Temple Bar, Dublin 8 (tel: +353 1 674 5707; www.sanctum.ie). The store also has a very gifted therapist, Rachel Walsh, who is a whiz at treating acne.

I grew up adoring Madonna in the eighties. At my Catholic boarding school I got detention for a) having a poster of her on my wall (too raunchy), and b) copying her make-up and dress sense on Sundays (too much eyeliner and lippy and were those earrings part of the standard uniform?). You can imagine how thrilled I was then, snuggled into the lush seats at Claridges, sipping tea and listening to make-up guru Laura Mercier explain that she had done the make-up on Madonna's Ray of Light video and that no, it wasn't possible for me to achieve that golden glowing skin without using some heavy duty industrial oil and liquid bronzer. 'If I did it for you, Gisèle, you would ruin sofas and chairs at every party. These looks are just created for videos and photo-shoots; for real life it has to be much more practical and easy to achieve.'

So, what's the secret to finding the perfect foundation? Cleanse your face before going shopping for new foundation. It has to be tried out on a bare cheek – this is the largest area that people see when they look at you straight on. Alternatively ask the make-up expert at the counter to cleanse the cheek area for you. Never test it on the back or inside of your arm or hand, it's pointless. After you've put it on, find a window in the shop that has natural light so that you can see its true colour. If it looks as though it has disappeared into your skin then it's the one for you.

How do you apply the perfect foundation? Your fingers are tools that should be used to build a perfect face, so learn to use them properly. Firstly, follow your skincare routine to cleanse your skin and make it ready for your make-up. Then apply your moisturizer with SPF or your sunscreen or serum, whichever you choose. Next put on a primer; this helps keep your make-up in place all day long. Primer is the ham in the sandwich, believe me! Next up apply your tinted moisturizer or your sheer foundation or a mixture of both. All of this should be done with your fingers, picking up a little product and then dabbing it gently into your pores. If you're using a heavy foundation apply it with a sponge, but never use a brush for sheer liquid foundation. A brush is only ever good for applying concealer or powder.

Laura Mercier with Madonna

Laura and me in Claridges

Does one foundation work for all seasons, Laura? Yes, but only if you're clever with it. There's no need to buy loads of different foundations, you just need one and you can add either a tinted moisturizer or a bronzing gel to it – to make it darker in the summer and lighter in the winter. For a polished summer look you should also illuminate by adding a little dab of my Mosiac Illumination over your tinted moisturizer on the cheekbones.

How do I get rid of imperfections? If you've imperfections like dark shadows or acne, apply my Secret Camouflage after your foundation. Pick up the product with the Secret Camouflage brush by dragging it across both pans, saturating both sides of the brush. Utilizing the back of your hand as a palette, use the brush to warm and mix the two colours until you find the shade that matches your skin tone. For dark eye circles, dab on a good rich eye cream (any one will do) and when it has soaked in use Laura Mercier's Secret Brightener, which is light-reflecting. Next add some concealer but be sure to choose the correct shade (too dark and you get racoon eye) and only use it on the darkest part of the ring under your eye, not around it – I've developed a concealer especially for this problem. I reinforce the concealer with my Secret Camouflage to keep everything in place and then I apply foundation to the rest of the face. For spots, broken veins and other imperfections, use concealer after your foundation, otherwise it'll just come off as you're applying your foundation over it.

How can I get that perfectly buffed shiny shins and shoulders look (like Madonna)? Fake tan, a good rich body cream and an oil with gold particles in it only after you've gotten dressed to go out. Fluide de Beauté 14 by Carita is a really good one and is very famous in Paris; it's available in London at Spa Illuminata, 63 South Audley Street, London W1 (tel: +44 20 7499 7777; or tel: +44 20 7402 9474 for Carita treatments and products in London, and tel: +353 1 822 2711 for salons and products in Dublin). There are also other illuminating products that you can apply. For the face, use a tinted moisturizer, a cream blush, an illuminating blush and a powder to set everything. Fifteen minutes after using your powder you'll see that dewy buffed look coming through. Stunning!

Make-up in Minutes

I was late for work, I had no make-up on and I was in a cab and due in a meeting in ten minutes. I needed an expert and I needed one fast. Why couldn't I look shiny and glossed and buffed like the girls on CSI? They have to deal with dead bodies all day and they still manage to look gorgeous, with perfect hair, perfect skin and perfect lippy. I called expert Emily Cohen of Pout to see if she'd help.

For ages I'd admired the fantastic, user-friendly nature of Pout products (you can apply most of the range using your fingers when you're in a rush), but would I get that perfect look so no one would suspect I did my war-paint in the back of a moving car? Emily didn't think it would be a problem – in the past she's touched-up celebrities' make-up on the way to premieres and openings – so we set off.

The first product Emily used was the After Glow Illuminator which had a pump-top rather than a cap, so there were no lids sliding under the seat to worry about, and no nasty leaks either. (So far so good and bonus marks for keeping my outfit clean.)

Next, Emily used Pout's translucent pressed powder, which comes in a compact complete with mirror and sponge – pressed so there's no risk of a powder explosion en route and designed to be applied without brushes. So nothing fiddly and, so far, no mess. Brilliant.

Next up was a chunky tube of blusher, like a big lipstick. Emily patted it onto my cheeks and spread it out using her fingers. Again, no tools in sight. Lips got a quick slick of plumping lip-gloss so no lipstick ended up riding down my face. Last of all, she tackled my eyes. She managed this more delicate task in stages: first, a quick rub of Pout eyeslick at the first red light (this product is amazing – it's easy-to-use creamy eye-shadow goes on like a dream and there's no creasing). At the second stop she added eye pencil, which twists up so you don't have to sharpen it and ruin your suit. The 'smudger' at the other end of the eye pencil helped to achieve a softer, more blended line. Finally, as we approached Covent Garden, she managed to get the mascara on without blinding me.

The results were natural, giving me a translucent glow, and lasted until late into the evening – and now I'm addicted to back-seat beauty; it gives me that extra twenty minutes in bed because, after all, every Goddess needs her beauty sleep.

Favourite smell? My son (13 months old) .
Favourite sound? Laughter.
Favourite taste? Rose.
Favourite to your sense of touch? Water.
Favourite colour? Peppermint green.
Favourite bird? Woodpecker.
Favourite flower? Sunflowers.
Favourite place? On the beach.
Favourite book? The Kite Runner by Khaled Hosseini.
Favourite piece of art? Reclining Nude by Amedeo Modigliani.
Favourite possession? 'Boris', my plant, which was my grandmother's – he's a Christmas cactus about 60 years old.
If you could have dinner with one person who would it be and what would you ask them? My grandmother, who died when I was 12, and who I miss dearly – I would ask her all about her life and what my mother was like as a child.

The kit
Little bag
Pout After Glow Illuminator
Pout Pressed Powder
Pout Flush Blush
Pout Plump
Pout Eyeslick
Pout Eye Pencil
Pout Mascara
Pout Plumping Lip-gloss

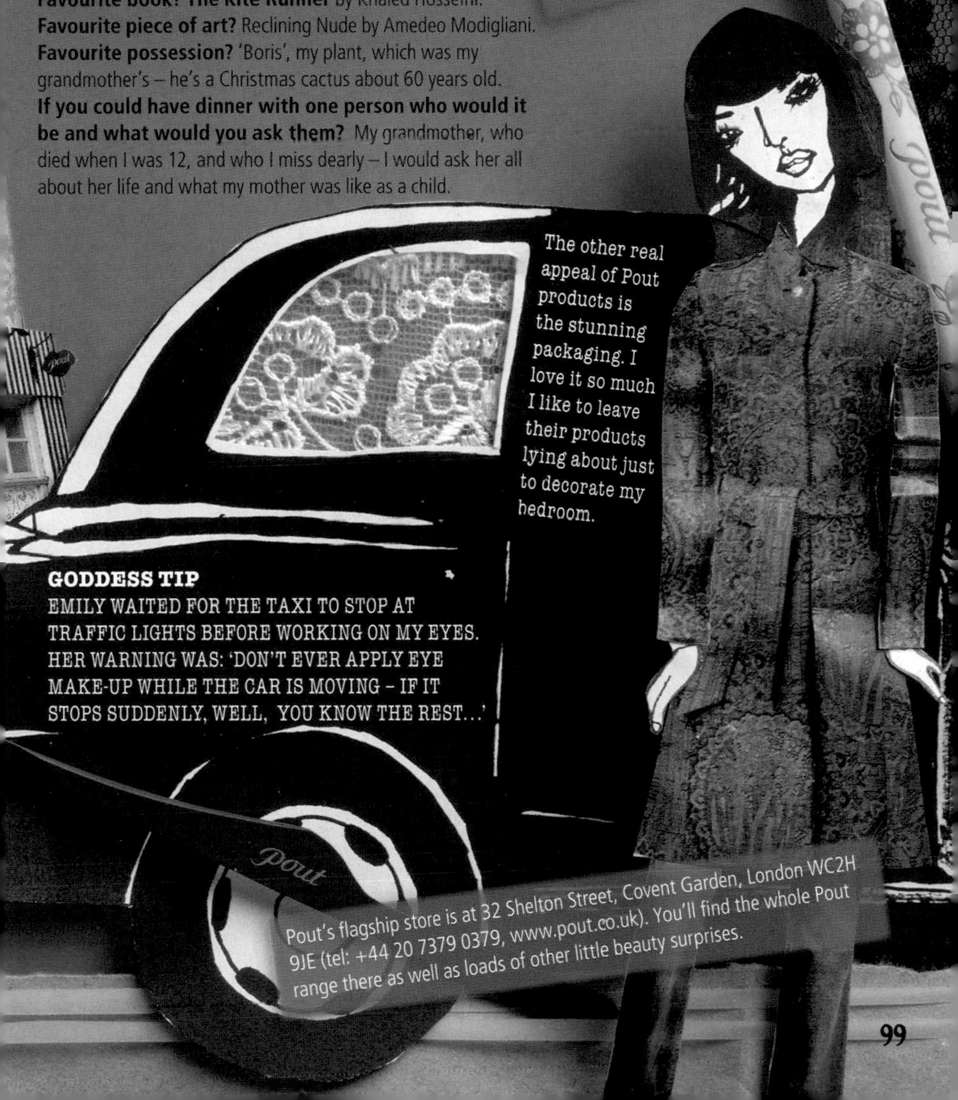

The other real appeal of Pout products is the stunning packaging. I love it so much I like to leave their products lying about just to decorate my bedroom.

GODDESS TIP
EMILY WAITED FOR THE TAXI TO STOP AT TRAFFIC LIGHTS BEFORE WORKING ON MY EYES. HER WARNING WAS: 'DON'T EVER APPLY EYE MAKE-UP WHILE THE CAR IS MOVING – IF IT STOPS SUDDENLY, WELL, YOU KNOW THE REST...'

Pout's flagship store is at 32 Shelton Street, Covent Garden, London WC2H 9JE (tel: +44 20 7379 0379, www.pout.co.uk). You'll find the whole Pout range there as well as loads of other little beauty surprises.

ALL DAY
ALL YEAR

soin essentiel
de jour

essential
day care

sisley
PARIS

NET WT 1.7 OZ (49 g 50 ml)

My favourite wash-off/exfoliating cleanser

Eve Lom, 2 Spanish Place, London (tel: +44 20 7935 9988, www.evelom.co.uk). Eve is a very accomplished therapist and her Eve Lom facial is excellent at cleaning out blocked pores and grimy city-trashed skin. She invented her own technique and ritual, and it's explained in a little pamphlet included in her Eve Lom Pomenade and muslin cloth (mail order tel: +44 20 8665 0112 or find them at Space NK, tel: +44 20 8740 2085). I use the system every night and sometimes even rub this on before getting in the bath and do the ritual while soaking – the steam in the bath really open pores up – buffing it off with the muslin cloth. Squeaky clean!

My favourite wipe-off cleanser

Sisley's cleansing milk with white lily (tel: +44 20 7491 2722, www.sisleya.com) is my favourite wipe-off cleanser. I love this product, it smells so good and it's so creamy. After a big night out with heavy make-up on it clears the lot, cleaning deeply, leaving skin dewy, glowing and lush. Dermalogica Ultracalming Cleanser (tel: +44 800 591 818) also suits all skin types and is a really great cleanser at a good price.

GODDESS TIP
DON'T HAVE THE WATER OR YOUR FACE CLOTH TOO HOT – IT CAN CAUSE BROKEN VEINS, IRRITATION AND DRY YOUR SKIN OUT.

Do I need a toner?

Toners

Alcohol-laced toners dry out skin and upset oily skin's balance, so ensure that if you tone you use a product that's completely alcohol free. My three favourites are Amanda Lacey's Persian Rosewater (tel: +44 207 351 4443, www.amandalacey.com), the Rose Floral Water by Neal's Yard (tel: +44 1747 834 634, www.nealsyardremedies.com) and Liz Earle's Instant Boost Skin Tonic (mail order +44 1983 813 913, www.lizearle.com), with its aloe vera juice, cucumber and calendula. Keep your toner in the fridge and let it soothe.

Moisturisers I love in the summer

All Day All Year by Sisley (tel: +44 20 7491 2722, www.sisleya.com) creates a genuine protective UV shield around the skin and protects it for up to eight hours while I'm sitting inside a window at my desk. It's my office must-have. B Kamins Day Cream SPF 15 (tel: +44 20 7379 0379, www.bkamins.com) is another great moisturising option. And for a more affordable moisturiser with SPF, Total Effects 7x Day SPF 15 by Olay really can't be beaten.

Moisturisers I love in the winter

Clinique Superdefense Triple Action Moisturiser is just amazing SPF 15. Also, Clinique CX soothing moisturiser SPF 25 is my secret weapon against wind and rain, and I take it with me everywhere when I'm travelling in the wintertime. It's a must for my skin before and after jogging in the cold. Chanel Hydramax Serum also does wonders and is really rich and good value for the amount of product you get.

Affordable moisturiser that suits everyone

Estée Lauder's Daywear Plus Multi Protection Anti-Oxidant Crème SPF 15 is £26 and is a great all-rounder. It suits everyone and comes as cream, lotion and even as a tinted moisturiser.

GODDESS TIP

DECLEOR'S AROMESSENCE NÉROLI OIL IS SUITABLE FOR ALL SKIN TYPES, EVEN SENSITIVE ONES. IT SINKS INTO THE SKIN AND DOESN'T LEAVE AN OILY FILM. WEAR UNDER YOUR MOISTURISER OR NIGHT CREAM.

Five steps to a home facial

You should be trying to give yourself a home facial twice a week. Try cleansing firstly with either Eve Lom (see opposite) or Cleanse & Polish Hot Cloth Cleanser by Liz Earle (mail order +44 1983 813 913, www.lizearle.com). It has eucalyptus and rosemary in it and suits all skin types, purifying your skin without stripping it and drying it out.

Put a few drops of Ole Henriksen's Inhalation Therapy (tel: +44 20 7235 5000 at Harvey Nichols) in a sink of hot water and soak your face cloth in it. This product also contains eucalyptus, which has an antiseptic quality and lifts your mood instantly when inhaled through your face cloth as you are washing off your cleanser. (You can leave this product out if you have particularly sensitive skin.)

Next I personally like to use Guinot's Gommage Biologique (see pp94) to slough away dead skin as a facial exfoliator; it's mild but effective and melts dead skin cells without causing irritation. You have to really rub this in and the heat of your face makes it melt in more. Wash this off again with your soaking face cloth, dry.

Apply Decleor's Aromessence Néroli facial oil (tel: +44 20 7402 9474) to puts natural oils back into the skin and to help your moisturiser to work deeper. Put a few drops of Decleor oil in your hand, warm it by rubbing them together and apply.

Then put Estée Lauder's DayWear Plus Multi Protection Anti-Oxidant Crème SPF 15 on over it. This product comes in several types: oil-free, with moisture, or there's even a tinted version which gives skin a really healthy glow.

GODDESS TIP

OLE HENRIKSEN'S NURTURE ME REPLENISHING CREME (TEL: +44 20 7201 5000 AT HARVEY NICHOLS) SHOULD HELP CALM ANY UNWELCOME IRRITATION AFTER A SALON OR HOME FACIAL.

Spots are caused by over-excited oil glands, which produce too much oil and clog the pores, a hormonal imbalance, stress or an unhealthy eating plan.

Acne and spot treatments

Cystic acne can be helped with prescription Roaccutane, but there may be unpleasant side effects. Prescription Retin-A lotions, which speed up the cell turnover in the skin, antibiotics, acid peels (see pp107), extractions and light treatments, which dry out the acne bacteria, may also help. Sunlight kills acne-causing bacteria so if spots continue to appear, try blue light therapy Omnilux Blue (tel: +44 870 8506 6550); the blue light is like sunlight but without the harmful rays. Alternatively, Dr Nick Lowe, consultant dermatologist at the Cranley Clinic, Harcourt House, 19a Cavendish Square, London W1 (tel: +44 20 7499 3223) uses cortisone injections, which even if administered twenty-four hours before a big do will reduce acne redness and swelling.

Acne and spot treatments at home

Don't poke at them; instead exfoliate twice a week with Dermalogica's Gentle Cream Exfoliant Cleanser (for UK stockists tel: +44 800 591 818 and Ireland tel: +353 1800 556 785; www.dermalogica.co.uk) and cleanse daily with Bio-Maple Hydrating Acne Wash by B Kamins Chemist (tel: +44 20 7379 0379 or www.hqhair.com) to unblock pores and clear out whiteheads and blackheads. Both products contain salicylic acid which is a natural anti-inflammatory. An excellent product to use after cleansing is PX Custom Concentrate Anti-Blemish Serum by Prescriptives (tel: +44 870 034 2566; www.prescriptives.com) and I would also recommend Acne Treatment gel cream by NV Perricone MD Cosmeceuticals (tel: +44 20 73329 2000; www.nvperriconemd.co.uk). Choose a light oil-free moisturizer such as Dermalogica's Special Clearing Booster (see details above) which zaps spots and can be worn under make-up. To cover spots opt for a medicated concealer like Galactic Shield! by Benefit (tel: +44 90 1113 0001). Try to avoid creamy foundations and instead choose one with an oil-free formula like Clarins True Radiance or Future Skin gel foundation by Chantecaille at Fenwicks (tel: +44 20 7629 9161). Alternatively, a powder foundation such as Inner Light Dual Foundation by Aveda (tel: +44 17 3023 2380) applied with a brush is best for very bad outbreaks. Keep brushes bacteria-free by washing in baby shampoo and warm water and leaving to dry naturally.

Spots – Need a little extra help?
Shenaz Sharif, Face & Body Clinic, Harley Street, London W1 (tel: +44 20 7436 3936), uses light to zap acne, rejuvenate skin and boost collagen in her Light Refinement Facial. A course of eight will really revive your skin. Beauty therapist **Julie Scarle**, 52 Abbey Gardens, London NW8 (tel: +44 20 7328 6616) helps banish spots with three months of cleansing and peels.

Acne scars, loose skin and puffy jowls
Over the past couple of years, the beauty industry has been moving away from surgical nip-tuck procedures towards non-invasive techniques that rely on lasers and light sources (see pp104) and radio-frequency energy (Thermage) to gently lift and tighten skin. Thermage is a procedure in which radio-frequency waves are administered to the skin while a coolant cools the skin at the same time – it's hot, hot, hot, and really only bearable under sedation. Uncomfortable as it is, it's superb for acne scars and loose skin on the face (jowly neck) and body as well as small wrinkles. Dr Nick Lowe, consultant dermatologist at the Cranley Clinic, Harcourt House, 19a Cavendish Square, London W1 (tel: +44 20 7499 3223) is an expert.

Alternatives to Thermage at home
NV Perricone Neuropeptide Facial Contour (tel: +44 20 7329 2000) remodels and recontours the face, neck, throat and jawline. Guerlain Success Model Lifting Serum Ultra Firming (tel: +44 19 3223 3909) is another great neck firmer and Crème de la Mer Lifting Face Serum and Lifting Intensifier (tel: +44 870 034 2566) visibly tightens the skin, especially around the neck and eye area (a lot less painful than Thermage!). For scarring Crème de la Mer Concentrate is especially effective at healing. It's expensive though!

Puffy jowls – Need a little extra help?
Guinot Hydradermie Lift Deluxeis facial at Guinot, 17 Albemarle Street, London (tel: +44 20 7491 9971, www. guinot.com) and in Dublin (tel: +44 818 719 303 to find a salon in your area) is excellent at toning up slack jowls.

Ladybirds love nettle aphids for dinner

Spots and acne can sting like nettles

103

SPIDER VEINS & ROSACEA

Spider veins

Spider veins (red squiggly lines) can appear anywhere but are most common on the face around the nose, on the legs and chest. Experts liken spider veins to weeds in the garden: you can weed them out all you like, but others will spring up in their place over time.

Lasers for spider veins

For open pores, facial hair, spider veins around the nose, IPL (intense pulsed light) lasers have been created to zap them so that there's little risk of scarring or colour change to the skin (see opposite page for more laser info). The Vasculight treatment at the SMG Laser Clinic (tel: +44 800 056 5929) or laser sessions with Susan Mayou at the Lister Hospital (see opposite) will get rid of the veins over time. Alternatively, sclerotherapy, where the vein is injected with an irritant which diverts blood flow and causes the vein to collapse, works as well. John Scurr at the Lister Hospital, Chelsea Bridge Road, London SW1 (tel: +44 20 7730 9563) specializes in these vein-zapping injections as does Dr Philip Bull (www.doctor-bull.com), vascular specialist at the London Vein Clinic. Combining both IPL and sclerotherapy gives excellent results.

Preventing and treating spider veins at home

Revive Sans Veins Body Repair Cream at Space NK (tel: +44 20 7299 4999) works well on leg veins, while Vitamin K Spray Plus for Legs by Jason Natural Cosmetics (tel: +44 20 7435 5911) also prevents thread veins from forming; it contains vitamin K which surgeons use to treat bruising and bleeding in surgery as it constricts the blood vessels. If you work outdoors in the elements chances are you'll get spider or broken veins on your face as well. To prevent them, wear a good moisturizer like Barrier Repair by Dermalogica (for UK stockists tel: +44 800 591 818 and for Ireland tel: +353 1800 556 785, www.dermalogica.co.uk), and apply Amanda Lacey's Oils of Provence, available at Harvey Nichols or by mail order (tel: +44 20 7351 4443, www.amandalacey.com), beforehand to help it sink deeper into the skin. Vein Away Plus by

Skin Doctors Dermaceuticals (tel: +44 800 298 9600) is another cream which helps reduce spider veins and I swear by Medik8 (tel: +44 845 673 2222, www.medik8. com), a fantastic product which contains vitamin K. Dermablend Cover Crème Foundation, available in 15 shades (tel: +44 24 7664 4356), with Dermablend Setting Powder applied over it, does a good job at hiding them.

Rosacea

Rosacea makes you look permanently embarrassed and skin is red, swollen and sometimes stings. It's exacerbated by hot or cold weather, alcohol, spicy foods, caffeine, stress and face creams or sun protection that contain too many chemicals.

Lasers for Rosacea

For rosacea, acne, unwanted hair, spider veins and melasma, lasers and light sources work wonders and Dr Andrew Markey and Susan Mayou at the Lister Hospital, Chelsea Bridge Road, SW1 (tel: +44 20 7824 5560), are the experts. There are several types of lasers used by doctors and dermatologists with different strengths for different jobs. For example ablative lasers burn off the top layers of skin and in effect give the same results as a peel. Ablative laser treatment can occasionally leave the skin dark in patches for up to two weeks. Non-ablative lasers diminish wrinkles and tighten and lift skin (like a face lift) and produce a little redness. Then for permanent hair removal, spider veins, pigmentation and rosacea there are the IPL lasers.

After any of these treatments use a mild cleanser (see below) and Clinique CX do an amazing moisturizer. B Kamins Revitalizing Booster Concentrate, available at Space NK (tel: +44 20 7299 4999) and HQ Hair & Beautystore, 2 New Burlington Street, London W1 (tel: +44 871 220 4141, www.hqhair.com), also soothes any irritation.

Alternative products for rosacea at home

Avoid heavy facials and only use products from skincare ranges specifically created for rosacea. My favourites, La Roche Posay's Rosaliac cleansing make-up removal gel and Skin Perfecting Anti-redness moisturizer, are excellent and available by mail order from Hickeys, O'Connell Street, Dublin (tel: +353 1 873 0427), or www. beautytarget.com will ship it to you from the US. Alternatively, try a cleanser and moisturizer from Cetaphil (tel: +44 19 2329 1033) or the very calming moisturizer Bio-Maple Booster Blue Rosacea Treatment from the B Kamins Rosacea range at Space NK (tel: +44 20 7299 4999) or HQ Hair & Beautystore, 2 New Burlington Street, London W1 (tel: +44 871 220 4141; www.hqhair.com). Other good choices are DDF Redness Relief Cream and DDF Organic Sunblock SPF 30 (tel: +44 20 7201 1699, www.the-berkeley.co.uk), also available at Harvey Nichols, as alternatives to chemical-laced products. To minimize redness while you're treating it, choose a pressed powder with peachy or golden yellowish tones (Laura Mercier does a good one) instead of pink or reddish tones which just accentuate an already red complexion.

OPEN PORES

Open Pores

Large open pores are more common if you have oily skin. The skin stretches to allow excess sebum to escape and doesn't return to its original shape. While you can't actually reduce the size of your pores, there are different ways to make them look tighter.

Microdermabrasion

A virtually painless alternative to chemical and laser peels, microdermabrasion is superb not only for open pores but also for blackheads, whiteheads, fine lines, wrinkles, sun-damaged skin, superficial age spots, hyperpigmentation, stretch marks (40-50 per cent improvement), oily skin and dry or patchy problems. A jet of aluminum-oxide crystals is aimed over the face to remove the uppermost layer of skin (feels like you're being pelted with sand). At the same time, a vacuum sucks away the dead cells to reveal finer, more refined pores underneath. Check out The Biofarm Clinic (tel: +44 20 7242 5749) for microdermabrasion, or you could try IPL laser (see pp105).

Alternatives to microdermabrasion for minimising pores at home

Blocked pores look bigger, so unblock them with Dr Brandt Microdermabrasion in a jar at Space NK (tel: +44 20 7299 4999) or Prescriptives Dermapolish System (tel: +44 870 034 2566). Alternatively, use the two-step MD Skincare Alpha Beta Daily face-peel system from Manhattan's king of peels Dr Dennis Gross, once daily for 30 days, for great results. For daily cleansing try Mario Badescu's Glycolic Foaming Cleanser from HQ Hair (see pp85) and then apply Phyto 52 by YonKa after your evening cleanse (see pp93). It breaks down oil in blocked pores and mixed with a few drops of YonKa's Dermol1 loosens blackheads and hydrates skin. To give pores extra strength you need to build up collagen, which makes the skin firm around them. Retinol 0.5 Night Refining Cream by SkinCeuticals (tel: +44 20 8997 8541) does just that. Meanwhile, to create a smooth complexion try Pore Minimizer Instant by Clinique (tel: +44 1730 232 566), and then apply your foundation over it. A dab of Benefit's Dr Feelgood (tel: +44 9011 130 001) also helps minimize them.

Use SPF on virgin skin

After a peel or microdermabrasion (even the home ones) your 'new' skin is fragile and has little protection against the sun and UV rays. Wear a sunblock such as Vichy Capital Soleil 50+ or La Roche-Posay Anthelios 50+ (see pp122).

HYPERPIGMENTATION

Hyperpigmentation or brown spots

Blotchy, unusual, brown spots are not freckles, they are hyperpigmentation surfacing as a result of sun damage decades before or hormonal changes due to pregnancy. You can treat brown spots with a peel, microdermabrasion or lasers, which may lighten the pigment on some skins but exacerbate it on others, so be wary. Apply factor 50+ (Vichy see pp106) and stay out of the sun to prevent further pigmentation in the future.

Peels

Peels get rid of dead skin cells, acne, acne scars and brown spots caused by the sun, pregnancy or the contraceptive pill (hyperpigmentation). Light glycolic peels or 'lunchtime peels' are performed when a doctor brushes 30 to 70 per cent glycolic acid onto your face causing the skin to peel off like sunburn after three to seven days. Before a peel (or indeed any procedure) I use Advantage Regimen 1: AM Moisturizer, from Harvey Nichols (tel: +44 20 7235 5000) to maximize my skin's healing process. I also apply Cicaplast Epidermal repair accelerator by La Roche Posay (mail order from Hickey's, O'Connell Street, Dublin, (tel: +44 353 1 8730427), or www.beautytarget.com will ship it from the US. Remède Post-Peel Skin-Calming Balm, used twice daily afterwards, is superb in calming any irritation. Dr Penelope Tympanidis, 19 Wimpole Street, W1 (tel: +44 20 7462 0030, www.renascence.co.uk) is particularly good at peels. Also recommended is the Jan Marini 40 Per Cent Glycolic Acid Peel, available at the Jan Marini Skincare Clinic (tel: +44 20 7935 0023, www.janmarini.com) and Laser Aesthetics, 87 Wigmore Street, London W1 (tel: +44 20 7935 3366) is also particularly good for peels.

Alternative to salon peels at home for brown patches

The baby sisters to salon peel treatments are both Lancôme Re-Surface Peel (developed by US dermatologist Tina Alster – a four-step glycolic treatment) and Elizabeth Arden Peel & Reveal Revitalizing Treatment. Each contain a much lower concentration of glycolic acid than the salon and both will help reduce brown spots over time. Dermalogica Skin Brightening System (three products) is extremely good at tackling them too (for UK stockists tel: +44 800 591 818 and for Ireland tel: +353 1800 556 785, www.dermalogica.co.uk). For purists, Hollywood facialist Ole Henriksen Face/Body Micro/Mini Peel System is a totally natural peel kit and is available at Harvey Nichols or HQ Hair & Beauty store, 2 New Burlington Street, London W1 (tel: +44 871 220 4141, www.hqhair.com). Alternatively, Intensive Holistic Lightener by DDF (tel: +44 20 7201 1699, www.the-berkeley.co.uk, or Harvey Nichols) delays brown spots from forming, and Yonka Crème 40 and Solution 46 (tel: +44 20 7518 8370) applied morning and night helps fade sun spots, freckles and can be used safely on pregnancy hyperpigmentation.

Need a little extra help?

Hyperpigmentation is a normal occurrence during pregnancy and facialist Una Brennan (tel: +44 20 7313 9835) recommends SkinCeuticals Phyto Corrective Gel under Hydrating B5 Gel (tel: +44 20 8997 8541, www.hqhair.com) to counteract skin discolouration. I bought these products and tried them for sun spots and they worked! Facials with Una are also excellent. Also, the DDF holistic lightening facial at The Berkeley Hotel, Wilton Place, Knightsbridge, London SW1X 7RL (tel: +44 20 7201 1699, www.the-berkeley.co.uk) is superb.

WRINKLES

A wrinkle is a tear in your skin which occurs because the muscle underneath is constantly hammering into it. Wrinkles are expression lines; without a few, a face can be bland and boring. Here are your options to get rid of the deep-seated ones.

BOTOX®

Dr Andrew Markey, The Lister Hospital, Chelsea Bridge Road, London, SW1 (tel: +44 20 7730 1219) administers BOTOX® in a very responsible manner. I totally disagree with frozen, expressionless brows and there's a reason that I chose Dr Markey above all others in London – he always stays the right side of natural. BOTOX® temporarily paralyses the muscles in the forehead, the sides of the nose and around the eyes, and because the muscles are relaxed, the overlying skin smoothes out and prevents new creases from forming. It wears off after three to four months. Personally, I've never had bruising, but if you're prone to it, for a few days before BOTOX® injections avoid blood thinners like Motrin, aspirin, alcohol and vitamin E. Afterwards apply Arnica cream (or take arnica pills) from The Organic Pharmacy, 396 Kings Road, London, SW10 0LN (tel: +44 20 7351 2232, www. theorganicpharmacy.com), which helps prevent bruising.

Alternatives to BOTOX® at home

Cosmetic companies discovered that argireline, a non-toxic chemical, replicates BOTOX®'s effects – on the surface at least. The ingredient is in Elizabeth Arden's Ceramide Plump Perfect and DDF Wrinkle Relax and DDF Anti-Wrinkle Eye Renewal Treatment at Harvey Nichols, or mail order from the Berkeley Hotel (tel: +44 20 7201 1699, www.the-berkeley.co.uk). Meanwhile, Eyecicles by Freeze 24.7 anti-ageing range (tel: +44 1877 373 3934, www.freeze247.com), available exclusively at Space NK, has a BOTOX®-like effect on mild crow's-feet around the eyes. Its bigger sister, Freeze 24.7, works to temporarily blur forehead fine lines. StriVectin-SD (available at Harvey Nichols), originally a stretch-mark cream, reduces wrinkles very successfully with its key ingredient oligopeptide. Strivectin-SD eye-cream has the same key formula, but has added soothing agents for the eye area which help reduce the appearance of fine lines, wrinkles and dark circles. They're both absolutely brilliant! Another topical cream, Prevage by Elizabeth Arden and Allergen, the company which produces BOTOX®, seems to melt away wrinkles within twenty minutes of application. It is available at Harrods (tel: +44 20 7730 1234). Also for wrinkles around your eyes, use Pro-collagen Wrinkle Smooth pen by Elemis (tel: +44 20 7499 4995, www.elemis.com) – it plumps up skin and therefore relaxes fine lines. Medik8 also has a great product, Medik8 Prelift (tel: +44 845 673 2222, www.medik8.com), which is an amazing eye-cream that not only helps fade dark circles, but also zaps lines and bags as well.

After the eyes, lips are the quickest to thin with age

THIN LIPS

Fillers

Hyaluronic acid gels injected into the lip tissue are currently used by experts to fill and plump them and the most famous of all of these is Restylane®. There's a whole host of hyaluronic acid gel wrinkle-fillers (Restylane®, Purogen, Hydrafill) for filling lines, wrinkles and contours (www.restylane.com). The permanent fillers are usually the ones responsible for the trout pouts. Restylane®, on the other hand, breaks down in the body over a three-month period so it's not usually a trout-pout culprit.

Treating thin lips at home with creams and plumpers

There are many beauty products on the market to help plump lips up and give temporary maximum volume. DuWop's Lip Venom (stings me like hell as the chilli extract in it works on drawing blood to the surface) or Freeze 24.7 Plump Lips and Freeze 24.7 Plump Lip Ice Sticks coloured glosses (tel: +44 1877 373 3934, www.freeze247.com), available exclusively at Space NK (tel: +44 20 7299 4999). Both of the Freeze products cause lips to instantly inflate, but feel like an army of ants crawling all over your mouth. I prefer Kanebo's Total Lip treatment (mail order tel: +44 845 130 2912, www.chemistdirect. co.uk) or Helen Rubenstein's Collagenist Lip Zoom, which are all are great treatments. And my favourite is Pout's Lip Plump (see pp99) – but I hate having to burst the beautiful packaging.

Treating thin lips at home with make-up

To create a fuller pout, outline your lips with a pencil that matches your natural lip colour, keeping close to your own contour around the corners (unless you want to resemble the Joker in Batman). Exaggerate the shape slightly around the Cupid's bow (the two triangles on your top lip). Fill in the rest of your lips with the same pencil and then add a touch of shimmer lipstick, a dab of one of Lancôme's Juicy Tubes or your favourite lip-gloss to the middle of your bottom lip and smack them together. It works!

CELLULITE & STRETCH MARKS

Cellulite

Cellulite is not a fat issue (even thin people have it), it's a circulation problem. Skin deteriorates because cells and blood vessels become weak and can't distribute enough nutrients. Fibres harden and contract around the underlying fat cells causing fat to pop through to the skin's surface and appear as the dreaded 'orange peel'.

Need a little extra help?

Try the Fennel Cleansing Cellulite and Colon Therapy Massage at Elemis every two weeks. Or, if your cellulite is particularly bad, try Endermologie – a deep-tissue massage given by a therapist using a machine that sucks and rolls the fat around in rollers. This increases the circulation of blood and oxygen and lymph drainage, and most salons do it.

Cellulite treatments: where to start

Read The Cellulite Solution: A Doctor's Program for Losing Lumps, Bumps, Dimples, and Stretch Marks by Howard Murad MD, published by Piatkus Books (www.murad.com). Dr Murad is the world's leading cellulite expert. He advises an eight-week nutritional overhaul which centres on a diet with supplements that reinforce blood-vessel walls from the inside. You can purchase the Dr Murad Firm and Tone Anti-Cellulite Supplement Pack from Beauty Experts (tel: +44 870 443 6031, www.beautyexpert.co.uk), which contains all that you'll need to carry out the programme. He advises that you take the supplements twice a day, morning and night.

GODDESS TIP
STRESS CAUSES CELLULITE BY DEHYDRATING THE BODY. RELAX MORE, HAVE A THERAPEUTIC MASSAGE, A WALK, DO SOME YOGA OR EVEN HAVE A WARM BATH.

PHYTO-SCULPT
Global anti-cellulite
amincit
lisse
raffermit

slenderizing
smoothing
firming

sisley
PARIS

5 US FL OZ

GODDESS TIP
ONCE OR TWICE A WEEK (NOT ON THE DAYS YOU DRY SKIN-BRUSH), USE AN EXFOLIATING SCRUB – CLINIQUE SPARKLE SKIN BODY EXFOLIATOR CREAM (TEL: + 44 870 034 2566) IS A GOOD ONE TO AID EXFOLIATION AND IMPROVE BLOOD FLOW TO THE EPIDERMIS.

Dry skin brush

Dry brushing the affected area, always in the direction of the heart, with a natural-bristle brush before bathing, will exfoliate dead skin and stimulate the lymphatic system – and your circulation. The Elemis Body Brush ((tel: + 44 20 7499 4995, www.elemis.com) is my favourite brush, but if you find it hard to reach the back of your thighs with this handheld model try a long-handled brush instead from Crabtree & Evelyn (tel: +44 20 7361 0499, www.crabtree-evelyn.co.uk) or Liz Earle (mail order tel: + 44 1983 813913, www.lizearle.com), who also stocks a great pair of exfoliating gloves. On the stomach, brush more gently in a circular, clockwise direction. Bathe immediately after a dry skin-brushing routine and then moisturise with Dr Murad's Firm and Tone Serum morning and night, available from Beauty Experts (tel: +44 870 443 6031, www.beautyexpert.co.uk).

Use an anti-cellulite product

Sisley Phyto-Sculpt Global Anti-Cellulite (tel: + 44 20 7491 2722) is the best anti-cellulite topical cream in my opinion. It has always helped improve the texture of my skin and it's super-hydrating. Christian Dior's Bikini Cellulite-Diet Body Refining Essence (tel: + 44 1932 233909) and Yves Saint Laurent's Total Fitness Ultra-Silky Slimming Gel (tel: + 44 1444 255700) are also quite good. Weleda's Birch Cellulite Oil (tel: + 44 115 944 8200, www.weleda.co.uk) or Dr Hauschka Blackthorn Body Oil are good natural alternatives.

Stretch marks

Stretch marks, or striae distensae as they're called in medical terms, are lasting incriminating evidence that the skin has been stretched too quickly, whether horizontally from a sudden weight gain or vertically from a growth spurt. The collagen and elastin splits, and marks form. Pregnant women are often left with these after childbirth. They turn from a pink to a purple colour and eventually a silvery white and can appear on hips, thighs, abdomen, calves, upper arms, breasts and buttocks.

Stretch-mark treatments

Pink stretch marks are new, and because of their strong pink pigmentation can be greatly improved with a treatment called pulsed-dye laser at Lasercare clinics (tel: + 44 800 028 7222, www.lasercare-clinics.co.uk), if treated within the first year of appearance. Older stretch marks are much more difficult to treat and may be improved by Fraxel laser treatments. Dr Jan Stanek and Dr Tom Bozek, 60 Wimpole St London (tel: +44 20 7487 4454, www.surgical-aesthetics.com) and Dr Karyn Grossman, 154 East 85th St, New York (tel: +1 212 879 9504, www.grossmandermatology.com) are Fraxel experts and half-hour treatments spaced at least a week apart to allow the skin time to recover will greatly improve skin condition. Skin is numbed and dyed blue for the laser to take effect – and the blue does wash off over time. Afterwards skin feels hot, like a case of mild sunburn, swells a little and stays pinkish for up to a week as it flakes off to reveal brand new skin. Dr Grossman prescribes Soothing Beyond Measure by Prescribed Solutions (www.prescribedsolutions.com): a great product which soothes inflamed skin while it heals. If you don't fancy the Fraxel treatment, you could try microdermabrasion (see pp106) or a peel (pp107) but both of these are less effective, in my opinion.

Alternatives at home

Stretch marks are difficult to treat once you have them so try to prevent them by keeping skin well moisturised with a good oil. Try Clarins L'Huile Tonic or Decléor's Aromessence Tonilastil Firming Aromatic Body Oil (tel: +44 20 7402 9474) or Bio-Oil (available at Boots). Elemis's Japanese Camellia Oil (tel: +44 20 7499 4995, www.clemis.com) is a really good choice and can even be rubbed on bump, bum and bust during pregnancy. Rodial also does a great bump-friendly, in other words totally natural, Body Polish and Cream (tel: +44 20 7565 8307, also at Harvey Nichols) and the range, which is packed with pomegranate, is the preferred beauty range at designer pregnancy store 9 London (www.9london.co.uk). Aromatherapy Associates' rose range is also bump-friendly and the Renew Nourishing Rose Body Oil (tel: +44 20 7371 9878) is one of the most popular stretch-mark preventers among those in the know. You could also treat yourself to an Elemis mother-to-be massage or an Aromatherapy Associates pregnancy massage (see pp88).

GODDESS
Beauty Kit

I've kept notes and drawings of beauty treatments, products and procedures for years now – I know, I'm a bit of a saddo. When asked about my favourites, I flick back through the years of doodles and get all gooey inside about the ones that have impressed me the most – the ones I've coloured in excitedly to make them stand out boldly. Here are the products and procedures that I use daily, the ones that have exhausted my markers, inks and watercolours…

Skincare kit
The ultimate lifesaver: Elizabeth Arden Eight Hour Cream is my addiction, (available nationwide). I've four tubes in the house at any one time. **Affordable night cream**: Olay's Total Effects 7x Night is an inexpensive choice as a regular night cream, or try Chanel's Précision Éclat Originel Radiance Revealing Serum or Lancôme's Absolute Night Recovery Treatment, for face, throat and décolleté. **Fill-in wrinkles**: Prescriptives' Invisible Line Smoother is a clear gel not unlike a morticians' wax. When applied it fills in lines – and make-up can then be applied straight over it. **Brighten skin**: Guinot Gommage Biologique Gentle Face Exfoliator (see pp94), melts dead skin-cells away instantly. Use every few days before applying SkinCeuticals Hydrating B5 (a moisturizing serum – see pp91), and then your favourite moisturizer (see pp101). To finish off the look, use Chanel's Bronze Universal on your face for a tan that appears in seconds. **To de-puff eyes**: As soon as you wake, steep a cloth in cold water and place it on your face, then drape two teabags, which you've first dipped in hot water and then chilled in the fridge, over your eyes for ten minutes. Then pat Hylexin or StriVectin SD eye cream, both at Harvey Nichols (tel: +44 20 7235 5000), or Dior's Capture R60/80 Wrinkle Eye Cream (tel: +44 19 3223 3909) around your eyes using your ring finger. Dr Sebagh For Your Eyes Only at Space NK (tel: +44 208 740 2085) is another great de-puffing product. **Boosting skin after illness or surgery**: Try using Guinot's Masque Energie Lift (see pp94), a face mask which instantly erases the signs of fatigue. Afterwards I like to moisturize with either Clinique CX Rapid Recovery Cream or Clinique CX Soothing Moisturizer (tel: +44 870 034 2566, www.clinique.co.uk). For scarring after surgery, or pasty complexion after illness use Crème de la Mer Concentrate (tel: +44 870 034 2566). **An intensive overhaul**: Sisleÿa Elixer (see below) four little pump containers used over a month will bring brightness back to your complexion in no time. Used twice a year it completely rejuvenates skin. **Anti-ageing serum**: Dr Andrew Weil for Origins Plantidote™ Mega-Mushroom Face Serum (tel: +44 800 7314039, www.origins.co.uk). **Anti-ageing cream**: Sisleÿa Global Anti-Age Extra-Rich (tel: +44 20 7491 2722, www.sisleya.com).

Peacock *n* a male peafowl, having a crested head and a very large fanlike tail marked with blue and green eyelike spots. *Coll. n* a muster of peacocks.

Make-up kit

BioCol Velvet Skin, available on the BioCol website, www.biocol.co.uk, or at Harrods, works wonders on uneven skin as a primer under make-up as does **Prescriptives Super Line Preventor** (tel: +44 870 034 2566, www.prescriptives.com). **Clinique Pore Minimizer, T-Zone Shine Control Gel** (tel: +44 87 0034 2566, www.clinique.co.uk), used over your moisturizer and under your make-up, perfects open pores and a shiny T-zone. **Becca Translucent Bronzing Gel** at Becca, 91A Pelham St, London (tel: + 44 20 7225 2501, www. beccacosmetics.com) gives a beautifully natural look as a foundation alternative, and **Becca Bird of Paradise Gloss** illuminates dull cheeks, lips and eyelids. **Clarins Beauty Flash Balm** (tel: +44 800 036 3558, www.clarins.com), worn over foundation, works as an instant pick-me-up before a big night out – or the morning after a hard night's partying. **Prescriptives** (see above) offers a 'Custom Blend' service in-store that will mix up foundation, powder and lipstick shades specifically to suit your skin tone. **Yves Saint Laurent Touche Eclat Radiant Touch** (tel: +44 14 4425 5700, www.ysl.com) hides dark shadows, fine lines when worn over foundation and is an absolute beauty essential. **Chantecaille Cheek Shade** (in Mood) at Fenwick (tel. +44 20 7629 9161) trims years off your face when brushed over your cheekbones. For blusher I also buy Yves Saint Laurent or Armani – they've no added glitter thankfully. Fix your make-up with **Poudré T. LeClerc** in the Banane colour (also at Fenwick): a light, rice starch powder which transforms you into a screen goddess when it catches artificial light. It comes in 22 colours. **Guerlain Divinora Eyeliner in Noir Ebène** (tel:+ 44 19 3223 3909, www.guerlain.com) gives really accurate lines. **Make Up For Ever 12 Flash Colour case** (tel: +44 20 8740 0808, www.makeupforever.com) has colours which smudge beautifully on the eyelids and lips. Also try Mac, Shu Uemura and Nars for eye-shadows. **Chanel's Cils à Cils in Marine mascara** (tel: +44 20 7493 3836, www.chanel.com) in blue makes eyes look whiter. To keep brows tidy, **Tweezerman Tweezers** (tel: +44 20 7237 1007, www.tweezerman. com) are the very best; and MAC's Brow Set (tel: +44 20 7534 9222, www.mac.com) helps to fill in over-plucked eyebrows. **Givenchy Baby Lips** (tel: +44 19 3223 3909, www.givenchy.com) palette contains a lip exfoliator, a balm and two shades of colour lips according to your natural pH.

Hands and feet

For hands I use **Delux Nail Scissors by Tweezerman** (www.tweezerman.com), Clarins Hand and Nail Treatment (tel: +44 800 036 3558), and Mavala for products, buffers and files (tel: +44 1732 459 412, www.mavala.co.uk). And for feet **Diamancel Foot File at Bliss** (tel: + 44 808 100 4151, www.blisslondon.co.uk) is the best at beating stubborn foot calluses. Clip nails straight across using **Nail Clippers from Mavala**. **Pedi-Cream from the DDF** range at The Berkley Hotel or Harrods is best for softening (see pp90) and **Jessica's Quick Dry polish** (tel: +44 20 8381 7793, www. jessicacosmetics.co.uk) sets in 60 seconds.

FITNESS WITH DAVID KIRSCH

It was deep winter in New York and the snow was piled high around the corner by the Flat Iron building, between 22nd and 23rd streets on Fifth Avenue. I'd jogged from Central Park for my gym session in nothing but a vest and trackie bottoms; my tummy was flat, my arms toned and my head clear. My secret? I'd been training with celebrity trainer David Kirsch (author of *The Ultimate New York Body Plan*, McGraw-Hill Education) for several weeks.

Back to my first ever session, and as I stepped, nervously, out of the lift at his Madison Square Club, 210 5th Avenue (tel: +1 212 683 1836, www.davidkirsch.com), David broke momentarily from a discussion with Linda Evangelista to greet me. He smiled reassuringly, handed me a towel and an iced water and lemon drink and returned to Linda and her lunges. (David also trains Liv Tyler, Heidi Klum and Sophie Dahl so you can imagine how I felt – it made me row harder just thinking about it.) I spent weeks doing squats, sidekicks, and excruciatingly deep lunges, to the sound of Kirsch's firm but supportive voice, "Straighten your spine. Sit deeper. Focus. Put your brain in your butt Gisèle." (Yeah right, between last night's Lombardi's pizza and this morning's feed of scones and jam.) His results were magnificent – I've never felt so fabulous – and his team of ten trainers, superb – they really do treat his clients like family. I stick with his programme in Dublin by buying his protein and vitamin supplements from www.davidkirsch.co.uk. For workouts, his book and DVD have helped me to keep up the regime on my own.

How can I get the Goddess look before a party, David?
Firstly, cut back on ABCs: that's alcohol, bread, starchy carbohydrates, dairy, extra sweeteners, fruit and trans fats, and go high protein, first that swims and then flies. Combine with steamed green veggies and mesculun salads. Try not to eat after 7p.m. and cut back on caffeine, salt, sugar and anything processed. Don't skip meals and instead supplement your diet with one of my shakes if you're on the run or tempted

to blow out on starchy carbs. Drink plenty of flat water to flush out toxins.

Right, so I've put a cork in my mouth after 7 p.m. every night; what next?
Always start your day with exercise. Even before you have your breakfast, walk around the block or do some push ups against a wall, or some squat thrusts in the kitchen whilst the kettle is boiling. If you do this for 15 minutes every morning, the elevation in your heart rate boosts your metabolism and you'll feel energized and focused for the day. Listen to your body – try only to eat when you're hungry. Enjoy preparing healthy and nutritious meals. Eat slowly. Chew your food.

What if I'm dining out, David? Any tips? *Make a game plan, Gisèle and keep to it! Go ahead and dine out but plan ahead. Choose a restaurant that offers healthy choices and know what you are going to order. There are plenty of healthy choices out there. If you simply can't do without a cookie or some chocolate, make sure it's good. A little of something good is better then lots of something bad.*

David's Dumbbell Wraparound

1.) From a seated position on your stability ball, walk your feet forward and slide your torso down the ball until you come into a bench press position, with your upper back and head against the ball, knees bent 90 degrees, and your feet on the ground. Grasp a dumbbell in each hand, with your arms extended toward the ceiling from your chest.

2.) Lower your arms behind your head.

3.) Once your arms are parallel with the floor with your palms facing up, bring your arms in a semi circle towards your hips, all the while keeping your arms parallel to the floor.

4.) Bend your elbows and squeeze your hands together above your navel, as if you are hugging your arms around a large oak tree with your palms facing each other. Return to the starting position and repeat 20-30 times.

Donkey Kicks

1.) Kneel on all fours with your hands under your chest and your knees under your hips. Place a medicine ball in the crease behind your left knee, squeezing your calf and thigh together to hold the ball in place.

2.) Bring your left knee in towards your chest.

3.) Exhale as you press your left foot towards the ceiling, continuing to hold the ball between your calf and thigh. Alternate between the positions 1 and 2 15-20 times.

4.) Pulse your leg upwards in a micro movement, reaching your left foot towards the ceiling over and over for about 15 seconds. Relax and repeat with the right leg.

Exercises taken from **The Ultimate New York Body Plan**, (McGraw-Hill Education).

David's Workout Tips
When working-out, ensure that your abs, arms and back muscles are exercised as this gives balance to the body. Allow yourself your vanity but don't be overwhelmed or eclipsed by it. Work towards your goal steadily and with patience.

GYM KIT

Running leggings

Stella McCartney running leggings at Adidas Performance Centre, 415-419 Oxford Street, London (tel: +44 20 7493 1886, www.adidas.com, or online ordering tel: +44 870 909 1200).

Running shoes

Asics Gel Nimbus at Run and Become, 2 Palmer Street, London (tel: +44 20 7222 1314, www.runandbecome.com) are excellent. Also check out Runners Need, 34 Parkway (tel: +44 20 7267 7525, www.runnersneed.co.uk) for superb staff advice.

Yoga

Try Sweaty Betty (tel: +44 80 0169 3889, www.sweatybetty.com), or Calmia 52-54 Marylebone High Street, London (tel: +44 84 5009 2450, www.calmia.com), for mats, and Orla Kiely, 31 Monmouth Street, London (tel: +44 20 7240 4022, www.orlakiely.com) for yoga bags.

Sore muscles

Roll on some This Works Muscle Therapy by This Works, 18 Cale Street, London (tel: +44 207 584 1887; mail order +44 8452 300499, www.thisworks.com, or at Harvey Nichols) or have a long soak in This Works Deep Calm Bath and Shower Oil. Alternatively, Elemis Aching Muscle Super Soak (tel: +44 20 7499 4995, www.elemis.co.uk), relieves tired stiff muscles after 20 minutes in the bath. Trust me you'll be needing them!

Professional Support up top

Shoulders Back tops (tel: +44 17 3770 0020, www.shouldersback.co.uk), correct posture and promote open chest breathing. Enell Sports Bras at Sheactive, 21/22 New Row, London (tel: +44 20 7836 6222, www.sheactive.co.uk, www.enell.com) provide guaranteed support during running.

Hair

If you have frizzy locks (and let's face it, who doesn't after a visit to the gym), then try John Frieda's Straight Ahead Shampoo and Conditioner and Serum – all part of the Frizz-Ease range (tel: +44 20 7851 9800, www.johnfrieda.co.uk). For ponytails I use my Mason Pearson Boar Bristle Brush (tel: +44 20 7491 2631, www.masonpearson.com) and Blax Snag-Free Elastic Bands at HQ Hair & Beauty store, 2 New Burlington Street, London (tel: +44 871 220 4141, www.hqhair.com).

Swimming

To protect your hair while swimming, wear a Silicone Speedo Swimcap from Sweaty Betty (see yoga). Before putting it on, comb through Philip Kingsley Swimcap Hair Protection (tel: +44 20 7629 4004, www.philipkingsley.co.uk); a product specially formulated to guard against chlorine.

Paraben-free deodorant

E Plus High C Roll On Deodorant by Aubrey Organics at The Organic Pharmacy (see pp91).

this works:
deep calm
bath and
shower oil

1.86 fl oz

BLAX

JOHN FRIEDA

FRIZZ-EASE

Hair Serum
ORIGINAL FORMULA

50 ml e 1.7

I asked Kathy Phillips, International Beauty Director for Condé Nast Asia and author of *The Spirit of Yoga* for her ultimate Goddess health and beauty tip:

Check out: www.you-are-beautiful.com

You use yoga to stay fit and healthy, what are its benefits?
I think it's important that each person finds their own yoga. That could be fishing, walking the dog, running, or even playing cricket, not necessarily yoga per se. The benefits of finding an exercise that puts you into a Zen space and restores your energy levels is incalculable. I believe that the Hatha Yoga I have done for the last 25 years oxygenates the blood, stimulates circulation, keeps the tissues healthy, keeps the nervous system balanced and the metabolism ticking over. They say when you need a teacher you will find one. Sadly the best teachers are the ones who keep quiet and look after their pupils and not the ones who get all the publicity. I have been very lucky in my teachers; my mentor, Mary Stewart started with B.K.S. Iyengar in the 60s. A "guru" in Sanskrit is merely a teacher who shows you the way. We should not get hung up on gurus at all. I try to explain all this in my book, The Spirit of Yoga.

what is beauty Kathy?

VOGUE
NIPPON

Dean Gisele,

I am writing this from Tokyo where Beauty, beheld by the Japanese eye, is undoubtedly quite different to mine.
Which just goes to show that " Beauty in things exists in the mind which contemplates them" – an observation by David Hume in the early 18th century, written long before the more hackneyed phrase- "Beauty is in the eye of the beholder".
"What is Beauty?" is a tough question to answer without sounding pretentious. In my opinion, Beauty gives pleasure and brings it- spontaneously.
It is not just about being perfect. It is idiosyncratic and individual to a person, place or thing.
For me it is a by-product of health, awareness, wisdom and serenity, more than it is a lucky accumulation of genes and beauty tricks. In a person it comes as much from the inside as the out – personified in an inner glow, an "energy", an aura.
Thanks to cosmetic scientists and pharmacists, reconstructive surgeons and dermatologists, make-up artists and hairdressers; we are increasingly trying to pursue Beauty as an aesthetic. This is not necessarily narcissism- it is the new art of the possible. But for me, it will never eclipse the unpredictable beauty of something or someone that is entirely natural.

x Kathy

117

3 TRAVEL

The first adventure I can remember happened one fresh spring morning when I was about five years old. Mum wrapped me tightly in my padded red wine coloured coat, tied the fur trimmed hood securely under my chin and Dad lifted me gently onto the little wooden seat he'd built over the toolbox on his grey Massey Ferguson 20 tractor. The seat was high up and Dad had even attached a cushion so that I could see out over the steering wheel while we explored the farm together. We chatted away happily over the shrill sound of the tractor's engine but when he wanted to explain something important he'd turn the throttle down, fix his eyes on mine and, with the engine ticking over, speak to me in his clear, kind voice. I listened intently to this great man's words as he carefully explained vital details about wild birds and animals. We talked, I always felt, as equals – our worlds undivided by experience, position or age.

Pointing to Michael Kelly's fields over the ditch behind the hayshed he told me that a man called Maurice Walsh had once lived just beyond them. Maurice had written many famous stories and Dad told me how his favourites were *The Quiet Man*, and *The Key Above The Door*; "*The Quiet Man* was filmed on the west coast of Ireland in Co. Mayo in 1952 and it starred two Hollywood greats, John Wayne (The Duke) and Maureen O'Hara." I remember wanting to go and see this place immediately but Dad said that Mayo was a very long way away and that perhaps I'd prefer to see Dingle (or An Daingean Uí Chúis as he called it), where Robert Mitchum starred in Ryan's Daughter in 1968. "Dingle is on the beautiful coastline along the Ring of Kerry," he reassured me, "so why don't we go there instead?"

From that day onwards I asked almost daily about the trip to Dingle. Dad explained that the summer's fine days had to be respected and used cleverly by farmers so promised when the hay was saved and safely stacked in the hayshed, and the turf was cut and brought home from the bog, we'd be able to go. "If you helped me Gisèle with the hay, I'd be quicker. I'll be going to Spancill Hill horse fair on the 23rd of June, so we'll go to Dingle a few days after that," he promised. (Every June he went to the Spancill Hill horse fair in Co. Clare and each October never missed the one in Ballinasloe in Co. Galway. To this day he hasn't missed either in 40 years.) Oh the anticipation of it all! I immediately started the packing. Dad made me more excited still by telling me that I'd be able to dangle my feet off of Dingle pier and dip my toes into the Atlantic ocean. Winking to my mother he said that if we looked hard enough into the distance we'd even be able to see the coast of America (weather permitting of course). "All we'll need," he laughed, "is a fine clear day."

As June dragged on, I looked longingly towards the bit of coast at the end of our road. My patience tested I convinced myself that I would be able to reach out and touch the Atlantic from the top of Tom Keane's ditch – I was sure that it was Dingle that I was looking at. One lunchtime, my mind made up, I packed my savings, dolls, teddies, Taytos, a drink and some chocolate in my dusty pink pram and planned my escape. After a hearty meal of pork chops, apple sauce, boiled celery, carrots, and potatoes, I slipped quietly out the front door, and headed in a straight line towards the coast.

With every step down the road the coast drew nearer – a bluey-white line drawn by an unsteady hand against the sky. I chatted to the dolls, informing them of our planned adventure, and their heads seemed to bob in agreement as the pram rolled along the baked-dry tarmac, bubbling and uneven in the heat. I passed the goats grazing and the lupins blooming at Tony Mulvihill's, and the sweet wild roses growing in Michael Kelly's ditch. I trotted to keep up with the pram as it rolled down the hill towards Nell Charlie's when a rustling in Michael Kelly's ditch stopped me in my tracks. I couldn't see anything so I carried on but soon realized that every time the pram wheels rolled an evil growling sounded from the bushes. Terrified, I turned the pram around and legged it for home.

That evening Dad explained sympathetically that there must have been a wild dog in the ditch at Kelly's. He also told me that the coastline wasn't Dingle at all but Ballybunion – a town I knew well – wet and grey in the winter months it blossomed in the summer (our very own Cote D'Azur!). As small children, we were happy to blend in with the sandy chaos on the beach at Ballybunion - with Loop the Loop stained lolly lips, and toes full of damp sand. And for ten years this was my idea of heaven – and much better than Dingle, where it rained when we finally got there and where all the squinting in the world didn't reveal America. Gutted.

These days Dad's tractor has been replaced by taxis, planes, trains and rickshaws. And, as I sink into deep, comfortable seats in foreign cities and am shepherded through cantankerous traffic as side streets and alleys flash past, I am once more that pampered child. When exploring, Dad taught me to seek out and welcome faces, marked walls and the tales that hide in the cracks that pepper pavements. He taught me to smell foreign air, query foreign light and inhale deeply the smell of foreign rain; to judge every new destination fairly and with equal objectivity. So, here are my honest opinions about the people and places I love around the world.

Prepare Yourself

Enlist the help of experts

A month before your trip, survey the damage. If you need to lose weight fast, read David Kirsch, author of **The Ultimate New York Body Plan** (book and DVD), www.newyorkbodyplan. com plan advice (see pp122-125). Fake tan will also help you look slimmer and the best prefessional application in my opinion is by St Tropez. Call Beauty Source tel: +44 115 983 6363. Another great pre-holiday option is The Holiday Countdown treatment at The Guinot Salon, 17 Albemarle Street, London W1S 4HP (tel: +44 20 7491 9971): they will give you a pre-trip buffed shine.

Tan your face

For the face, Lancôme Flash Bronzer or Clarins Radiance-Plus Self Tanning Cream-Gel give flawless results. Always exfoliate face and neck first as fake tan will stick in creases and adhere to dry patches. Use a fine-grain gentle scrub like Dermalogica Daily Microfoliant (for UK stockists tel: +44 800 591 818 and for Ireland tel: +353 1800 556 785, www.dermalogica.co.uk). Wait two days after waxing or laser facial-hair removal to tan your face, otherwise results will be blotchy. Swipe a cotton ball underneath the cheekbones, which makes the cheekbones stand out and gives a natural sun-kissed look.

De-fuzz

Shave, wax, or have it lasered using IPL (see pp104). Bare Necessity (tel: +44 800 027 2029) offer great laser treatments, and just one session every six weeks for seven months will totally eradicate hair. For waxing see Heidi Klein right, or other experts (pp89). And if you experience ingrown hairs, MD Formulations Pedi-Cream is excellent, as is Bliss Ingrown Hair Eliminating Peeling Pads at Harvey Nichols. I use Chanel's Calming Emulsion to soothe and calm my skin after laser, waxing or shaving and remember that any hair removal (even shaving) must be done a few days before you plan to apply fake tan.

One-stop holiday shops

Biondi, 55B Old Church Street, London (tel: +44 20 7349 1111, www.biondicouture. com) stocks a huge range of holiday treats from cashmere slippers and pillows to passport covers and bikinis – you can even design your own bikini. Heidi Klein, 174 Westbourne Grove, London, W11 (tel: +44 20 7243 5665), and Pavilion Road, SW1 (tel: +44 20 7259 9418) are also two great pre-holiday stores. I buy Melissa Odabash's amazing range of beautiful bikinis (designed to specifically flatter each body shape) from here. Check out the range at www.odabash.com. Heidi Klein also offers body scrub, massage, manicure and pedicure: it's a one-stop holiday shop and Amy Jones, the waxer there, is one of the best!

BRITISH AIRWAYS

Tan your body

My favourite body tanner is St Tropez Autobronzant cream and I use a cosmetic sponge to apply it to problem areas. Before application, I exfoliate with Clinique's Sparkle Skin Body Exfoliating Cream, concentrating on elbows, knees and the backs of ankles, and then moisturise with Kiehl's Crème de Corps (tel: +44 20 7240 2411). I take a bath twelve hours before tanning with Aromatherapy Associates Deep Relax Oil (tel: +44 20 8569 7030, www.aromatherapyassociates.com) – it conditions the skin. The day after self tanning I go back and spritz St Tropez spray downwards on love handles and upwards on my butt cheeks to slim them.

Carte d'accès à bord Boarding pass

Ultimate holiday footwear

I love my havianas! 450,000 pairs are made every day in Brazil, in a gazillion different colours. In London you can get them at Coco Ribbon (tel: +44 20 7229 4904).

Immunise

Check out www.medicineplanet.com: it gives country-specific info and has tons of advice from doctors on immunisation and disease risks in different countries.

Bag the best seat

www.seatguru.com shows the seat plans for most airlines. So get that extra leg room before anyone else does.

In-flight Essentials

Cleanse with **Sisleÿa Cleansing Milk** (see pp100), then apply **SkinCeuticals B5 Gel** (see pp91) under **Prescriptives Super flight Cream** (tel: +44 870 034 2566, www.prescriptives.com). **Optrex Brightening Drops** rehydrate parched, post-flight peepers and **This Works Travel Kit**, containing 8 skin-saving goodies, including one which combats in-flight germs called **Breathe In** (see pp240) – an in-flight must-have.

Don't forget...

Bose QuietComfort 2 Acoustic Noise Cancelling earphones: these are really comfy and reduce external noise for when you're snoozing or just listening to your music (tel: +44 139 242 8388, www.bose.co.uk); **Passport Cover** by **Smythson** (see pp243); **Ballantyne Cashmere Blanket:** deliciously soft and luxurious (see pp55); **Muji Mini Bottles** for decanting skincare products from www.muji.co.uk; **Tumi Electric Adaptor:** works in over 150

countries and is available at www.tumi.com or in all major department stores; **Babyliss Whisper Jet Travel Dryer:** a powerful 1800 watt hair-dryer complete with fold-out handle from www.hqhair.com; my favourite candle from **Hotel Costes** (see pp142); and if you want to nourish your cuticles on the go, **Dr. Hauschka's Neem Nail Oil Pen** (tel: +44 1386 792 642, www.drhauschka.com), won't spill all over you or your luggage.

Beach kit

La Roche Posay Anthelios Cream (SPF 20, 40 or 50+): the highest protection against UVB (known to cause burns) and UVA (causes premature ageing and skin cancer) rays, (see pp105). **Institute Esthederm Extreme Bronze Repair:** an anti-wrinkle, tanning cream – go to www.esthederm.com or visit Space NK (tel: +44 208 740 2085, www.spacenk.com). **SkinCeuticals CE Ferulic** and **SkinCeuticals Serum 10:** applied under sunscreen these products prevent skin damage and

stimulate repair (see pp91). **Yves Saint Laurent Baume D'Ete Tinted Lip Balm** with SPF 10 is available at department stores and **Matrix Biolage Protective Hair Oil:** protects locks from salt, chlorine and the sun – at www.salon-collective.co.uk. **Liz Earle Sunshade Botanical Aftersun Gel** (see pp100). **Silhouette Sunglasses** (model 8592): light and comfortable, and they never fall off (www.silhouette.com). **Florentine Milliner's Grevi Hat:** wide brimmed and soft this even folds up in your bag, available from Fenwick, www.fenwick.co.uk.

Travel Must Haves

MD Skincare Hydra-Pure™ Intense Moisture Cream: this cream strips away the heavy metals found in foreign tap water which sit on the surface of the skin, and also increases the efficacy of your other skincare products. **Nuxe Huile Prodigieuse:** a nourishing oil which leaves skin and hair illuminated with prismatic golden particles (tel: +44 1932 827060 for stockists).

How to pack your bags!

Travel notebook
Packing takes planning so I always make a list in my travel notebook and tick off the items as they're laid out on my bed. This is also very helpful when I'm packing to come back home: it means I leave nothing behind me as I tick off the items on the list in a different colour.

The kit – Tissue paper
Tissue paper and plastic sheets are a Goddess's best friend. Have you ever wondered why shop assistants wrap your purchases in tissue paper inside a square bag? Clothes only crease if they come in contact with sharp edges, like those on a suitcase, for instance. Wrapping your items separately before packing in tissue paper prevents wrinkles and creases: buy it in department stores or use dry-cleaning plastic instead.

Chopper vision
With each item laid out on my bed I have an aerial view of what I'm about to pack. I survey the outfits, mixing and matching as often as I can, and then I ask myself do I really need a million pairs of shoes and thirteen different hair products? I take one pair of trainers, a pair of havianas and a pair of Christian Louboutin stilettos as footwear. I fasten all jackets and shirts as it helps them keep their shape and it's a good way of checking that all buttons and zips are working. I also like to take some padded hangers, as wire ones ruin clothes.

The kit – Muji
Buy some Tocca Laundry Delicate Wash from Pout in Covent Garden and decant along with all of your other favourite products into Muji bottles (www.muji.co.uk). Muji also do mesh bags, which come in a few different sizes and are perfect for socks, bikinis and trinkets. Ziplock bags are also great for used underwear if you don't fancy washing.

The kit – Miller Harris
Also, Miller Harris does very small glass bottles with mini funnels for decanting your scent. Pick up a citron candle and some citron shower gel for some zesty goodness if you're heading for the sun.

The kit – Toothbrush
Toothbrush covers are a must for keeping your toothbrush clean – buy a pack of four at John Lewis.

The kit – bubble wrap
Bubble wrap, light and voluminous, can be used to fill up loose space on the way out and then to wrap your souvenirs on the way back.

GODDESS TIP
IF YOU'RE GOING ON A SHOPPING TRIP, PACK YOUR SMALL SUITCASE WITH YOUR CLOTHING IN IT INSIDE A LARGER ONE. YOU'LL HAVE THE USE OF THE BIGGER ONE ON THE WAY BACK TO CARRY ALL OF YOUR NEW PURCHASES. OR TRAVEL WITHOUT YOUR BAGS BY SENDING THEM AHEAD WITH FIRST LUGGAGE, A SERVICE THAT WORKS IN CONJUNCTION WITH FEDEX (WWW.FIRSTLUGGAGE.COM).

Luggage
Tanner Krolle (www.tannerkrolle.co.uk), Valextra (www.valextra.it), Pickett (www.pickett.co.uk) and Tumi (www.tumi.com) are my favourite luggage labels.

Packing

If you're a frequent traveller, keep your washbag packed and stocked in your bathroom at all times, ready just to put in your suitcase. Pack your shoes first, fill the holes and gaps with socks, lingerie and swimwear. Lay a few sheets of bubble wrap over this layer and cover with white tissue. Place the legs of your trousers together and lay them down so that the top and the hem drape out over the edges of your case. Layer your tops down one by one, folding them perfectly in tissue (enjoy that crinkle, mmmmm). For larger long-sleeved items, lay them down in layers, one by one, leaving the excess to spill over the edge of the suitcase. Use your washbag as a core, wrap it in tissue and fold your items in around it. Fill any spaces with lingerie, socks or crumpled-up bubble wrap. With no sharp edges or places to move your clothes will arrive at the other end intact.

Perspiration Pads

If you're planning on wearing your best silk dress in a very hot climate you don't want it ruined by sweat stains. Buy some perspiration pads from John Lewis's haberdashery department. They come in disposable or washable and you simply stick them or sew them into the underarm of your dress and they soak up the perspiration.

Lighten up

Weigh your suitcase before you buy it, as this will eat into your luggage allowance on every single trip.

Label your luggage

To avoid the mix-up with another identical black bag, order some personalised straps from Mini-Labels (www.minilabels.co.uk). Or Smythson, 40 New Bond Street, London W1S 2DE (tel: +44 7318 1515, www.smythson.co.uk) do some beautiful card labels, or leather ones if you want to treat yourself.

125

JET LAG

I love dreaming of places

Learn to Fly Here!

BOSE

What is jetlag?

The cause of jetlag is simple: as the body crosses time zones its circadian rhythms (the internal body clock that tells us when to sleep), becomes disrupted. Deprived of exterior stimuli (light, dark or day-to-day routine), our body clock becomes confused. As a general rule, it takes one day to recover from every hour lost, or gained. I suffer most flying to and from London and New York, and particularly when returning from Los Angeles or Sydney. I've also learned the hard way that I feel more jetlagged flying East, than I do flying West.

How can you cure it?

The golden rule is that you should try and book a flight which allows you to sleep while it is night at your destination. That way, immediately upon arrival, you can get some daylight and try to enjoy a full day's activities. The table on the right, compiled by Dr David O'Connell, a jetlag expert and author of Jetlag: How to Beat It (Ascendant Publishing), available to buy from his clinic at 41 Elystan Place, Chelsea Green, London SW3 (tel: +44 207 584 9779, www.drdavidoconnell.co.uk), should help you when booking your flight times.

On board

A window seat on a flight makes snoozing much easier. Eat something light, like dried fruit or nuts, or have a yogurt. Also remember to avoid booze, caffeine and salty snacks and to drink plenty of water.

Plan your flights to combat jetlag.

New York
Depart from London, late afternoon.
Return from New York on an 8 p.m. flight.

Los Angeles
Depart from London, around lunchtime.
Return from Los Angeles on a lunchtime flight.

Sydney
Depart from London at midday.
Return from Sydney on a 9 a.m. flight.

Phuket
Depart from London, no later than 4 p.m.
Return from Phuket on a midnight flight.

Goa
Depart from London, before 6 p.m.
Return from Goa on a midnight flight.

Caribbean
Depart from London, late afternoon.
Return from the Caribbean on an 8 p.m. flight.

Before you fly

To see what products you should be using before and during your flight see pp122.

First night: perk up a jetlagged body

Upon arrival I try to exercise and spend some time outdoors – a brisk walk usually does the trick. Before bed I use Dermalogica Body Hydrating Cream, applying it to legs, arms, bum, boobs and stomach (for UK stockists tel: +44 800 591 818, or for Ireland tel: +353 800 556 785, www.dermalogica.co.uk). Then, using wet hands, I massage a few drops of the organic Weleda Lavender Relaxing Body Oil (mail order tel: +44 115 944 8200, www.weleda.co.uk), which always ensures a beautiful night's sleep – and I even wake up with an amazing sheen on my skin. Lastly, I pop Bliss Sleeping Peel Mask on my face which gently cleans clogged pores, and has my skin squeaky clean by morning.

Second night: sleep in a bottle

If I'm still feeling grotty by the second night of my trip I turn to my late-night skin saver, Guorlain Issima Midnight Secret (tel: +44 19 3223 3909). Dubbed 'sleep in a bottle', just three pumps before I go to bed and I feel a changed woman by the time morning comes around (more than one application is not recommended).

Organic jetlag remedy

Arnica/Cocculus 30c, from The Organic Pharmacy, 396 Kings Road (tel: +44 20 7351 2232, www.theorganicpharmacy.com), provides natural relief before, during and after your flight.

Pillow menu

When I stayed at The Benjamin Hotel, 125 East 50th Street, New York (tel:+1 212 715 2500, www.thebenjamin.com), I had a choice of 11 luxury pillows on a 'pillow menu' in my room. There was a hypoallergenic one to relieve sneezing, itchy eyes, sinus congestion and morning headaches, and a Gelly Neckroll that could be heated or chilled depending on what was required (a hot Neckroll works well for neck ache, muscle spasms and upper-back tension whereas a cold one is good for migraines). My two favourites were the NASA memory foam pillow and the Buckwheat pillow – a crunchy, cuddly bag of scrunchiness, which smelled like a field full of freshly cut hay. You can buy the pillows directly from their website. Their sleep concierge, Eileen Gill also recommended a massage, hot milk and cookies, and an aromatherapy-laden, lukewarm bath.

THE BENJAMIN
An Executive Suite

THE BENJAMIN

127

LONDON

First Impressions

The scent of Mimosa as I dash past Liberty; an overwhelming sense of frustration at the lists and lists of amazing things to do and see in Time Out, and the lack of hours in the day in which to do them; creators with new haircuts, new ways of dressing; raw, urban-style literature on the underground; the stifling heat on the tube at rush-hour; suits drinking beers at lunchtime; aromatic ducks displayed in windows in Chinatown; and lots and lots of pigeons.

Lunch and watch life go by

Busaba Eathai, 106-110 Wardour Street, Soho, W1 (tel: +44 20 7255 8686). Grab a seat at the window and watch Soho drift by while sampling some really great Thai food. (Try the green curry and jasmine rice.)

Sunday lunch

Take your pals to St John Bread & Wine, 94-96 Commercial Street, E1 (tel: +44 20 7251 0848, www.stjohnrestaurant.co.uk) and have the whole roast suckling pig (feeds up to 16 diners). You have to pre-order the little fella a week in advance, at a cost of £320, but he's well worth the wait.

Great Italian pasta

Assaggi, 39 Chepstow Place, Notting Hill Gate, W2 (tel: +44 20 7792 5501). A non pretentious, authentic little Italian in Notting Hill that serves the best tagliatelle and scallops in town. With only a dozen tables, booking is essential.

Great duck and fabulous decor

The French food at Les Trois Garçons, 1 Club Row, Brick Lane, E1 (tel: +44 20 7613 1924, www.lestroisgarcons.com), is exquisite. And the decor? The stuffed swan on the bar wears a tiara and the bulldog a set of fairy wings. Currently my favourite restaurant in London.

Steak and cabaret

Bistrotheque, 23-27 Wadeson Street, E2 (tel: +44 20 8983 7900, www.bistrotheque.com) serves some great dishes upstairs in the stark white warehouse and some great cabaret and mojitos in the club downstairs.

Healthy lunch

Leon, 35 Great Marlborough Street, W1 (tel +44 20 7437 5280) for fast, healthy food. Try the falafel, pitta bread and a raw juice. Heaven is a morning spent poking around Liberty before heading to Leon for falafel or chicken with aioli. Mmmmmm!

Catch a movie

The Electric Cinema, 191 Portobello Road, W11 (tel:+44 20 7908 9696, www.electriccinema.co.uk) has soft leather seating, food and drink, and a slick programme of movies so there's no more need to slum it, gals.

Breakfast

The Wolseley, 160 Piccadilly (tel: +44 20 7499 6996, www.thewolseley.com) great, strong, coffee, freshly baked croissants and a beautiful room that stays open on weekdays until 12 p.m

Glitzy Afternoon tea

Sketch, 9 Conduit Street, London W1 (tel: +44 870 777 4488) is amazing! The cakes are displayed like jewels, the decor is ravishing and after several pots of white jasmine tisane, visiting the very eclectic little girls room is an adventure.

Check-in luxury... and afternoon tea

Ever since I stayed at Claridge's Hotel, Brook Street, London W1A (tel: +44 20 7629 8860, www.claridges.co.uk), I've dreamed of the Art Deco opulence, cedar-scented closets and fluffy pillows. And when I'm having tea in the tearoom with my best mate Anne, I love encouraging the piano player to play louder and louder – so that no one can hear our dirty little secrets.

G-Spot

I love the V&A Museum, Cromwell Road, South Kensington, SW7 (tel: +44 207 942 2000, www.vam. ac.uk). The Gamble Room, the original tearoom since 1868, is one of the most elegant places on the planet.

Sushi

Right, so we all dream of hanging out at Nobu but for a more authentic Japanese dining experience (and more reasonably priced), it's got to be En Ten Tei for me, every time: 56 Brewer Street, London W1 (tel: +44 20 7287 1738).

Celebrity haven

Don't let the celebs put you off (as if they would). The food and service at the Ivy, 1 West Street, London WC2 (tel: +44 20 7836 4751) is excellent. Try the bangers and mash (if you can bag a table) for nourishment, starfucker!

G-Spot

Take a picnic to Richmond Park or Kensington Gardens and see if you can spot the wild Ring-necked Parakeets. You can't miss them – they're bright green and squawk very loudly. They first appeared in the city in the 1970s and their origin is mish-mash of urban myths – some say they escaped from the set of an exotic film being shot at Shepperton Studios, others think they escaped a quarantine holding at Heathrow airport. It's estimated that there will be upwards of 100,000 of them in London by 2010.

Invent your own ice cream

Pop into Harrods and have the experts at Morelli's Gelato (tel: +44 207893 8959), help you to create your very own flavour ice cream. After 24 hours your new ice cream will be ready for you to take away.

Check-in midrange

Soho Hotel, 4 Richmond Mews (off of Dean Street), London W1D (tel: +44 20 7559 3000, www.sohohotel.com). I've had the greatest little get-togethers here with my pals in the downstairs sitting room area. The location just can't be beaten but the following morning's booze bill sure hurts.

THE SOHO HOTEL
London

My favourite local haunts

Diptyque, 195 Westbourne Grove, London W1 (tel: +44 207 727 8673, www.diptyque.tm.fr). Parisian chic comes to London with this gorgeous boutique's scented candles. I love the Baies, Leather and John Galliano the most. **Playlounge**, 19 Beak Street (tel: +44 20 7287 7073, www.playlounge.co.uk) for limited edition action figures, gadgets and books. **Phonica**, 51 Poland Street, London W1 (tel: +44 20 7025 6070, www.phonicarecords.com) for Hip Hop, Electro House, Breaks/Dubstep on vinyl. **Magma**, 8 Earlham Street, London WC2 (tel: +44 20 7240 8498, www.magmabooks.com) I don't just go to Magma to buy books, I go there to realise fabulous, colourful dreams. **Rosie's Deli Café**, 14e Market Row, Brixton SW9 (tel: +44 7815 76 12 83, www.rosiesdelicafe.com). The chilli jam and scrambled eggs are scrumptious, and regulars even get their own mug which hangs on a hook below their name on the wall. **Royal Court Theatre**, Sloane Square, London SW1W (tel: +44 20 7565 5000). There's always something worth seeing at the Court – you can even stand in the slips for 10 pence on a Monday night. **Ginger Pig**, 8-10 Moxton Street, London W1 (tel: +44 20 7935 7788). Organic meat by friendly butchers. At **46 Lots Road**, London SW10 (tel: +44 20 7352 9883) you can find the most fantastic reclaimed hardwood home and garden furniture. **Cassie Mercantile**, 14 Addison Avenue, London W11 (tel: +44 20 7610 4000) is store for the vintage purist – book an appointment with Graham Cassie and he will help you pinpoint your vintage fantasy. **Gerry's Wines and Spirits**, 74 Old Compton St, London W1 (tel: +44 20 7734 4215). With over 150 types of vodka, 90 tequilas and 80 different rums, this is the best place to shop for ingredients for my favourite Mojitos. **Labour And Wait**, 18 Cheshire Street, London EC2 (tel: +44 20 7729 6253, www.labourandwait.co.uk) sells the most amazing home wares, wooden pencil boxes, and authentic stripey tops, Parisian-style. **Topshop** I can never walk by the Oxford Street branch of Topshop, London W1D (+44 20 7636 7700, www.topshop.com), without going in; this shop is simply addictive.

Design genius

My favourite Paul Smith store is at Borough Market, 13 Park Street, London SE1 (tel: +44 20 7403 1678, www.paulsmith.co.uk). For stripy Paul Smith tableware, try Thomas Goode, 19 South Audley Street, London W1 (tel: +44 20 7499 2823, www.thomasgoode.co.uk).

I love B-store

I remember being totally blown away last year by an installation by Christian Wijnants in the window of B-store, 24a Saville Row, London W1 (tel: +44 20 7734 6846, www.buddhahood.co.uk). It was a knitted Virgin Mary sitting on a chair, cradling baby Jesus in her arms. I ventured in and found clothes by Boudicca, Karen Walker, Bernhard Willhelm, Christian Wijnants, Eley Kishimoto, as well as shoes from owner Jose Neves' Buddhahood line.

My favourite store in London

Beyond the Valley®, 2 Newburgh Street, London W1 (tel: +44 207 437 7338, www.beyondthevalley.com), is one of the hippest shops in town. A shop-come-gallery, they specialize in showcasing raw design talent and art. This shop is a pandora's box of goodies.

+44 (0)207 437 7338
...re@beyondthevalley.com
www.beyondthevalley.com

Beyond the Valley
PILOT STORE

My favourite buys

Konditor and Cook, 10 Stoney Street, London SE1 (www.konditorandcook.com), is a delicious cake shop that makes loads of beautiful little pink 'love' cakes. I love everything by **Vivienne Westwood**, 44 Conduit Street, (tel:+44 20 7935 7788, www.viviennewestwood. co.uk); adore trousers by **Stella McCartney**, 30 Bruton Street, London W1J (tel: +44 20 7518 3100, www.stellamccartney.com), and can't leave Mayfair without visiting **Claridges**, (see pp129), to pick up a bottle of their signature musky bath oil – in its elegant Art Deco bottle, with the lid shaped like the hotel's bathroom taps.

Bring Home

Antique linen sheets from **The Cloth Shop**, 290 Portobello Road, London W10 (tel: +44 20 8968 6001); a peeling gilt chair from **Core One**, Gasworks, 2 Michael Road, London SW6 (tel: +44 20 7371 5700); an antique lamp from **James Worrall**, 2 Church Street, London NW8 (tel: +44 020 7563 7181, www. jamesworrall.com); a lush, embroidered cushion, fashioned from old British flags by **Becky Oldfield's Lost and Found** label (tel: +44 7958 331030, www. lostandfounddesign.co.uk); athentic ballet shoes and slippers from **Gandolfi**, 150 Marylebone Road, London NW1 (tel: +44 20 7935 6049, www.gandolfi. co.uk); Campbell's Tea, English Mead, Dundee fruitcake and a jar of St John and Dolly Smith's Brinjal Indian-style pickle, all from **A Gold**, 42 Brushfield Street, London E1 (tel: +44 20 7247 2487, www.agold.co.uk); a grapefruit candle from **Jo Malone**, 150 Sloane Street, London W1 (tel: +44 20 7730 2100, www. jomalone.co.uk); Latte per II Corpo Body Lotion from **Farmacia Santa Maria Novella**, 117 Walton Street, London SW3 (tel: +44 20 7460 6600); ribbons and birds from **VV Rouleaux**, 6 Marylebone High Street, London W1U (tel: +44 207 224 5179, www.vvrouleaux.com); and magazines and fashion books from **RD Franks**, Kent House, Market Place, London W1 (tel: +44 20 7636 1244, www. rdfranks.co.uk). Diaries and notebooks from **Smythson**, 40 New Bond Street, London W1 (tel: +44 20 7629 8558, www.smythson.co.uk).

Bargain vintage

Beyond Retro, 112 Cheshire Street, London E2 (tel: +44 20 7613 3636, www.beyondretro. com) is by far the largest. It houses over 10,000 garments at any one time, from cowboy boots to old-skool trainers, and it's all cheap as chips.

Fashion must

A stylist for Italian Vogue and L'Uomo and Casa magazines, Ann Shore stocks an eclectic mix of finds at Story, her shop at 4 Wilkes Street, London E1 (tel: +44 20 7377 0313). Open 12 p.m. to 6 p.m. on Sundays, and weekdays by appointment only.

Pigeon *n* any of numerous related birds having a heavy body, small head, short legs and long pointed wings. *Coll. n* A flock of pigeons.

TRACEY EMIN:
LONDON'S TRUE
URBAN GODDESS

Tracey Emin's *Strangeland* is the first book I've completed in years. What egged me on towards the finish in this book was the honesty, beauty and freedom in Emin's prose. It seemed appropriate to me, somehow, that the author herself later confessed to me that, 'I read three books at any one time myself and don't get to the end of any of them. Ever.' I've admired and respected her as an artist, and writer, for years now. Her work speaks volumes to me and women of my age – not unlike the way Irvine Welsh's voice strikes a poignant chord with young men.

My God, but Tracey Emin is totally sexy in person; dressed casually in jeans and a little cardigan she just can't help it, it just bubbles through her pores. She offers me tea and we chat and giggle, her eyes dancing when she talks about robins, the smell of Docket (her cat), about hair, perfume and bras. She tells me that she buys flowers for herself all the time and hates receiving them as a present because it deprives her of the joy of choosing them.

That was way back in December and what I've learned of her since has just endeared her to me more. She tugs gently at my heart strings with her artistic sincerity. She's London's Urban Goddess in her purest form.

So London's your home. What's the one thing overall you love about the city? *Text messaging and my sovereignty.*

What can you get in London that you can't find anywhere else? *Docket, because he doesn't travel very well.* (See next page for Tracey's letter.)

Any favourite watering hole? *The Golden Heart, with Sandra in front of the bar.*

Do you have a favourite shop and why? *I don't like material objects but I love shopping. That's why clothes are good for me – when I go to heaven I won't need any.*

Do you prefer buying clothes or books? *Clothes. Clothes more than anything.*

Do you collect anything? *Scotsmen and small chairs!*

Do you use the tube? *Yes. I have an Oyster card. It takes me ten minutes to get into central London. It takes 45 by taxi depending on traffic. I'm not stupid!*

You also own a house by the sea now. Why do you love the sea? *Because I love having pure space.*

Do you ever miss Margate? *No, not now I've got a house there.*

In your book *Strangeland* **I love your recipe for the perfect fish finger sandwich, and I can't pass a supermarket shelf with strawberry Nesquilk on it without thinking of your advice. Do you have another little recipe that you love making at home?** *Chicken soup. Docket and I love chicken soup.*

Favourite smell? *The back of Docket's neck.*
Favourite sound? *The sea.*
Favourite to your sense of touch? *I like the feel of fur, on humans.*
Favourite colour? *I'm very confused about colour at the moment. I'm not sure whether it should exist. We should have purity of thought. Mondrian made his life about that.*
Favourite bird? *The robin. Sarah Lucas and I used to have a shop. The shop was called The Birds, The Shop, The Shop, The Birds.*

133

My home –

My house was built in 1729 – Its very beautiful, there is not one straight door, one straight stair – Everything is crooked, its like living on a ship –

It has five floors, My bedrooms at the top and the kitchen is at the bottom – I spend a lot of time running up and down – Sometimes when I came home drunk, I don't actually make it up the stairs – I just collaps – and wake up with the mark of the kitchen flag stones – in a cross shape on my face –

The street where my house is, has a grade one listed church – It was built by ~~Hawksmare~~. Hawksmoor – In the church yard stands a tree – Tall and Majestic – I like the tree a Lot,

Behind the tree a Long way off in the distance is the Pink and Blue neon of the ~~the~~ Ibis Hotel – Its a fantastic

view — like it was created especially
for me — My Cat and I spend a
Long time - Staring at of the window —
He sits on the Ironing board in my
dressing room — Accationaly a bird will
fly past, The church bells will chime —
and we will hear a Faint call to prayer —
it's all pretty ~~veny~~ Magical.

Tracey Emin 2006.

First impressions

The beat of the Mute swans' wings, as they rise from the 'aul' canal.
The smell of Butlers coffee on Nassau Street.
Conversation drifting out of the open doors of pubs; race form, weather, football results wafted along on the warm, earthy smell of Guinness.
Painters, poets and bards locking horns in Grogans.

Mute swan *n* any of various large aquatic birds, having a long neck and usually a white plumage. *Coll. n* 1. a herd or bevy of swans 2. when flying in a 'V' formation – a wedge of swans. Mute swans have poor forward vision and have been known to crash into bridges and buildings in Dublin and even into cliffs on the coast. Mute swans hiss when attacked and peck if provoked, but overall are much gentler than the other two species of swan found in Ireland, namely Bewick's and Whooper swans, which arrive in November and leave in March. Mute swans don't migrate.

'bell-beat of their wings' – W. B. Yeats from *The Wild Swans at Coole*

See my favourite giraffe

I often visit the Natural History Museum, Merrion Square West, Dublin 2, (tel: +353 1 677 7444, www.museum.ie), to stare at the eyelashes of Spoticus, the museum's prize giraffe. So mesmerized have I been by them all this time that I forgot to check whether it was a boy or a girl. I called the museum and asked the security man to run upstairs and have a peep for me. Five minutes later he returned with his verdict: 'Spoticus is most definitely a boy!'

Check-in luxury

The Morrison, Lower Ormond Quay (tel: +353 1 887 2400, www. morrisonhotel.ie). Great food and a really nice bar. It's also in a great location because if you duck around the back of it, down Smithfield, you can see really old and unspoilt parts of Dublin. Five minutes away down Henry Street is where all the high-street bargains are to be had.

Francis Bacon's Studio

Dublin City Gallery, The Hugh Lane,
Charlemont House, Parnell Square North, Dublin 1,
(tel: +353 1 222 5550, www.hughlane.ie).

Francis Bacon, one of the greatest artists of the twentieth century, died in 1992, and it wasn't until the contents of his studio at 7 Reece Mews, South Kensington, London, were uncovered that the long-held secrets of the way he worked were revealed. His whole studio right down to the last scrap of paper has been relocated to this gallery so you can see how he created his masterpieces: he used corduroy trousers, cut up into pieces, to pattern his paintings, and corduroy imprints are even evident on his studio door, suggesting that he first applied paint to the door before dipping the corduroy in this makeshift palette and then applying it to the canvas. Bacon also used cashmere sweaters, ribbed socks and cotton flannels to similar effect. Absolutely amazing!

Park life

Imagine you have a rich aunt in the country with a huge house and a garden with a maze and you get an idea of what the Iveagh Gardens in Clonmell Street (off Harcourt Street) are all about. An idyllic little hideaway in the centre of the city, this is where I go to dream.

Sweet talk

The monthly gatherings at the Sugar Club, 8 Lower Leeson Street, Dublin 2 (tel: +353 1 6787188 have now reached cult status. Taking place from 7–11 pm, it's one of the hottest tickets in town. International designers, artists, DJs, photographers and creatives descend on the Sugar Club to give an insight into their designs, doodles and drawings. Check out the very hip and happening www.candyculture.net for details and be inspired by these wonderful creators. This is the gig to help you meet like-minded creative hipsters. Wicked!

Retro grooms

Look in the dusty windows of the Irish Yeast Company, 6 College Street, (tel: +353 1 677 8575, at the plastic brides and grooms (they're so old they're wearing bell-bottoms). This shop has been selling yeast to Dublin's bakers for more than a hundred years.

Drinks

Hip

If you're looking for a young, arty crowd, The Globe, 11 South Great George's Street, Dublin 2 (tel: +353 1 671 1220), is perfect.

Grogans

Artists, poets, writers and Dublin's young talent converge on this city centre joy. Grogans, 15 South William Street, Dublin 2 (tel: +353 1 677 9320), is everything a good pub should be and more.

Guinness

Drink the best pint of Guinness in the world at Mulligan's, 8 Poolbeg Street, Dublin 2 (tel: +353 1 677 5582). Forget your black velvets (Guinness and champagne) and have it virginal – it's burgundy when held up to the light. And you thought Guinness was black, didn't you? Walk up James's Street towards the Guinness Storehouse, St James's Gate, Dublin 8 (tel: +353 1 408 4800, www.guinness-storehouse.com), and smell the hops in a fresh April breeze.

Old world

The Long Hall, 51 South Great George's Street, Dublin 2 (tel: +353 1 475 1590). This is one of my favourite pubs in Dublin. It feels so old and noble, I love relaxing here with my pals.

Hideaway

The stag's head above the door is 112 years old – a good start to what will be a private day's relaxing in the Stag's Head, 1 Dame Court, Dublin 2 (tel: +353 1 679 3701). The beautiful stained-glass windows offer protection from the inquisitive pedestrian traffic outside.

Eats

French cakes and breakfast

La Maison des Gourmets, 15 Castle Street, Dublin 2 (tel: +353 1 672 7258), not only does lovely tea, huge croissants and French pastries, but the waffles, bacon and maple syrup are my favourite breakfast treat.

Real Italian pizza

Run by true Italians, The Steps of Rome, 1 Chatham Court, Dublin 2 (tel: +353 1 670 5630), just off Grafton Street, serves delicious pizza slices to eat in or take away. I particularly like to order the potato and rosemary one and window shop at Muji (next door) and Kitchen Confidential, across the street, which has everything you'll ever need to bake that famous Irish soda bread.

Bangers and mash and backgammon

Gruel, 68 Dame Street, Dublin 2 (tel: +353 1 670 7119), serves great bangers and mash and you can always lounge around afterwards and play scrabble or backgammon over a brownie and tea.

Afternoon tea

The scones might be tiny, but the sumptuous sofas, fine bone china, good tea and impressive art collection (even on the way to the bathroom) makes the Merrion Hotel, Upper Merrion Street, Dublin 2 (tel: +353 1 603 0600), my favourite place in Dublin for afternoon tea.

Fish and chips

Join the queue snaking down the road outside Leo Burdock's fish and chips shop on Werburgh Street, around the corner from Christchurch Cathedral, then sit on the steps of Dublin Castle and enjoy your tea.

A great steak

Irvine Welsh loves this place for its steak. Shanahan's, 119 St Stephen's Green (tel: +353 1 407 0939, www.shanahans.ie), serve the thickest and juiciest steaks in the country. Check out the Original JFK Rocking Chair from Air Force One and have a drink in the Oval Office bar in the basement before dinner.

Sunday lunch

This is my local and I have to cope with the beautiful aroma of roasts and gravy every time I pop out to buy a newspaper. Roly's, 7 Ballsbridge Terrace (tel: +353 1 668 2611, www.rolysbistro.ie), serves a wonderful Sunday lunch. The food is French in style and I've only ever had great meals here. The Clonakilty black pudding with sweet potatoes and apple is particularly good.

Dublin Bay prawns

This is a real treat on a Saturday for me. We hop on the DART which runs along the coastline and alight at Sandycove/Glasthule for seafood at Cavistons Restaurant, 59 Glasthule Rd, Sandycove, Co. Dublin (tel: +353 1 280 9120, www.cavistons.com). It serves everything from oyster shots and baked black sole on the bone with black butter to perfectly char-grilled sardines. It's so fresh they practically tell you each fish's address!

Sunday brunch

Odessa, 13-14 Dame Court (tel: +353 1 670 7634), has great food and great service. Sunday brunch is a must, to either dissect your night before or plan your night ahead.

Special dinner

If it's a special someone you're taking to dinner then go all out and treat yourselves at L'Ecrivain, 109a Lower Baggot Street (tel: +353 1 661 1919). The food here is totally exquisite and the wine list absolutely divine. I can't rave enough about their degustation (ten-course taster menu), at €120 per person - this doesn't include drink but you get to taste the best of what Dublin has to offer, food-wise.

Dance

Friday: Monkey Tennis at Anseo, 18 Camden Street Lower, Dublin 2 (tel: +353 1 4751321).
Saturday: Pogo at The Pod, Old Harcourt St. Train Station, Dublin 2 (tel: +353 1 4780225, www.pogo-dublin.com).
Monday: Strictly handbag at Rí-Rá, Dame Court, Dublin 2. (tel: +353 1 6711220,www.rira.ie).

My favourite local haunts
Jenny Vanders (1), 50 Drury Street, Dublin 2 (tel: +353 1 677 0406). Vintage finds, bags and jewellery. **Butlers Chocolate Cafés (4)**, (www.butlerschocolates.com). There are branches around the city – try the chai latte. **Brown Thomas**, 88-95 Grafton Street, Dublin 2 (tel: +353 1 605 6666). As well as stocking a huge range of international fashion labels, they have an amazing selection of shoes from Christian Louboutin to Jimmy Choo. **Smock**, 20-22 Essex Street West, Temple Bar, Dublin 8 (tel: +353 1 613 9000) This tiny boutique, stocks Veronique Branquinho and a host of other contemporary designers **Greene's Bookshop(2)**, 16 Clare Street (tel: +353 1 676 2554). For second-hand books and that odd rare little treasure, upstairs should be your first port of call. Downstairs there's a post office, perfect for stamps for your diary to remind you of your trip. **Organic Food Market (3)**, Temple Bar Meeting House Square, Temple Bar. Held on Saturdays and good for oysters, organic sausages, olives, vegetables and cheese. **Butchers: Doyle Bros (5),** 138 Pearse Street, Dublin 2. 100 per cent Irish beef, lamb, chicken and pork – the best meat in Dublin. **Cheese: Sheridans Cheesemongers**, 11 South Anne Street, Dublin 2 (tel: +353 1 679 3143). For cheeses that will make your smorgasbord stand out. I also buy smoked meat, cured ham and salamis here, along with olives, organic pasta, home-made jam and honey. **Vegetables, nuts and berries: Roy Fox**, 49a Main Street, Donnybrook, Dublin 4 (tel: +353 1 269 2892). **Deli: Magill's,** 14 Clarendon Street, Dublin 2 (tel: +353 1 671 3830). The oldest deli in Dublin. **Food Hall: Fallon & Byrne (6)**, 11-17 Exchequer Street, Dublin 2 (tel: +353 1 472 1010). Dublin's answer to Dean & Deluca

My favourite buys

A wool blanket from **Avoca Handweavers**, 11-13 Suffolk Street, Dublin 2 (tel: +353 1 677 4215, www.avoca.ie), and a wallet or bag from **Chesneau**, 37 Wicklow Street, Dublin 2 (tel: +353 1 672 9199, www.chesneaudesign.com). **Ferguson Irish linen** from House of Ireland, on the corner of Nassau and Dawson Street (tel: +353 1 671 1111, www.houseofireland.com). I love Ferguson's single and (especially) double damask sheets, also available at www.fergusonsirishlinen.com. You'll also find **McCaw Allen linen** at the House of Ireland – excellent for beautifully plain sheets.

Buy

GODDESS TIP
IF YOU'RE CALLING FROM OUTSIDE IRELAND ALL NUMBERS IN DUBLIN ARE PREFIXED BY 00353 1

Bring Home

A first-edition book from **Cathach Books (1)**, 10 Duke Street (off Grafton Street), Dublin 2 (tel: +353 1 671 8676, www.rarebooks.ie). For first-edition Joyce, Yeats and many other rare titles. **Barry's Irish Tea (2)**, (www.barrys-tea.com), which can be found downstairs in the supermarket of Dunne's Stores in St Stephen's Green shopping centre at the top of Grafton Street. Gold blend is my favourite. Also stock up on **Tayto crisps (3)** and **Jacob's Kimberley (4)** and **Mikado (5)** biscuits while you're at Dunne's. **Powers Irish Whiskey (6)** and **Bailey's Irish Cream** from The Celtic Whiskey Shop, 27-28 Dawson Street, Dublin 2 (tel: +353 1 675 9744, www.celticwhiskeyshop.com).

Didn't get there?

Check out Dublin hipsters **Angry (7)** (tel: + 353 1 478 9299, www.angry-associates.com) and their alive and kickin' t-shirts, hoodies and sweaters. Sweet!

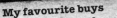

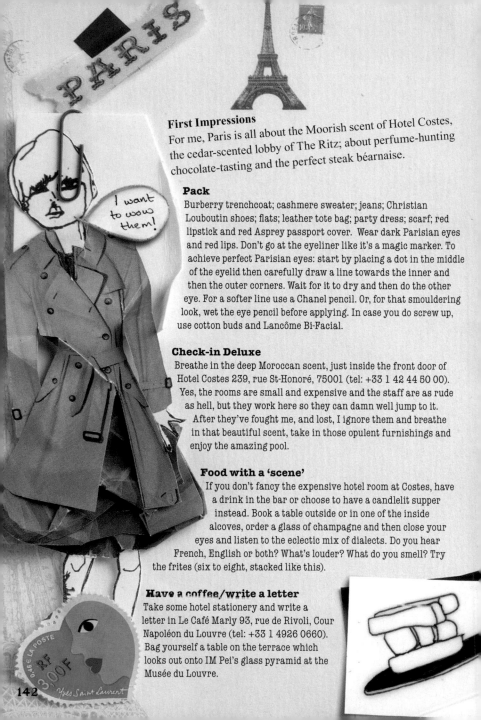

PARIS

I want to wow them!

First Impressions
For me, Paris is all about the Moorish scent of Hotel Costes, the cedar-scented lobby of The Ritz; about perfume-hunting chocolate-tasting and the perfect steak béarnaise.

Pack
Burberry trenchcoat; cashmere sweater; jeans; Christian Louboutin shoes; flats; leather tote bag; party dress; scarf; red lipstick and red Asprey passport cover. Wear dark Parisian eyes and red lips. Don't go at the eyeliner like it's a magic marker. To achieve perfect Parisian eyes: start by placing a dot in the middle of the eyelid then carefully draw a line towards the inner and then the outer corners. Wait for it to dry and then do the other eye. For a softer line use a Chanel pencil. Or, for that smouldering look, wet the eye pencil before applying. In case you do screw up, use cotton buds and Lancôme Bi-Facial.

Check-in Deluxe
Breathe in the deep Moroccan scent, just inside the front door of Hotel Costes 239, rue St-Honoré, 75001 (tel: +33 1 42 44 50 00). Yes, the rooms are small and expensive and the staff are as rude as hell, but they work here so they can damn well jump to it. After they've fought me, and lost, I ignore them and breathe in that beautiful scent, take in those opulent furnishings and enjoy the amazing pool.

Food with a 'scene'
If you don't fancy the expensive hotel room at Costes, have a drink in the bar or choose to have a candlelit supper instead. Book a table outside or in one of the inside alcoves, order a glass of champagne and then close your eyes and listen to the eclectic mix of dialects. Do you hear French, English or both? What's louder? What do you smell? Try the frites (six to eight, stacked like this).

Have a coffee/write a letter
Take some hotel stationery and write a letter in Le Café Marly 93, rue de Rivoli, Cour Napoléon du Louvre (tel: +33 1 4926 0660). Bag yourself a table on the terrace which looks out onto IM Pei's glass pyramid at the Musée du Louvre.

Perfect steak béarnaise

Chez Georges 1, rue du Mail 75002 (tel: +33 1 42 60 07 11), serves the most perfect steak béarnaise and skinny frites you'll find in Paris, expect good old fashioned service.

See the Mona Lisa

Stroll around the Louvre, side-stepping the Da Vinci Code fanatics, then cross over onto the Louvre des Antiquaires 2, Place du Palais-Royale, and browse the antiques. Bring some cash and you can haggle down the prices.

Macaroons

Indulge in a hot chocolate at the shrine to the macaroon, Ladurée 75, avenue des Champs-Elysées (tel: +33 1 40 75 08 75). Then, a few doors down, post your letters in a tiny post office with beautiful Parisian stamps and buy extra for your travel diary. Ladurée on rue Bonaparte (tel: +33 1 44 07 64 87, www.laduree.fr) has the most beautiful 19th century inspired interior. Pierre Hermé 72, rue Bonaparte (tel: +33 1 43 54 47 77) is a fave of the fashion pack. See pp211 for more macaroon G-Spots.

Check-in mid-range

Just as aromatic as its bigger sister Hotel Costes, but without a restaurant, a bar or the high tariffs, Hotel Bourg Tibourg 19, rue du Bourg-Tibourg 75004 (tel: +33 1 42 78 47 39, www.hotelbourgtibourg.com) is small but perfectly formed and situated in the Marais. I like room thirty-five the best.

Local food

Pop across the road to Le Coude Fou 12, rue du Bourg-Tibourg (tel: +33 1 42 77 15 16) for good traditional French food – the artichoke starter and the rabbit main course are flawless and the atmosphere is fabulous too.

GODDESS TIP

CHILL WITH FRIENDS AT ANDY WAHLOO (TEL: +33 1 42 71 20 38), SIT ON AN EMPTY COKE CRATE, PROP YOUR DRINK UP ON AN ARABIC ROAD SIGN AND PUFF AWAY ON A HOOKAH. FOR AMAZING MOROCCAN FOOD, GO NEXT DOOR TO 404, 69, RUE DE GRAVILLIERS (TEL: +33 1 42 74 57 81), AND CHECK OUT THE TINY ROOM UPSTAIRS.

Christian Louboutin's Paris

Do you have a favourite dining spot?

Brasserie Lipp 151 Boulevard St-Germain, 70006 (tel: +33 1 45 48 53 9). Queues snake out the door – you can't book – but I love their pot au feu.

Do you do the galleries?

I like to visit L'Institute du Monde Arabe, 1, rue des Fosses-St-Bernard (tel: +33 1 4051 3953). It has great exhibitions and a comprehensive bookshop. I'm also a huge gardener and love La Maison Rustique near St.Germain des Prés, 26, rue Jacob, 75006 (tel: +33 1 42 34 96 60), for books on flowers and gardening. Galignani, 224, rue de Rivoli (tel: +33 1 4260 7607) is good for art books.

I'm looking for beautiful ribbon where should I go?

Mokubu, 8, rue Montmartre, 75001 (tel: +33 1 40 13 81 41). They also have branches in New York and Tokyo.

Have you any shopping weaknesses?

Hermes, 24, rue du Faubourg Saint-Honore (tel: +33 1 4017 4717).

Secret hideout?

A little Danish restaurant called Flora Danica, 142, avenue des Champs-Elysées (tel: +33 1 44 13 8626). I love the venison and red cabbage and it has an indoor garden. Shhh!

My favourite buy

My favourite summer floral perfume is a bottle of Lys Méditerranée created by nose Edourd Fléchier at Editions de Parfums Frédéric Malle 37, rue de Grenelle (tel: +33 1 42 22 77, www.editionsdeparfums.com). Christian Louboutin told me about this shop and the perfumes it sells created by the world's greatest perfume noses.

Ritz Paris

My favourite shop
Colette, 213, rue Saint-Honoré (tel: +33 1 55 35 33 90, www.colette.fr) is a great concept store selling books and magazines. I love Colette's CDs released on their own label.

Fashion staples
Bags – Jamin Puech, 68, rue Vieille du Temple 75003 (tel: +33 1 48 87 84 87, www.jamin-puech.com) stock the most beautiful bags by Benoit Jamin and Isabella Puech. **Denim – A.P.C.** For straight-legged, classic dark jeans and really hip casuals, you can't get better than A.P.C. 3, rue de Fleurus (tel: +33 1 40 37 41 55). Check out the store's website before you fly at www.apc.fr.

Super labels
L'Eclaireur (tel: +33 148 87 10 22) Dries Van Noten and many more superb fashion buys. **Antik Batik**, 18, rue de Turenne (tel: +33 1 44 78 02 00) eclectic beading. **Sonia Rykiel**, 70, rue du Faubourg Saint-Honoré (tel: +33 1 42 65 20 81, www.soniarykiel.com) one of Paris's most creative designers. **Isabel Marant**, 1, rue Jacob 75006 (tel: +33 1 43 26 04 12) get rock star chic at amazing prices. **Paul & Joe**, 64/66, rue des Saints-Peres, 75007 (tel: +33 01 42 22 47 01, www.paulandjoe.com) beautiful!

New shoes
Hot-foot it to **Christian Louboutin**, 19, rue Jean-Jacques Rousseau, 75001 Paris (tel: +33 1 42 36 05 31, www.christianlouboutin.fr) for stunning scarlet-soled creations which have long sold out in New York and London.

Champagne
Have a glass of champagne at **The Ritz**, Hôtel Ritz Paris, 15 Place Vendôme, 75001 (tel: +33 1 43 16 30 30, www.ritzparis.com). Check out the 1001 facts on the website before you go. Love the song on the website!

My favourite local haunts
Table De Fes, 5 rue Sainte-Beuve, 75006 (tel: +33 1 45 48 29 94) the best Moroccan restaurant in Paris. **A la Mère de Famille**, 35, rue du Faubourg Montmarte, 75009, Chocolates, jams and dried fruit in beautiful packaging. **Aux Pipalottes Gourmandes**, 44, rue Rochechouart, 75009, a wonderful deli. **Barthelemy**, 51 rue de Grenelle, 75007. Cheese! **Bellota Belotta**, 18, rue Jean Nicot, 75007, Ham specialists. **Bertrand**, 7, rue Bourdaloue, 75009, a tea room with amazing cakes. **Izrael**, 30, rue François Miron, 75004, Like a bazaar in Istanbul. **La Crémerie**, 9, rue des Quatre Vents, 75006, a gorgeous old charcuterie. **Le Comptoir de la Gastronomie**, 34, rue Montmartre, 75001) Chocolate cake and foie gras. **La Maison des Trois Thés**, 33, rue Gracieuse, 75005) A thousand different teas. **Le Moulin de la Vierge** (105, rue Vercingétorix, 75014) A divine bakery.

TÉLÉPHONE (33) 01 43 16 30 30 - E-MAIL MANAGEMENT ; mgt@ritzparis.com

AX RÉSERVATION (33) 01 43 16 36 68 / 01 43 16 36 69 - TÉLÉFAX (33) 01 43 16 31 78 / 01 43 16 ... 572 219 913 - SIRET 572 219 913 00017

Visit the Eiffel Tower

(And take a little one home). The Eiffel Tower is located on the Champ de Mars (tel: +33 1 44 11 23 35, www.tour-eiffel.fr), and stays open until 11pm, or midnight in August. Go at night to avoid the crowds and enjoy the romantic atmosphere.

Stationery

I discovered the most beautiful correspondence cards and stationery at Melodies Graphiques, 10, rue du Pont Louis Philippe (tel: +33 1 42 74 57 68) and Clin D'Oeil, 8 rue du Pont Louis Philippe (tel: +33 1 42 74 06 05). For diaries, pop down the street to Papier Plus, 9, rue du Pont Louis Philippe (tel: +33 1 42 77 70 49).

Breakfast and a walk

Oscar Wilde had breakfast every day at Les Deux Magots 170, Boulevard Saint-Germain (tel: +33 1 45 55 25) during his year-long exile in Paris. After breakfast, go out to Père-Lachaise and pay a visit to his grave.

Do the art thing and then eat

Do not miss the Musée Rodin, 77 rue de Varenne (tel: +33 1 44 18 61 10, www.musee-rodin.fr) or the Musée d'Orsay, 1 rue de la Légoin d'Honneur (tel: +33 1 40 49 48 14, www.musee-orsay.fr). And make sure you pass by the breathtaking Place de la Concorde and the Pompidou Centre, 3615 Beaubourg (tel: +33 1 44 78 12 33), where you can relax over an apéritif in the chic top floor restaurant. Take lunch at Benoit, 20, rue St Martin 75004 (tel: +33 1 42 72 25 76) – they serve great foie gras and rabbit.

Hip Stores

Madame André at 34, rue du Mont-Thabor (tel: +33 1 42 96 27 24) is a really cute little boutique in Paris. It's stuffed with quirky jewellery, Japanese finds and beautiful pieces. I really love this shop. The name refers to street artist André who runs Black Block, at Palais de Tokyo, 13 Avenue du Président Wilson, 75516 (tel: +33 1 47 23 37 04, www.blackblock.org), a Pandora's box of art objects (which incidentally is another of my favourite shops in the city). Check out his club night at Le Baron, 6 Avenue Marceau; an exclusive retro rock club.

Beautiful pharmacies

There are beautiful pharmacies hidden all over Paris: Pharmacie Centrale, De L'Ile St Louis, Paris (tel: +33 1 43 54 45 28) is well worth the visit, if only to stock up on the sublime Roger & Gallet toiletries.

Vintage market

Head to Le Marché aux Puces, where you'll find quite literally thousands
of stalls selling vintage – from Louis Vuitton and Hermes to Levi's. The
market is situated in the 20th arondissement in St. Ouen and runs on
Saturdays, Sundays and from 9.30am until 6pm on a Monday. Broken
up into a bazaar and several mini markets, I say make a beeline for the
covered Marché Serpette – it's a vintage bonanza. Also look out for Olwen
Forest's stall selling Chanel, Schiaparelli and Balenciaga jewellery, vintage
Vuitton and original Hermes Kelly bags. Try rue des Rosiers for vintage
Levi's, Burberry raincoats, flapper-style slips and Pucci printed dresses.

Bring home

Ballet shoes: Repetto, 22, rue Paix 75002 (tel: +33 1 44 71 83 12),
as worn by Paris's ballerinas. **Music: Virgin**, 52, avenue des Champs-
Elysées (tel: +33 1 49 53 50 00) and **Colette** or **Costes. Linen and
scent: Fragonard Boutique**, 196, boulevard St-Germain 75007
(tel: +33 1 42 84 12 12, www.fragonard.com) **Sweets: G. Tetrel
Confiserie**, 44, rue des Petits Champs, sweets the way they're meant to
be. **Vintage magazines: Les Archives de la Presse**, 51, rue
des archives, 75003 (tel: +33 1 42 72 63 93) **Wine: Legrand
Filles et Fils**, 1, rue de la Banque, 75002 (tel: +33 1 42 60
07 12, www.caves-legrand.com). Just look up at the ceiling.
And, for the best wine opener, cross the way to their wine
accessories' boutique.

Didn't get there?

Aimé in London, 32 Ledbury Road, W11 (www.aimelondon.com) stock a
host of French fashion labels. For French antiques and garden implements
visit Appley Hoare Antiques, 30 Pimlico Road (tel: +44 20 7730 7070,
www.appleyhoare.com). Turn to pp237 for on Parisian scent shopping.

147

BARCELONA

First Impressions: A big metal fish, smoked horse meat, secrets on walls, the doughnut man on the beach and Unilever/Miko lemon sorbet Cornettos. Absolutely gorgeous!

Check-in luxury
Hotel Banys Orientals, Carrer de l'Argènteria, 37 – 08003 (tel: +34 93 268 84 60, www. hotelbanysorientals.com). The most expensive duplex loft is €125. The design in this place is really slick.

Check-in mid-range
Inside BCN, Carrer Espartería, 1 – 08003 (tel: +34 93 268 28 68, www.inside-bcn.com). Great quality apartments from €85 a night. Centrally located in the Gothic Quarter, the hippest part of Barcelona, and most have wireless broadband.

Street-art gallery
Iguapop Gallery, Carrer Comerç, 15 – 08003 (tel: +34 933 100 735, www.iguapop.net) – a neat gallery with shows by some of my favourite street artists including Borris Hoppek and Miss Van. Also keep your eyes peeled for these artists' work on Barcelona's street walls (see Art pp173).

Art
Maxalot, Carrer de la Palma de Sant Just, 9 – 08002 (tel: +34 93 310 10 66, www.maxalot. com) brings together graphic design, iconography, street art and all the hybrids in between to create exhibitions which have included Obey, Michael C. Place, Designers Republic, and Joshua Davies.

Limited-edition prints and clothing
Farm4, Baixada de Viladecols, 3 – 08002 (tel: +34 93 319 01 82, www.farm4.com) a graphics and design lab and shop filled with clothing, objects and limited editions by local designers and artists.

A drink with the locals
Cal Pep, Plaça de les Olles 8 (tel: +34 93 310 79 61, www.calpep.com) is a bar G-Spot. In the know locals get here early to chill at the tapas bar and we all know that the locals are never wrong. Pep takes your order in his friendly way and the tallarines (wedge clams in broth), botifarra sausage with beans and trifásico - fried whitebait, squid rings and shrimp, all lightly battered to accompany your favourite tipple make for a great night out with friends. Pity it closes each August when Pep goes to the beach.

Look out for Miss Van on the streets

CUPÓN DE PASAJERO / PASSENGER COUPON

Spain means land of the rabbit

NOMBRE DEL PASAJERO / NAME OF PASSENGER
SCANLON/GMS

DESDE / FROM
DUBLIN

BARCELONA

Animal farm

Charcuteria Arantxa, Calle Tallers 5 – 08001 (tel: +34 93 412 72 86). I had the Jamon Iberico de Bellota, from the most pampered of pigs raised on acorns and love. The darker meat that I gobbled three helpings of, I later learned was horse. Neeeeeeever would have guessed!

Must dos

Climb to the top of the Sagrada Familia church steeples and inhale deeply the grooves and waves of Antonio Gaudi's design or lie and stare up at the sky on the roof of his La Pedrera.

My favourite local haunts

La Estrella de Plata, Pla del Palau 9 (tel: +34 93 268 06 35, www.estrella-de-plata.es). I love this tapas place, even though it's madly expensive. **Cerveceria Catalana**, Carrer Mallorca 236 – 08008 (tel: +34 93 216 03 68): the best fish tapas and beers. **Bar Joan**, Santa Caterina Market 108: tapas and the beauty of the huge market interiors – the wall tiles and roof reflect the fruit and veg, and it's like one huge, beautiful painting. **Cacao Sampaka**, Carrer Consell de cent, 292 – 08007 (tel: +34 93 272 08 33, www.cacaosampaka.com), or Carrer Ferran 43–45 – 08002 (tel: +34 93 304 15 38): divine chocolate bars and chocolate drinks in these cafés in a gazillion flavours including Madagascar, Venezuela, Papua New Guinea and rose. **Pappa Bubble**, Caller Ample 28 – 08002 (tel: +34 93 268 86 25, www.pappabubble.com): a crazy sweet shop where you can watch them make all their own sweets from sugar water and glucose.

Bring home

Hand-made espadrilles from **La Manual Alpargatera**, Carrer d'Avinyó, 7 – 08002 (tel: +34 93 301 01 72, www.lamanualalpargatera.com): bring in your own fabric and they'll create espadrilles for you, or choose from the shop's stock and customize with your own coloured ribbons. Jeans from **Overales & Bluyines**, Carrer Rec, 65 (tel: +34 93 319 29 76) including many limited editions and a huge supply of second-hand denims. Beautifully packaged chocolate from **Xocoa**, Vidreria 4 – 08003 (tel: +34 93 319 63 71, www.xocoa-bcn.com), created by the amazing graphic-design duo Marc Català and Pablo Juncadella. A music box, puppet or mask from **El Ingenio**, Rauric, 6 08002 (tel: +34 93 317 71 38, www.el-ingenio.com). This 160-year-old store also has a workshop where they make scary puppets. Eeeeeek!

Didn't get there?

Combining his chocolate with saffron, red pepper, vinegar, and even, in the case of 'caramelo-cola', a pleasant after-taste of Coca-Cola, Barcelona-based **Enric Rovira**, Josep Tarradellas, 113 – 08029 (tel: +34 93 419 25 47, www.enricrovira.com) is a chocolate genius. His creations are also available in London at **Brindisa**, 32 Exmouth Market, London EC1R 4QE (tel: +44 20 7713 1666, www.tapas.co.uk).

CAROUSEL

I was in Geneva and it was raining. Hunched on a street corner, lost, I looked through the rain and saw a carousel on top of a steep hill. The music spilled down the hill, towards me, like the tune that raced in my heart as a child when Mum clasped my hand tightly and demanded that Dad take us all to see the circus.

I followed the music like a helpless little girl all the way up to the top of the hill. The carousel spun faster and faster; a cacophony of colour as the horses whirled round and round. The rainwater ran down a handwritten, laminated sign hanging on a piece of string under the canopy, which read 'Carousel' 2.50CHF (2.5 Swiss Francs). I poked around for some change in my bag and fought the rainwater as it tried to claim everything inside. Eventually I found the correct currency among the relics and coins of past adventures and I offered the old man, his hand never moving from the big metal wheel that turned the carousel, my money, and just a few pence extra for his time. He looked up at me and smiled graciously, reached out his carousel-calloused hand and pulled me up and onto his menagerie. I clambered onto a white plastic pony with red paint and chipped ears. Clutching my soggy bags, I suddenly felt the pony turn into a rearing horse beneath me, rising and falling to the music. The old man turned the wheel making us spin faster and faster.

The rain pounded on the roof but inside the carousel the music played on and I was safe; safe from the rain, safe from the city, safe for as long as the music sounded. I found my camera at the bottom of my handbag, wet and ailing, and dried it with my scarf. I stretched my hand out to try and take a snap but the up and down movement of the horse made it too hard to balance. The old man left his post and came towards me, gesturing to pass the camera his way. After a bit of fiddling with the buttons (and a lot of pigeon Fren-glish on my part), he attempted to take the shot. After a few tries he had mastered the zoom and with a nod he took aim and got the picture. The carousel creaked to a halt and he rushed quickly back to man it. I went to dismount but he beckoned for me to take another ride.

Two well-dressed French couples in their forties stopped and stared at my obvious excitement; my legs and arms flayed around uncontrollably as I jumped up and down with glee. I felt so free, so happy, so honest. Wrapped in heavy mackintoshes and wearing huge designer shades, they stared dryly at me. One of the men pulled out his leather wallet and threw 10 centimes in the old man's direction. He bent down and picked the money off of the ground before fumbling for change in his pockets and helping the gentleman's lady on board. She perched elegantly, side-saddle, on a horse in front of me and nodded to her friends as the carousel started. "Bravo, bravo!" they cheered as she flew quickly past them. "Vite, vite!" her partner shouted, waving his beret in the air. She looked unmoved and stared silently into the distance. How could anyone know this freedom and not smile?

The old man continued to turn the handle with one hand and to search his pockets with the other. Eventually, happy that he had found the correct amount, he left the wheel and offered the man his change. The man refused to take it, saying, "It's very little, it's nothing. Keep it!" The old man returned solemnly to his wheel, his eyes filled with a look of both resentment and shame.

Behind the carousel stood a candy-striped market stall selling knick-knacks and manned by a red-cheeked young Indian woman. The torrential rain ran unforgivingly along the gutter, and into her broken leather shoes. It bubbled and spat its journey downhill, showing little mercy even to the shiny brown cobbles. She was cold, soaked to the bone, and yet smiling. The old man left his wheel, crossed the street towards her and handed over the rich man's 7.50. She bowed graciously and offered trinkets in exchange. He plucked a pair of bright yellow laces and some red plastic clothes pegs from her wares. Then he returned to his resting horses and helped the cold lady down.

TIPPING

SOHO GRAND HOTEL
Salon
10 West Broadway
NYC, NY 10013

HOXTON APP
16 HOXTON
TEL NO 02
REG.

The tip came in at around the same time as restaurants in the eighteenth century; since then, however, it has mutated into something unrecognizable. It's supposed to be a 'discretionary' show of gratitude, but in reality, it's not that at all. In US hair salons rolled-up tens, twenties and fifties change hands so quickly that it puts crack dealers on street corners to shame. Cough up or have your hair destroyed next visit with a chainsaw. In restaurants in Europe 12.5 per cent is added to your food bill, which you inevitably pay by credit card. Does the waiter or waitress get this money or is it used to make up the rest of the staff's wages?

Restaurants everywhere

I ask the waiter where the service charge on the bill goes. Does he/she get tips or is the tronc (a French word for the box in which cash tips used to be kept before being divvied up at the end of each night among the restaurant staff) used for uniform laundry bills, staff taxes or, worse still (and totally immoral), to make up all the staff's wages backstage? I make a rule of asking for the 12.5 per cent to be removed from the bill and instead I give it in cash to the person who has waited my table – that way I know that he/she is getting it and it's not being spent on something or someone else.

Tipping-free zones

Sweden – a service charge is automatically billed into everything.

Tokyo – you never tip in Japan: restaurants and hotels add 10–20 per cent.

The Concierge

Concierges don't live off tips; a handwritten note is the best way of showing your gratitude.

Hotels

In Europe only tip at the luxury ones and give the bellboy €1 per bag. If a doorman hails you a cab give him €2. In the US, the bellboy usually gets $3 to $5 per bag, based on size. Hotel doormen get $3 (for a quick cab flag-down) or $10 (if he's found you a cab down the street in the rain). Cabbies get $1 and bartenders $1 per drink.

Room Service

Recently, most hotels have been including a gratuity of 15 to 19 per cent on room service, which means you don't have to tip on top of that. Having said that, if someone runs downstairs for milk for your porridge or a sewing kit, and comes back within five minutes, bank on parting with $5. On the other hand, give $10 if he offers to sew the button in for you.

Hair salons

I've been exposed to it all here, from hairbrush drawers left open next to my salon chair – just wide enough for me to spot the glaringly obvious tip envelopes stuffed with notes of high denominations – to the bags full of boxes from Prada, piled high behind the reception desk of one Manhattan salon. Who's to say that these weren't all planted by the stylists themselves to help me part with my cash? In one well-known Broadway establishment I was even handed a bunch of those yucky brown tip envelopes with my bill. When I poked about in my purse and didn't have enough notes to fill the envelopes, reception advised that I take a junior stylist next door to a Duane Reads to help me find a cash machine. Embarrassed and guilty, I did just that – after all I didn't want to appear mean. It was total exploitation and the whole bill came to $450 with $125 on the tips alone.

How much?

The hard and fast rule? Anyone who touches you must be tipped! So how much does each little elf get? An employee who brings you a coffee and magazines and introduces himself/herself by name is doing so in order for you to remunerate him/her later on a clearly named yucky brown envelope – for these employees a few dollars will suffice. On top of that, $2 is the going rate for a shampoo, $5 for a head massage. Another $5 to $10 goes to the assistant who assists the blow-drier (you know, holding hairbrushes, clips, bits of hair and all of that). And then the blow-drier will be expecting a $10 tip, so all in all your wash and blow-dry will cost you an extra $20 upwards in tips. Stylists and colourists expect 20 per cent or more of your total bill.

In hair salons slipping money into stylists' back pockets is frowned upon – they're not strippers.

What's expected?

In the US it's all about putting out and then putting out some more on special occasions to ensure that you'll be squeezed in at the last minute for that haircut, waxing or manicure. Remembering your stylist's cousin's Bar Mitzvah, his sister's love of perfume and his boyfriend's passion for the theatre all gain you insurance. And what can you expect in return? The certainty that your hair will be cut straight, that your colour won't go green and that he'll slot you in for a last-minute blow-dry. Not much else.

NEW YORK

First impressions
August's searing heat, mixed with the smell of melting tar, gasoline, salted pretzels and sun cream. The smell of November's salted snow piled in heaps along the street mixed with noodle soup and roasted nuts on a breeze that'll cut your face in half on Fifth. The constant sound of car horns!

Check-in, luxury
For me, the Mercer at Prince & Mercer (tel: +1 212 966 6060, www.mercerhotel.com) in Soho is my favourite hotel in New York when I want action. I book room 507 for a summer visit, open the windows and enjoy the sounds and smells of bustling Soho below. It's got all of my favourite stores within a few minutes' walk.

Check-in, mid-range
Chambers, 15 West 56th Street (tel: +1 212 974 5656, www.chambershotel.com) is stuffed with artworks (more than 500 to be precise), and the hallway on each of the fourteen floors has its own installation. Rooms are loft-like spaces with good linen and shower-heads the size of manhole covers. It's only a five-minute walk to Fifth Avenue.

Business brekkie, lunch or martini
If you don't fancy paying the price for a room in The Four Seasons, 57 East 57th Street (tel: +1 212 758 5700 or go to www.fourseasons.com), schedule a power breakfast there instead. It's the best place in town if you want to impress a client. Its opulence, five-star service and the famous martini menu is a must on every Luxury Goddess's 'to do' list. I stayed here when I had my teeth veneered: you can soak in the bath (it fills in five minutes) and watch telly at the same time. Staff provided tea, tampons and a complimentary car (drops you off within a two-mile radius from 8 a.m. to 11 p.m.). A member of staff even went out to Duane Reads and had my prescription filled. They also welcome pets, who receive a special bowl, snacks and a sleeping pillow. Awwwh! Their service is consistently excellent. When booking, ask for a park or city view (fifty per cent of the rooms have one).

Limited-edition vinyl toys
Every Urban Goddess needs to visit KidRobot, 126 Prince St (tel: +1 212 966 6688, www.kidrobot.com). I love their limited-edition vinyl toys, mini-figures and Dunnys – they've the best selection in the world.

Big treats
Marc Jacobs Store, 163 Mercer Street (tel: +1 212 343 1490) and little treats at the Marc Jacobs shop dedicated to accessories on 385 Bleeker Street (tel: +1 212 924 6126, www.marcjacobs.com): pencils, cashmere socks and affordable little things. Just three minutes down Third Avenue you'll find...

Eclectic
Butik, 605 Hudson Street (tel: +1 212 367 8014) is the most beautiful little store belonging to model and photographer Helena Christensen and Leif Sigersen, stocking metal garden furniture, clothing, tools and even hot-water bottles and gardening things. They source designs and items from Denmark, Sweden and France, yet another reason for me to be obsessed with New York.

Hot chocolate/ice cream
Have a gelato (the italian for ice cream), chocolates filled with marshmallow or the best hot chocolate in New York at The Chocolate Bar, 48 Eighth Avenue (tel: +1 212 366 1541, www.chocolatebarnyc.com).

All things Asian
Takashimaya, 693 Fifth Ave, near 54th Street (tel: +1 212 350 0100) is a specialty store devoted to all things Asian, including orchids, saki, silks and over 150 teas.

For interiors and inspiration
Moss, 146 Greene Street (tel: +1 212 204 7100 or go to www.mossonline.com) is one of my favourite design stores in the world. The way in which each item is displayed is art in itself. Murray Moss is truly a genius, and I could stay here for hours. Then I go to the Deitch Gallery, 76 Grand Street (tel: +1 212 343 7300, www.deitch.com) and my day is complete.

Best New York Marilyn moment
The triangular shape of the Flatiron Building (skyscraper on 23rd Street) produces wind currents that make women's skirts billow and caused police to create the term '23 skidoo' to shoo away would-be onlookers. Put on your best panties and a skirt, and give it a try. Oooops!

The Big Apple? More like the big banana if you ask me!

Most American car horns sound in the key of F

155

Stationery

I love poking around Kate's Paperie, 561 Broadway (tel: +1 212 941 9816, www.katespaperie.com). Paper Presentation, 23 West 18th Street (tel: +1 212 463 7035, www.paperpresentation.com) is a paper megastore. Papivore, 233 Elizabeth Street (tel: +1 212 334 4330), has handmade notepaper and monogramming; and if you're craving a British fix head to Smythson of Bond Street, 4 West 57th Street (tel: +1 212 265 4573, www.smythson.com).

Get sober

Have a cwoffee New York style, half-caff skinny hazelnut mochaccino, hold the foam? Oh, go back to the planet of Feng Shui haircuts and over-sized breast implants, you screwed-up Angeleno. You need to scope out a plain cwoffee, one milk (and sugar if you so desire), from the orange Mudtruck parked on 6 Astor Place or in Wall Street (check out www.themudtruck.com). They also have a sit-down coffee place called Mudshot, 307 East 9th Street (tel: +1 212 228 9074) with a great back garden. The Mudtruck serves the best cup of coffee in town.

Get wasted

At one New York fashion week a movie producer took me to Siberia, 356 West 40th Street, in Hell's Kitchen (tel: +1 212 333 4141), for a drink. I thought I'd been abducted. There's no sign, just big black doors with a red light-bulb above them. I will never forget that night: off-duty cops, off-duty strippers and a very famous rock star playing dirty games in the corner. Dark, dingy and dirty, it's a real rough dive – definitely a must for the cool Urban Goddess.

Steak

Peter Luger, 178 Broadway in Brooklyn (tel: +1 718 387 7400, www.peterluger.com) has been around since 1887. The giant porterhouse is perfect surrounded by the restaurant's trademark steak sauce.

Have a quality hot dog and a great papaya drink

Try Papaya King, 179 East 86th Street, corner of Third Avenue between Third and Lexington (tel: +1 212 369 0648, www.papayaking.com).

New York breakfast

Okay, forget judging the décor, just go to Barney Greengrass, 541 Amsterdam Avenue at 86th Street (tel: +1 212 724 4707, www.barneygreengrass. com) on a Sunday morning for breakfast. Order the scrambled eggs with dark, caramelised onions and their lox with a toasted bagel, and you're stuffed for the day. I first learned what a bialy was here (it's a yummy Polish roll).

Have proper pizza

'Real' New Yorkers have an inbuilt talent to be able to balance pizza, walk and eat at the same time, and there are many mainstream pizza joints to oblige them with a single slice. For first-timers, avoid molten hot yellow lava cheese and orange grease by leaning forward as you try this feat. For a sit-down pizza, Lombardis, 32 Spring Street (tel: +1 212 941 7994, www. lombardispizza.com) serves a whole pizza, which is by far the best in Manhattan. If you want gourmet then DiFara's, 1424 Avenue J, Brooklyn at East 15th Street (tel: +1 718 258 1367) is indisputably the best, if you fancy schlepping out to Brooklyn for it.

Have a pastrami on Rye

Katz's Deli, 205 East Houston Street at Ludlow Street (tel: +1 212 254 2246) serve a sandwich as big as your head. It's the oldest deli in New York.

Meet a sushi master

A good friend suggested I try an omakase (a Japanese tasting menu while in New York). I tracked down Yasuda, 204 East 43rd Street (tel: +1 212 972 1001, www.sushiyasuda. com) and booked a night when Yasuda himself could serve me behind the sushi bar. The sashimi – sea eel, toro tuna, yellowtail, sea urchin roe and shark – all served at room temperature and the rice slightly warm (hallmarks of perfect Japanese preparation) were sublime. This is the best old-school sushi and sashimi I've ever had. Please, please go here to experience what sushi should taste like.

Flash-fried river crab and cosmos

At Sushi Samba 7, 87 Seventh Avenue (tel: +1 212 691 7885, www. sushisamba.com). I love the flash-fried little river crab with a cosmo. The menu is Japanese/Brazilian and I've consistently had great meals here. The staff are some of the best in New York, helpful, friendly and educated about the food. The best place in town to go with a group of friends for cocktails and dinner.

Dance

I had my first ever DJ lesson from Q-tip at Table 50 two years ago. It changed hands in 2006 so now I go to Marquee, 289 10th Avenue at 27th Street (tel: +1 646 473 0202 to dance instead.

Read

Rats: A Year with New York's Most Unwanted Inhabitants by Robert Sullivan. The author spends a year in a garbage-strewn alley in lower Manhattan with a notebook and night-vision goggles to study the little buggers. Aaaaaaaahhhhhhhhh! It was here that I learned that one pair of rats has the potential to breed over 15,000 descendants in one year.

My secret place

Sakagura, 211 East 43rd Street, B1, between Second and Third Avenue (tel: +1 212 953 7253, www.sakagura.com). Go through the lobby of the office building, down the stairs to the cellar and through the plain door. This Asian late-night place is great to bring friends who've never been to Tokyo. It has over 200 brands of sake and really tasty snacks. Worth the search (watch the prices as you get drunk!).

Marvin Scott Jarrett's shopping G-spots

(for jeans see also pp48) At **An Earnest Cut & Sew** in New York's Meatpacking District, 821 Washington Street (tel: +1 212 242 3414, www.earnestsewn.com), you can have an expert make you a pair of jeans. It's here that Scott Morrison, founder of Paper Denim & Cloth, has created a concept store with a bespoke service that invites you to pick your denim, rivets, button (how does 24-carat gold sound?), pockets, thread colour and extras (your favourite proverb on the pocket? Your beloved's name inside the fly?). **Barneys Madison**, 660 Madison Avenue (tel: +1 212 826 8900, www.barneys.com) for interesting labels. **Nom de guerre**, 640 Broadway, Lower Level (tel: +1 212 253 2891, www.nomdeguerre.net) located in a multi-level subterranean space on the corner of Broadway and Bleecker, and invisible to the naked eye, this space is like an underground bunker packed with underground hip labels.

Bring home

Vintage Christmas baubles: Mr Pink, 223 West 16th Street (tel: +1 646 486 4147, www.mrpinkinc.com) sells 1950s glass and things for the kitchen as well as tinsel Christmas trees and vintage decorations. **A rubix cube**: Restoration Hardware, 23 Fifth Avenue (tel: +1 212 260 9479, www.restorationhardware.com). **Underground labels**: Jane Mayle's clothes shop, 242 Elizabeth Street (tel: +1 212 625 0406) carries the hottest New York labels, which you won't be able to find at all in London. **Delicious interiors prints**: Hable Construction, 117 Perry St (tel: +1 212 989 2375, www.hableconstruction.com). **Movie Scripts**: Look out for the guy with the stand on Union Square. **Knickknacks**: Walgreens, 350 Fifth Ave & 33rd Street (tel: +1 212 868 5659, www.walgreens.com): this pharmacy sells everything from tiny screwdrivers for your glasses to plastic travel bottles for your cosmetics. **Jeans**: Cantaloup Destination denim, 1359 Second Avenue (tel: +1 212 288 3569) stocks Tsubi, Hudson, Oliver Twist, Blue Cult, Sacred Blue, Oligo Tissew and Fins.

My favourite local haunts

Pastis, 9 Ninth Avenue, corner of Little West 12th Street (tel: +1 212 929 4844, www.pastisny.com), I love sitting outside and watching life go by in the Meatpacking District while having the penne. **Craft**: 43 East 19th Street (tel: +1 212 780 0880, www.craftrestaurant.com), build your meal one ingredient at a time, I love the scallops and the toffee-steamed pudding with freshly made rum and raisen ice cream for afters. Mmmmmm! **In God We Trust**, 135 Wythe Avenue, Brooklyn (tel: +1 718 388 2012, www.ingodwetrustnyc.com), a treasure-trove of trinkets and fashion treasures. **Poppy** 281 Mott Street (tel: +1 212 219 8934) for edgy fashion. **Domsey**, 431 Kent Avenue, Williamsburg, Brooklyn (tel: +1 718 384 6000) thrift store with really super pieces. **Arthritis Thrift Shop**, 121 East 77th Street (tel: +1 212 772 8816) and **B-6 Flea Market**, 93 Avenue B (tel: +1 212 529 5804) for more thrift. **Hell's Kitchen Flea Market** is located on 39th Street between Ninth and Tenth Avenues (www.hellskitchenfleamarket.com) superb for antiques and one-off designer items. **The Yarn Connection**, 218 Madison Avenue, 36th Street (tel: +1 212 684 5099) for knitting things. **Magnolia Bakery**, 401 Bleeker Street (tel: +1 212 462 2572) for cupcakes. **Classic Kicks**, 298 Elizabeth Street (tel: +1 212 979 9514, www.classickicks.com) for trainers. **K Trimming & Co.**, 519 Broadway (tel: +1 212 431 8929) stocks the most lace I've ever seen in my life. It's truly amazing. **Pearl Paints**: 308 Canal Street (tel: +1 212 431 7932, www.pearlpaint.com) art supplies, unusual paper and hard-core pencils and paint. Fabulous!

My favourite buys

The Journey is the Destination: The Journals of Dan Eldon at Strand Book Store, 828 Broadway (tel: +1 212 473 1452 or go to www.strandbooks.com). My friend Gerry was raving about this for ages, and when I finally did get a copy it was everything he had said and more. This store has 18 miles of books. Oh, and anything by Zac Posen!

STRAND BOOK STORE
828 BROADWAY
NEW YORK, NY 10003
212-473-1452

QTY   PRODUCT   DEPT   PRICE

1 T JOURNEY IS THE DE190800   21.00

PEARL

rt, craft & graphic discount

stablished 1933

CAMPING

My first-ever experience of camping came courtesy of my parents for my First Holy Communion. We all dressed up to the nines (me in my green maxi) and went for a huge picnic by the stunning lakes of Killarney about fifty miles away from our home. Dad would point out red deer in the woods and Mum would show us huge stone monuments and crosses along the roadside that her uncles had carved by hand (they were sculptors). It was pure adventure and we couldn't wait until there was a big occasion to get going to Killarney again. Now and then we'd see red, blue and yellow tents nestled among the tress or tucked away in the corner of woodlands. These looked so exotic to us as kids – I always wondered what secrets lay inside those bright nylon flimsy triangles.

Putting up a tent

A week before my first adult camping trip I was itching to be surrounded by nature, a bottle or two of good vino, a few toasted marshmallows, trips to the local town for fresh supplies and some really stimulating company to share my tent with – all any Goddess needs. For entertaining male company in a field you'll need a stellar tent to save you from the elements. To ensure that I would be safe and protected, I decided to do a little research into my tent's strength and durability in my own back garden.

I ordered what an adventure fanatic advised me was the safest tent on the market – 'the North Face's VE-25 is the tent for extended camping on the Himalayas'. Made by North Face (www.northface.com) it was guaranteed to withstand harsh environments, so within ten minutes of dragging it out and getting it up in the back garden I asked Peter to test it with the garden hose. Zipping myself in, I waited for the torrential downpour,

Michael Eavis has no favourite cow on his farm

Michael Eavis and me in the rain

but the cosy nylon igloo didn't spring one single leak – that is until I stuck my head out of the front to investigate the rustling in the bushes. My neighbours were watching bemused as Peter power-hosed me to death – knowing better than to ask what we were up to (this week), they just smiled a knowing smile.

Stay dry yourself

So, if the rain is pelting down outside, the safest place for you and your belongings is in a waterproof tent. But what if you don't want to miss any of the festival action? I asked the fabulous Michael Eavis of Glastonbury fame for tips on staying dry. As the owner of the farm where Glastonbury is held, he's seen his fair share of rain over the years. Of all people, he'd know best how to stay snug and dry. Without a moment's hesitation he asked me if I owned a pair of good wellies. It was raining on the day we met and he explained that 'Wellington boots or waterproof shoes are the single most important item to have at a festival.' Walking for any length of time at all in wet mud or water can cause trench-foot, a painful condition where your feet soak up the water and crack open. It takes ages to heal, so wellies are a must. Eeeeeek!

Don't Forget

Tent (check pegs/lines/ poles/groundsheet)
Sleeping bag/mat/pillow
Sunglasses/contacts
Ear plugs/cotton wool
Towel/soap
Toiletries (toothbrush/paste, tampons, shaving items, loo roll, wet wipes, make-up)
Sun cream
Contraceptives
Barry's tea bags
Torch/batteries
Mobile phone
Camera/film
Drugs (prescription)
Next-of-kin notification
Personal ID/travel tickets
Festival Ticket!
Driving licence
Money/cards
Shorts/jeans/dress
Socks/underwear
Boots/wellingtons
Waterproofs
Hoodie/Hat
Clean clothes to go home in
Bags (for dirty clothing and footwear)

> **GODDESS TIP**
>
> IF YOU CAN'T GET THE TASTE OF COFFEE OR SOUP OUT OF YOUR FLASK, FILL IT WITH WARM WATER AND ADD A FEW TEASPOONS OF BICARBONATE OF SODA OR TWO DENTURE-CLEANING TABLETS. LEAVE TO SOAK OVERNIGHT AND WASH WITH WARM SOAPY WATER THE NEXT MORNING. ALWAYS STORE YOUR FLASK WITH THE LID OFF AND A SUGAR CUBE IN IT OR A FEW GRAINS OF RICE TO KEEP IT FRESH AND AERATED.

g did not take this -
Martin Parr

Martin Parr

I've always adored Martin Parr's work (www.martinparr.com): his bright-coloured ice creams, beach scenes and shots of ordinary everyday mundane things show the world in all of its simplistic and colourful glory. Although he has published several books, his Fashion Magazine, which I bought in Colette in Paris, is my favourite. It's really clever. He photographed all of it – the shoots, the ads, everything in it – himself. He captures the world through a child's eyes, never going for the big picture, but always concentrating on the smaller elements, details that grown-ups sometimes choose to ignore.

Within ten minutes of meeting him he'd told me that I was 'Interesting. Ditzy… in a good way. Not your usual boring encounter. Different!' Sitting there all Geography teacher-like in his shirt and sweater I felt like he was scolding me for being late for school. I'd just read his book *The Photobook: A History volume I* (Phaidon) and it was really fantastic – a must-read collection of Martin's favourite photobooks from around the world.

What makes a good photo, Martin? *I like mistakes – they make pictures much more interesting, like a photo of someone at the beach and it's just a foot in the water. Spontaneity is more important than a perfect shot for me. There are no rules when it comes to taking a good photo.*

Check out www.zachgold.com to see everything from flying sausages to 50cent I love his amazing illustrations too.

Zach rocks!

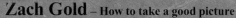

Zach Gold – How to take a good picture

I would like to preface my answer to this question with the caveat that my answer is not the truth but only the thoughts I had on the matter one Saturday morning sitting on my couch in Brooklyn. I think of taking a really good picture in two ways. The first is a picture that is part of a tradition, that is to say that there exists a history of pictures before it to which it refers but that it adds something fresh. The second is an original picture. The work there is to be done when taking an original picture starts with disregarding anything you might like when you look through the lens and see something familiar. This is the 'this is good because it looks like something that has already been accepted as good' phenomenon. Your familiarity benchmark should be replaced by something more inclusive in order that you can open yourself up to what is really in your heart and to why you are taking pictures in the first place. Is it to simply record your friend getting married, having a laugh in a bar and throwing up in her apartment afterwards? Or is it to infuse that picture with who you are and how you feel about the world? And of course to be able to do this you need to spend some time asking yourself these questions – at least for as long as it takes... to take a photograph.

'Oscar Mayer Army Rations', Zach Gold

163

4

HOME

My first home was my grandparents' cottage in Glouria, eight miles outside the Co. Kerry town of Listowel, on my father's farm. My parents brought me up there with my brother and sister, for the first few years of our lives and we savoured a clear view of the ocean in the daytime and the dancing shadows of the brambles and hedgerows in the moonlight. At bedtime the wind howled in from the Atlantic, rattling the slates on the roof and battering the Rhododendron bush in the garden. Its creaking worried me and so I'd look out the window and up at the distant galaxies to take my mind off of the frightening noise. Darting from shape to shadow my eyes searched for the security of the Great Bear (or Big Dipper), the huge plough-like formation – a lidless floating saucepan – that commanded the most respect in the night sky. I would count up the string of stars that made up the handle (three) and bowl (four) of the saucepan. The two stars at the end of the bowl were the "Pointer Stars" because if a line were to be drawn between them and continued onwards and outwards into space it would eventually hit the star at the tip of the handle of the Little Dipper. This star was called Polaris or the North Star. Satisfied at finding it, my eyelids would grow heavy and I'd drop off to sleep – always facing north.

We'd awake each morning to excited talk of building – plans laid out on the kitchen table amidst cups of strong tea, thick slices of buttered bread, home cured rashers and fresh farm duck eggs. My parents were building a house so that my sister my brother and I could each have our own room. Auction dates were circled in thick red marker on the calendar in the hallway – a gift to my father at Christmas from the local building supplies company – and week after week we'd visit auctions to buy furniture. Month by month our new house, two fields up the road, grew taller and taller. Mum had all of the new furniture stored safely in the attic wrapped in cardboard and blankets; the boards in the ceiling were buckling under the weight. The contents of our new life forever expanding, it spilled out through the doorway until the attic could fit no more.

In the new house everything was shiny, the windows were polished and the pillars and railings painted white. Brass pots were hung from hooks on a rail over the range inside the entrance to the kitchen, and Mum excitedly unwrapped chopping boards, two breadbins, a kettle and her wedding china from boxes strewn across the floor. Dad handbuilt a wooden library in the livingroom and around the time of our moving in we spent a whole day in Dublin, shopping for books and the perfect knife block and sharpener. Our day ended in Easons bookshop where we stocked up on volumes about horses, gardening and D.I.Y. We also bought a huge cookery book which had new and exciting recipes from different parts of the world.

The antiques that were scattered around the house were flavoured by other people's experiences: an old leather camel-shaped footstool smelled of the thinkers and readers that had used it before us, and an inlaid, ink-stained table bore the evidence of letters of both love and remorse. The move was finally completed when the floors were put down and the child of Prague was put halfway up the stairs, on a back window. Dad had said it would become a true home when the swallows came to nest in the front porch – and sure enough, with a bit of coaxing that April, they too moved in.

September, and as we were returning to school so too were the swallows to Africa; autumn was coming – darker, colder evenings were creeping in. It was time to heat the house and light the two open fires in the living and sitting rooms to keep out the dampness. Baskets of turf were stacked in each and piles of firewood were drawn from the forest and stored in a log hole in the kitchen, by the range. The firewood crackled and spat bright splinters across the still new carpet while the smell of resin rose from sizzling logs as the sap escaped and ran hissing down the grate. That smell was the first hint that Christmas was coming.

Last year, a few nights before leaving for my parents' house for Christmas, I sat in my own sitting room in Dublin watching the reflection of the flames in the chandelier; they bounced off the frames of artworks by friends of mine, nestling gently against the dark damask wallpaper, and finally came to rest on the gold-leaf spines of my childhood World Book Encyclopaedias, stacked alphabetically in a perfect row against the wall. Everything was looking lovely and Christmassy. I'd trawled the world for unique doorknobs and beautiful candles and the previous August Mum had given me my childhood angel for the top of my Christmas tree because she was doing a big clear out. I switched off the lights and climbed the stairs to my bedroom. I felt safe and secure, and as I turned back my fresh, clean bed linen I felt responsible for all of this and happy; only then did I realize that this was really my home.

Where's my ring? I'm always losing it...

Brushes and dishcloths
It can be difficult to find cleaning-up products that look, well, stylish – that is, until you log on to Moose and Spoon at www.mooseandspoon.co.uk. Their long-handled wooden dustpan and brush is the cat's whiskers and their dishcloths? Divine! RE (tel: +44 1 434 634567, www.re-foundobjects. com), also has a great selection of lovely things but my favourite is a rack of Swedish wooden-handled cleaning brushes.

Clean oven
Keep your oven clean by placing a sheet of aluminium foil at the bottom, making sure it doesn't touch the heating element. Clean up any spills as soon as they occur. If the oven is still warm, sprinkle salt or baking soda on the spill. Alternatively, if the spill is completely dry, wet it slightly, add some dishwashing powder and cover with wet paper towels. Leave for two hours and then wash with hot water.

Pots

Le Creuset pots are cast iron and come in beautiful colours: visit www.lecreuset.co.uk. They are also available at John Lewis and Debenhams. Most department stores and good cookwear shops have a wide selection of pots to choose from. I like to check how comfortable the handles feel before buying pots, rather than buying them online. However, these brands are all superb: Stellar at www.topcookware.co.uk, Meyer at www.pots-and-pans.co.uk, Fissler at www.espitech.com and a wide range at www.divertimenti.co.uk.

Pestle and Mortar

Trawl Asian markets for a big heavy mortar and pestle – they'll be much better value than designer ones.

Floor Cleaner

Combine 2 cups of vinegar with 6 cups of warm water. Wash floors, using a floor cloth, and leave to dry. This solution is also good for cleaning counters. To keep things stylish, use an enamel bucket from John Lewis or Wares of Knutsford, Cheshire (tel: +44 845 612 1273, www.waresofknutsford.co.uk).

Squeaky clean

Want your conscience to be squeaky clean? The Natural Collection (tel: +44 0870 901 4547, www.naturalcollection.co.uk), stocks a range of scrubs, tablets, detergents and powders that are all eco-friendly. Or you could make your own (see pp168).

Bread bin

Cucina Direct (tel: +44 870 420 4300, www.cucinadirect.co.uk), has a really great white one.

Pans

A copper frying pan, butter/sauce pan and pot will bring a professional touch to your kitchen. The Cuprinox range at David Mellor, 4 Sloane Square, London, (tel: +44 20 7730 4259, www.davidmellordesign.com, is to die for. Also try mail order company The French House on (tel: +44 870 9014547, www.thefrenchhouse.net), for great copper cookware and tea towels.

GODDESS TIP

IF YOU REMOVE YOUR PRECIOUS RINGS FOR COOKING, ATTACH THEM TO A SAFETY PIN WITH A LOCK AT THE TOP AND PIN IT TO YOUR CLOTHES.

Kettles

Check out Gill Wing Cookshop, 190 Upper Street, Islington, London N1 1RQ (tel +44 20 7226 5392), for an amazing range of pastel-coloured kettles, buckets and earthenware. Or try Wares of Knutsford, Cheshire on (tel: +44 0845 612 1273, www.waresofknutsford.co.uk).

Display packaging

Hunt down interesting and attractive packaging and tins to add character to your kitchen, at Mortimer & Bennett, 33 Turnham Green Terrace, London, W4 (tel: +44 20 8995 4145, www.mortimerandbennett.co.uk).

Stay clean

Buy a Brabantia brushed-steel touch bin from John Lewis or a Kickboy bin by Wesco at Amaroni (tel +44 1205 260384, www.amaroni.co.uk).

GODDESS TIP

CLEAN YOUR COPPER PANS BY RUBBING WITH HALF A LEMON COVERED IN SALT. (THIS WORKS FOR CHOPPING BOARDS TOO.)

Broken something?

Match and replace broken or discontinued china patterns and complete your dinner service at Lost Pottery, (tel:+44 1325 718 590, www.lostpottery.com).

SPRING CLEAN

Ahh Spring! Fresh, clean rain, snow drops and daffodils; baby lambs, baby birds and the annual spring clean! From carpets and curtains and windows and woodwork to cluttered closets and shelves, everything needs to get the once over and if you're like me you probably hate it more than anything else! What I do love is experimenting with powders and potions passed onto me by my granny – these home cleaners really do work.

Windows

A spray bottle filled with half vinegar and half water dissolves grime fast. Polish with newspaper, a cloth nappy or coffee filters which are all lint free. A spray of club soda adds sparkle. Don't wash windows on a sunny day, the solution dries quickly and causes big white streaks.

Carpets

Make scented baking soda by adding 3-5 drops of essential oils to 2 cups of baking soda. Mix well and let it air dry, then sprinkle onto your carpet as both a cleaner and an odour buster. Let it sit for 15 minutes and vacuum clean. To really give your carpet a lift, sprinkle with salt leave for 15 mins and then vacuum.

Rugs

Vacuum rugs and if they need spot cleaning, use vinegar. Check label for wash details and if suitable bung in the machine. If it needs gentler cleaning, hang it on an outside clothesline and give it a good hosing and wash with dishwashing powder. Then leave it on the line to dry in the sun. Leave expensive Persian rugs to the experts.

Cute vacuum

You can spruce up your own vacuum cleaner by sprinkling several drops of Penhaligon's Lavandula oil (tel: +44 20 7590 6111, www.penhaligons.com) onto half a tissue or cotton ball before letting the vacuum suck it up. If your vacuum cleaner has a water reservoir, add a few drops of oil into it.

Pests

The first thing to attract pests is an unclean house scattered with food scraps and waste. If you haven't been the best of Home Goddesses here's how to get rid of the nasty little buggers if they creep in.

GODDESS TIP
WHEN VACUUMING THE HOUSE DON'T FORGET TO GET WELL UNDER THE FURNITURE. IT WILL HELP KEEP YOUR QUOTIENT OF CREEPY-CRAWLIES LOW.

Get a cat

Postman Pat and Bob the Builder both have furry feline pals. Cats make perfect reading companions and an added benefit is that even a snoozing moggy is enough to send book-gnawing mice and pesky rats packing their bags and looking elsewhere for B&B.

Cat *n* a small domesticated feline mammal having thick soft fur and occurring in many breeds. *Coll. n* a clowder/clutter of cats. Did you know that cats can't taste sugar or salt?

Fly *n* any common dipterous insect that frequents human habitations, spreads disease, and lays its eggs in carrion, decaying vegetables, etc. *Coll. n* A business/swarm of flies. The housefly hums in the middle octave, key of F and jumps backwards as it takes off for flight.

Fly traps
Fly spray stinks, so I use elderflowers hung in bunches inside my back door instead. London based aromatherapist Danièle Ryman has a little eucalyptus tree to keep houseflies at bay.

How do I get rid of pests?

Mouse *n* any of numerous small long-tailed rodents that are similar to but smaller than rats. *Coll. n* a nest of mice. A mouse can fit through a hole in the wall the width of a normal pen.

Mouse trap
Hunger is why he's arrived, so keep the kitchen free of scraps. Set a "Live Capture" mouse trap – order on www.gardens.perfectbuy.co.uk and bring him in alive. Unharmed you can then release him a mile down the road. If you're just too lazy to try any of these solutions, you could just leave the job to a cat. Meow!

GODDESS TIP
FILL A HOT WATER BOTTLE WITH BOILING WATER, CLOSE IT AND COVER WITH DOUBLE-SIDED STICKY TAPE. DRAG IT ACROSS YOUR PET'S BEDDING AREA AND THE FLEAS (IF THERE ARE ANY) WILL HOP ONTO IT AND BE STUCK FAST TO THE TAPE. GOTCHA!

Rat *n* any of numerous long-tailed Old World rodents, that are similar to but larger than mice and are now distributed all over the world. *Coll. n* a swarm/plague of rats. A rat can survive for longer than a camel without water. Leave rat catching to the experts. (Eeeek!)

Funny Smells

Some foods can pong really badly in storage, while you're cooking them or if discarded in the bin. Here are a few tips to keep those nasty ickle foody smells at bay.

Onion

It's the oil in an onion which causes eyes to water. Pop it in the fridge for an hour before chopping and this will calm down the oil's pungency. Then strip the onion of its dry bits plus the light slippery skin outside the flesh (this contains the oil). Burn a candle nearby when chopping to dull the pong and if your hands smell strongly, try rubbing a stainless steel spoon, massaging a little mustard powder into them or steeping them in milk. If you intend frying onions, a wet piece of newspaper placed beside the cooker will absorb the fried oniony smell.

Fish

Always clean fish on newspaper, then wrap up the waste and put it in the bin. To clean a fishy chopping board, rub on mustard or mustard powder and rinse. To remove a fishy smell from your hands rinse them in lemon juice. When frying or poaching fish add celery to the pan to dilute the whiff. A few tablespoons of vinegar added to the washing water removes fish smells from pots and plates, and, after baking fish, why not sweeten up the kitchen by popping some orange or lemon peel in the oven for twenty minutes at 180°C.

Boiled vegetables

A few caraway seeds, a bay leaf or a slice of white bread torn into pieces and added to the pot minimizes the smell of cooking cabbage, cauliflower or sprouts. Add bits of red pepper when boiling broccoli. Alternatively, a small bowl of vinegar near the hob also does the trick.

Burnt pots

I always seem to burn milk when boiling it. A new trick I've learnt is to wet the bottom of the pot with water before putting the milk in. If it's very badly burnt, leave vinegar and water in it overnight. If it has a black crust, soak some cold tea or Coca-Cola in it for a few hours.

what's that smell?

Smelly teapot

Leave a sugar cube or a tea bag in your unused dry teapot to keep it nice and safe from smells.

The bin

Every time I chuck something in the bin I throw a few bits of dried lavender in with it but you can also use a few fresh herbs to prevent unpleasant bin pongs. Keep a sweet-smelling lavender bag near the bin – it works a treat.

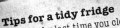

Tips for a tidy fridge

When is the last time you cleaned out your fridge? I make a million excuses a week to try and get out of cleaning mine! Once I even convinced myself that cleaning the fridge was bad luck because my horoscope said 'avoid the colour green'. Raw meat, poultry or fish should always be stored wrapped in paper or in a sealed container on the bottom shelf of your fridge so it can't touch or drip onto other food. Cooked meat should be stored on the shelves above it, loosely covered in foil, cling-film or greaseproof paper. Try to store cheese in an airtight box with a sugar cube to keep it fresh. And milk and eggs (keep their pointy ends down – it makes them last longer), are best stored on shelves rather than in the door as it's the least cold part of the fridge and is best used for condiments and make-up.

Fridge smells

Zap bad fridge odours with a saucer of roughly broken-up charcoal, an orange spiked with cloves or a piece of cotton wool soaked in vanilla food essence. Store a natural sponge in your salad drawer to keep fruit and veg crisp. Keep your fridge smelling sweet by washing it with 1 tablespoon of bicarbonate of soda dissolved in two pints of warm water, weekly.

Kitchen Pong

If the kitchen is musty and stale wring a cloth out in white vinegar and swing it through the air or boil a few cloves in ½ a cup of vinegar and 2 cups of water for twenty minutes.

FAVOURITE GODDESS TIPS

IF YOU KEEP YOUR NAIL POLISH IN THE FRIDGE IT WILL DRY MUCH FASTER. ALSO TRY CHILLING YOUR EYE PENCIL BEFORE SHARPENING IT TO STOP IT CRUMBLING.

D*Face

ART

When we decided to put art up in our house, we had very little money, so we relied solely on gifts and trade-offs with friends around the globe. Two artists we did spend money on, however, were talented street artists D*Face and Faile. Why? Because we loved their work, simple! To get real value from art in your home, it has to be work that you personally respond to every day. What's the sense in buying a print or a canvas if you can't get enjoyment out of it when you're having a really crummy day?

Dave the Chimp

My favourites

D*Face (www.dface.co.uk) I love this diamond dust on Jean-Michel Basquiat's wings. He does a mean queen print and cites Warhol as an influence.

Galo (www.galoart.net) A modern-day Picasso.

Mysterious Al (www.mysteriousal.com) Beautiful prints of characters with attitude.

Calma (www.stephandoit.com.br) Brazilian brilliance!

Faile (www.faile.net) Iconic imagery manipulated in the cleverest of ways.

Swoon (www.wearechangeagent.com/swoon/) Taking imagery from around her on the streets, she creates the most beautiful paper cuts and wood-block prints you'll ever see. Respect!

Miss Van (www.missvan.com) Sexy, sexy, sexy girls.

Dave the Chimp (www.fotolog.com/chimp243) A really talented illustrator. It took him a week to carefully paint the 'Love' piece above.

Elph (www.akaelph.com) Pure Scottish genius.

Boris Hoppek (www.borishoppek.de) Tiny painted wood blocks, hand-made dolls and little chalk men drawn on the street who look like they're sleeping in matchboxes.

The London Police (www.thelondonpolice.com) Chaz draws the best freehand circles on the planet – better then Einstein.

Asbestos (www.theartofasbestos.com) Check out the beautiful but scary dolls' heads.

Jon Burgerman (www.jonburgerman.com) One of the cleverest illustrators I know.

Muteid (www.muteid.co.uk) See his beautiful canvas on the next page.

Adam Neate (www.adamneate.co.uk) Leaves his art on the streets of East London for one and all to take home, go fetch!

Calma

Asbestos

Miss Van

Muteid

I love Tracey Emin's sketches and after meeting her in her studio in London and seeing how she creates, her eclectic space, her tools, the workings of her wonderful brain, it makes her work even more special to me now.

Boris Hoppek

Elph

Asbestos

Faile

Buying mainstream

Try www.habitat.net or Own Art who offer interest-free loans of up to £2,000 through the Arts Council (www.artscouncil.org.uk) to enable you to buy art in any Arts Council gallery. Conditions include paying back the money you borrow in ten equal instalments. The Affordable Art Fair at Battersea Park, London (tel: +44 20 7371 8787, www.affordableartfair.co.uk) exhibits the work of 130 international galleries. Prices range from between £50 to £5,000. Also check out www.eyestorm. com for the work of Damien Hirst and others.

Hanging it

Firstly, get the light right and you're onto a winner. Too bright and it'll bleach your works; too dull and they'll look murky. Hang smaller pictures in a group or box-frame them since a small picture in the middle of a wall can look lost on its own. To hang small pictures, attach two screw rings to the frame one third of the way down on each side and slip the picture onto two hooks in the wall – this avoids you having to adjust them all the time. For large pictures, use plate hooks a third of the way down the frame and attach them to picture chains which you can easily adjust. For frames either shop at Habitat or have them made at John Jones, 4 Morris Place, off Stroud Green Road, Finsbury Park, London N4 3JG (tel: +44 20 7281 5439, www.johnjones.co.uk).

Jon Burgerman

Colour your space

G-Spot

I really love wallpaper. It was an old piece of flock wallpaper from my childhood that inspired the cover of *The Goddess Guide*. Cole & Son in London tops my list because it's the prime source for entirely authentic period wallpapers printed by original methods and it is the only company in the world to make hand-made flock wallpapers in the traditional way (I love it so much I got my cover flocked). They have the most magnificent archive of block prints, screen prints and original drawings from designers including A. W. Pugin, Lucienne Day and Eduardo Paolozzi. Check out the whole range at Cole & Son, Ground Floor 10, Chelsea Harbour Design Centre, Lots Road, London, SW10 0XE (tel: +44 20 7376 4628, www.cole-and-son.com).

This Cow Parsley print (item code 66-7046) is available to buy from Cole & Son's New Contemporary collection. Isn't it gorgeous? Cole & Son wallpaper is so hip, that interior designer Amanda Masters, successfully transformed the LA Oscar Villa into a stylish outpost for Soho House VIP guests during Oscar week, with three of the company's wallpapers including this Cow Parsley print.

GODDESS TIP
USE A PANEL OF WALLPAPER TO BRIGHTEN UP A FORGOTTEN SPACE LIKE A STAIRWELL OR LITTLE BATHROOM WHICH ISN'T USED MUCH. (PAPER IN A MAIN BATHROOM WILL DISINTEGRATE QUICKLY WITH CONDENSATION.)

How can I make my room really different?

176

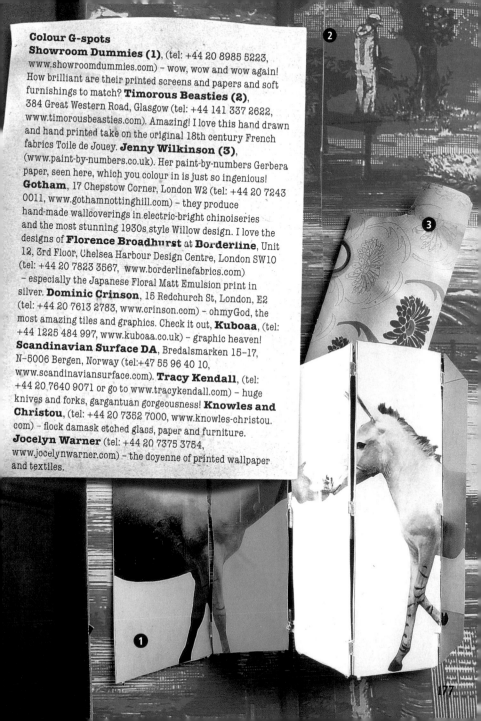

Colour G-spots

Showroom Dummies (1), (tel: +44 20 8985 5223, www.showroomdummies.com) – wow, wow and wow again! How brilliant are their printed screens and papers and soft furnishings to match? **Timorous Beasties (2)**, 384 Great Western Road, Glasgow (tel: +44 141 337 2622, www.timorousbeasties.com). Amazing! I love this hand drawn and hand printed take on the original 18th century French fabrics Toile de Jouey. **Jenny Wilkinson (3)**, (www.paint-by-numbers.co.uk). Her paint-by-numbers Gerbera paper, seen here, which you colour in is just so ingenious! **Gotham**, 17 Chepstow Corner, London W2 (tel: +44 20 7243 0011, www.gothamnottinghill.com) – they produce hand-made wallcoverings in electric-bright chinoiseries and the most stunning 1930s style Willow design. I love the designs of **Florence Broadhurst** at **Borderline**, Unit 12, 3rd Floor, Chelsea Harbour Design Centre, London SW10 (tel: +44 20 7823 3567, www.borderlinefabrics.com) – especially the Japanese Floral Matt Emulsion print in silver. **Dominic Crinson**, 15 Redchurch St, London, E2 (tel: +44 20 7613 2783, www.crinson.com) – ohmyGod, the most amazing tiles and graphics. Check it out, **Kuboaa**, (tel: +44 1225 484 997, www.kuboaa.co.uk) – graphic heaven! **Scandinavian Surface DA**, Bredalsmarken 15–17, N–5006 Bergen, Norway (tel:+47 55 96 40 10, www.scandinaviansurface.com). **Tracy Kendall**, (tel: +44 20 7640 9071 or go to www.tracykendall.com) – huge knives and forks, gargantuan gorgeousness! **Knowles and Christou**, (tel: +44 20 7352 7000, www.knowles-christou.com) – flock damask etched glass, paper and furniture. **Jocelyn Warner** (tel: +44 20 7375 3754, www.jocelynwarner.com) – the doyenne of printed wallpaper and textiles.

Customize your walls

Stella McCartney's walls at 30 Bruton Street, Mayfair (tel: +44 20 7518 3100, www.stellamccartney.com) are dripping with vintage pieces of jewellery, postcards, feathers and crystal beads either glued in place or pinned onto the wallpaper print with tailor's sewing pins. The Matthew Williamson shop a few doors up at 28 Bruton Street, Mayfair (tel: +44 20 7629 6200, www.matthewwilliamson.com) is also a perfect example of beautifully executed wall customization. He took a Chinoiserie wallpaper in an Earlham print on an emerald-green silk background by de Gournay, 112 Old Church Street, Chelsea (tel: +44 20 7823 7316, www.degournay.com), and embellished the birds' tails with a thin brush and fluorescent paint to make them stand out more. He then added brooches to the birds' beaks and pinned them onto different branches of the trees in the print for sparkle. Divine! There's nothing stopping you also having this print in your bedroom and painting on the birds' tails yourself. And The Stencil Library (tel: +44 1661 844 844, www.stencil-library.com) stocks both stencil brushes and Liquitex acrylic paint if you decide to add your own colour. To paint bird tails and make them glow like Williamson's, you'll need a thinner brush than a stencil brush and you'll get a stunning result if you use Bro-Glo paints by J. W. Bollom (tel: +44 20 8658 2299). Check antique stores or charity shops for brooches and add to lampshades and wallpaper to get the extra G-factor.

Add birds

Sketch or photocopy birds and plants from books, cut them out, paint them and stick 'em up around your room to make it more special and individual. Or contact Deborah Bowness (tel: +44 7817 807 504, www.deborahbowness.com) to have the most beautiful bird themed wallpaper prints in your bedroom. If you're a huge bird fan then Claire Coles stitched bird wallpaper (tel: +44 20 7371 7303, www.clairecolesdesign.co.uk) is scrummy! Also have a look at her stitched cups and saucers. Beautiful! Louise Body (tel: +44 7734 907 357, www.louisebodywallprint.com) also stocks a stunning range of cute birds.

Touch-up tips

If you've hired painters to paint your house then ask them to leave a tin of paint with you when they go so that you can make minor repairs and touch-ups throughout the year. If your paintbrush hasn't seen the light of day in ages, soften it in hot vinegar for a few minutes, then wash it in soap and warm water and let it dry before use.

Add flowers

These flower sticker sets from Rachel Kelly at Interactive Wallpaper (tel: +44 20 7490 3076, www.interactivewallpaper.co.uk) will really bring a girly twist to your walls. Rachel also gave me a few little pieces of her Sex & the City wallpaper when I met her in London. Leaving Sex & the City in the past, this print seen here is a must-have for any shoe-loving Goddess. (It costs £165 per five-metre roll, so maybe do one wall in your bedroom with it.) I love it so much I even used it to back Narciso Rodriguez's Musk story (see pp57). Well it is very New York after all.

Putting it up

Invite some friends around and have a wallpaper party – tea, cake and wallpapering, what could be more fun than that? On www.diyfixit.co.uk there are clear details on how to wallpaper your wall as well as tons of other DIY tips – everything from stripping walls to wiring a plug. If it's proving to be a bit of a pain go to Homepro at www.homepro.com. It has access to over 2000 professionals – you email your request and they find the appropriate pro for the job within 24 hours in the UK.

Interior Design Sticker Kit

To Apply: Peel application film and sticker from carrier paper. Position sticker, then smooth with strong pressure to adhere. Carefully peel back application film to leave sticker in position.

The kit

Ladder
Pasting table
Bucket
Pasting brush
Wallpaper brush
Craft knife
Big scissors
Spirit level
Pencil
Patience
Plumb line

How do I put it up?

GODDESS TIP

IF YOU DO EXPERIENCE ANY BUBBLES, CUT THE BUBBLE WITH A CRAFT KNIFE AND IT SHOULD LIE FLAT. IF YOU MESS UP, ROLL UP A PIECE OF WHITE BREAD AND USE IT TO 'ERASE' MARKS ON THE WALLPAPER. IT REALLY DOES WORK.

Bedroom

The bed

I'm a huge fan of antique bed frames and I trawled antiques markets for ages looking for the one. If you're after a reproduction Laura Ashley (tel: +44 871 9835 999, www. lauraashley.com) does a really good one. You might even consider adding a French bed canopy from Cox & Cox (tel: +44 870 442 4787, www.coxandcox.co.uk).

Candles

I save my favourite candles for the mantelpiece in my bedroom. These are red candles in black glass containers, made from a mixture of rose, coriander, lavender, laurel, wood, incense and musk, which I buy at Hotel Costes (see pp142). I always make a secret promise to myself that when they burn out I'll return to Paris to replace them. And even though you can buy them in Browns, 23–27 South Molton Street, London W1K (tel: +44 20 7514 0016 www.brownsfashion.com), I keep my Paris promise to myself instead!

Get a girly phone

Buy this pink, reconditioned telephone for long girly chats on your bed at Planet Bazaar, 397 St John Street, Islington, London (tel: +44 20 7278 7793, www.planetbazaar.co.uk).

The mattress

Vi-Spring naturally filled mattresses (available at Selfridges or www.vi-spring.com), are the crème de la crème of pocket-sprung heaven. If your budget won't stretch to this try Hypnos, available at John Lewis (tel: +44 18 4434 8200, www.hypnos.ltd.uk).

Lighting

Attain the perfect low lighting and you instantly create a place of peace, tranquility and rest. I have learned through trial and error that low lighting is best achieved with bedside lamps – overhead lights are nasty, harsh and not conducive to serenity – and the right lampshades.

Bed linen

I'm a huge fan of monogrammed white, crisp, heavy sheets and pillowcases from Volga (tel: +44 1728 635 020, www.volgalinen.co.uk), or Cabbages & Roses, 3 Langton Street, London, SW10 (tel: +44 20 7352 7333, www.cabbagesandroses.com). For the summer, The White Company (tel: +44 870 900 9555, www.thewhitecompany.com) offers beautiful plain white sheets and duvets, but during the winter I like some colour, so a sweet French Toile de Jouey quilt, and pillow cases from The French House (tel: +44 870 901 4547, www. thefrenchhouse.net), brighten things up. For striped linen, Cologne & Cotton, 88 Marylebone High Street (tel: +44 20 7486 0595/ +44 1926 881 485, www.cologneandcotton.com) offers divine duvet covers. And for a real Goddess treat there's nothing as beautiful as antique monogrammed sheets from Jane Sacchi (tel: +44 20 7349 7020, www.janesacchi.com), or Egyptian cotton sheets from The Egyptian Cotton Store in West Sussex (tel: +44 845 226 0098, www.egyptiancottonstore.com).

Put a pea under your mattress and dream of being a Goddess...

Store linen in a beautiful chest

At Claridges (see pp131) I slept with the doors of the closets wide open, surrounding myself in the comforting smell of cedar all night long. Why did this deep, cedar smell make me feel so safe? Well, I discovered recently that my gran kept all of her important books in a cedar-wood chest in her bedroom, packed tightly in with the pillowcases and sheets she used to put on our beds. I've set my heart on finding a cedar chest with this exact smell for my own linen. Meanwhile, Shiseido's Féminité du Bois (see pp231) on my pillows helps me relive this memory.

Goddess Tip

A drop of essential oil on your light bulbs will release the scent of the oil and keep your room smelling nice.

Goddess Tip

Keep a notebook and pen by your bed to jot down your dreams.

LAUNDRY

If you can't dedicate a whole room to your laundry at least remember when creating a cupboard for it that you'll need a skinny, tall section to accommodate your ironing board, vacuum cleaner, broom and mop. Other than that all you really need is good shelving and a drying rail. On the bottom shelf store your shoe-cleaning products, linen spray, vacuum bags and starch. Check out Moose and Spoon (tel: +44 870 005 2533, www.mooseandspoon.co.uk) for shoe cleaning brushes which are not only useful but also look really cute, and why not store them with your shoe things in a customized little cardboard box? On the middle shelf of your cupboard, store your lingerie and clothing before ironing, and have a rail to keep damp clothes separated and elevated. Store bed linen and towels on the top.

Yellow armpit stains

If you allow your antiperspirant to dry before dressing it reduces your chances of getting yellow underarm stains. To remove yellow armpit stains, try soaking your garment in warm water with liquid peroxide (suitable for white T-shirts and shirts), then wash in the hottest wash allowed on the garment's label. If the stain is still there after the wash, dampen it and sprinkle it with meat tenderiser. Let it stand for about an hour and then wash it again.

Gum

To remove gum, place the item in a plastic bag in the freezer – remove from the freezer after an hour. Bend the fabric in half through the centre of the piece of gum and it should crack off. If not, try chipping at it with a butter-knife. If that doesn't work, let the gum return to room temperature, rub it with peanut butter, then try to take it off with the knife. Afterwards wash your garment as usual.

GODDESS TIP
STICK AN OLD EMPTY PERFUME BOTTLE OR A TUMBLE-DRIER SOFTENER SHEET IN THE BOTTOM OF YOUR LAUNDRY BAG TO COUNTERACT THE PONG OF SOCKS AND DIRTY, SWEATY CLOTHES.

GODDESS TIP
I SEARCHED FOR SO LONG FOR A CLOTHING AIRER WITHOUT SUCCESS AND THEN EVENTUALLY FOUND THE MOST BEAUTIFUL TRADITIONAL BEECH ONE AT BAILEYS HOME AND GARDEN (TEL: +44 1989 561 931, WWW.BAILEYSHOMEANDGARDEN.CO.UK). THE WEBSITE ALSO CARRIES A RANGE OF THE MOST GORGEOUS PACKAGED WAXES, POLISHES AND BRUSHES, AND IF YOU WANT TO HANG YOUR CLOTHES OUT IN THE GARDEN THE TIMBER DOLLY PEGS ARE DIVINE!

Ink

First try hairspray (but not on acetate). If that doesn't work then make a paste of dry mustard and water, spread over the stain for fifteen minutes, then wash and rinse. For white fabrics moisten with salt and lemon and then hold over steam. Felt-tip pen should be treated with methylated spirits.

G-Spot

For the ultimate ironing-board cover try Cath Kidston (tel: +44 870 850 1084, www.cathkidston.co.uk). She also stocks a beautiful floral-printed laundry basket, laundry bags, clothes-peg holders, aprons and tea towels.

Wax

Chip off as much as you can with a butter-knife, then place several layers of paper towel over the wax that still remains and apply a warm iron to it. Keep changing the paper towels as the wax soaks off and is absorbed.

Grass

Place a cloth under the stain inside the garment and sponge with methylated spirits, then wash in the usual manner.

Blood

Soak the item in salt and cold water. For older blood stains use the salt and water and then add a few drops of ammonia to the water. Or apply a cold paste of cornflower and cold water, leave to dry, brush off and then launder.

Stains in clothing

When applying stain-removing solutions to fabric, apply from the back of the fabric and not the front. This way the stain won't spread any deeper.

Macs

Baby wipes usually get stains off mackintoshes – especially make-up.

GODDESS TIP

YOU CAN REFRESH YOUR BLACK CLOTHES BY ADDING STRONG COFFEE OR TEA (2 CUPS) TO RINSE WATER.

GODDESS TIP

ELIMINATE STATIC BY STROKING YOUR CLOTHES WITH A WIRE HANGER. THIS ALSO WORKS IF YOU'VE GOT STATIC IN YOUR HAIR.

Stiff sheets and towels

Wash with less detergent and add 1 cup of white vinegar (a natural fabric softener) to the rinse cycle. This also works on any lingering odours. For very smelly clothes, steep in baking soda and water for an hour before washing, wash and then add vinegar to the rinse cycle.

BATHROOM

Mind your jewellery
Place some hooks inside your bathroom cabinet so that you can store your jewellery away from ominous gaping plugholes.

GODDESS TIP
KEEP A GOOD BOOK BY THE LOO OR A NOTEBOOK AND PEN TO DOODLE AND JOT DOWN IDEAS.

Chair
A chair or a stool in the bathroom is much more comfortable than sitting on the edge of the bath when applying beauty products.

Add mirrors and lights
Poke around junk shops for different-sized mirrors, attach pretty ribbons to them or frame them and display them randomly on a wall. Fit lights above mirrors to help when you are carrying out tasks. Switches should be on pull-cords only – electric sockets in a bathroom are bad news.

Ventilate
To prevent mould your bathroom should have a window, or if that's not possible then an extractor fan. Also keep the radiator on in the winter to prevent dampness from setting in.

Decorate with soaps
Claus Porto soap company was set up in 1887 in Portugal. I adore their Ach Brito Claus Mimosa, Magnolia, Violet, Rose and Fig and Grapefruit soaps – the latter two are pictured here (tel: +44 20 8735 2882, www.npw.co.uk). Alternatively the black and white flocked box of soaps by Tricia Guild from the Designers Guild new Fragrant Home range (tel: +44 20 7351 5775, www.designersguild.com) looks chic against whiter than white walls.

Fresh air
Place lemon slices in an open bowl in the bathroom to keep the air citrus fresh, and if you're a fan of lemony scent keep a bottle of Annick Goutal Eau d'Hadrien eau de toilette (tel: +44 20 7730 1234 or see pp237) in the lavatory and have a spritz as a treat when you visit. Add a couple of drops of your favourite essential oil to the inside of the cardboard toilet-tissue roll. With each turn, fragrance is released into the room.

Add knobs and hooks

Chloe Alberry, 84 Portobello Road, London W11 (tel: +44 20 7727 0707, www.chloealberry.com) has the most beautiful range of door hooks and crystal knobs. And look no further than Carden Cunietti, 81-83 Westbourne Park Road, London W2 5QH (tel: +44 20 7229 8630, www.carden-cunietti.com) for drawer and door handles made from shells.

Face cloth

Face cloths can be fiddly. It is better to buy two and sew them together to make a mitt, which is much easier to use in the bath.

Towels

If you want to personalise your bath and hand towels then Biju (tel: +44 1903 610267, www.biju.co.uk) offers an embroidery service for the towels and bathrobes that they sell.

CLEANING UP

Hairbrush and comb

Run your comb through your brush and then pop them in the sink for half an hour with warm water and add either clarifying shampoo or baking soda. Rinse afterwards and allow them to dry naturally.

Mildew remover

Dissolve a half-cup of vinegar with a half-cup of Borax in warm water and use to clean and disinfect mildew on a bathroom mat. Sprinkle it on and scrub it off. Keeping your mat dry between uses prevents this.

Sticky labels

To remove decals, sticky labels and glued-on price tags steep a cloth in hot vinegar and squeeze it to saturate the glue.

Bath rings

Use Borax for removing hard-water stains. Just sprinkle some onto the offending area, let it sit for a few minutes, then wipe with a damp sponge.

Tub and tile

Mix 2 cups of baking soda and water to make a smooth thick paste. Apply the paste to the tub or tile and let it sit for 20-30 minutes. Rinse off with a soft rag, moving in a circular motion. Once the paste is off, spray the tub or tile with a 50/50 vinegar/water rinse. The rinse will remove any residue and disinfect the area as well.

The toilet

Next time you are cleaning your bathroom, drop two Alka-Seltzer tablets into the toilet and let the bubbles go to work for 30 minutes, then brush clean. In addition, pouring 2 cups of vinegar into the bowl and letting it sit overnight will eliminate toilet rings. For best results do this once or twice a month.

Washing the floor

To disinfect your bathroom floors pop a few drops of lavender essence from Summerill & Bishop, 100 Portland Road, London, W1 (tel: +44 20 7221 4566, www.summerillandbishop.com) into a big bucket of hot water and mop. Never have carpet in a bathroom – too unhygienic.

Washing your smalls

Hand wash your smalls in Durance en Provence hand wash, and if you're a real stickler for perfection iron them using the Linen Water ironing spray. They come in a whole range of scents, but my favourites are orange flower and lime blossom. Available from Decordance, 126 Talbot Road, Notting Hill, London (tel: +44 20 7792 4122).

5 GARDEN

The most relaxing hours of my life took place lying flat on my back, arms splayed out in an angel position in Doolin's little green field. The daffodils bloomed, little bundles of springtime and happiness, as I lay there under the ash, or was it an oak, or a sycamore?

A bumble bee broke my concentration. Where did she come from? What key was she buzzing in? She made that unique noise that only bumble bees makes as she clumsily bashed againts tree trunks. My Dad would surely know the answers to my million and one questions... Then suddenly the bell to tell everyone to return to their classrooms would sound, and I'd wait twenty more minutes before clambering across the ditch, skippping back across the dusty road and hopping in over the school wall.

Now that I live in the city I suffer from severe cravings for the countryside. I'm obsessed with the small green patch that is my simple back lawn. And despite having dismissed the idea of 'twitching' in the past (I couldn't help but associate it with anoraks and trainspotters, computer geeks and rocket scientists), I found myself rushing out to buy a bird table within hours of spotting a small crow through my living room window, or was it a rook or a jackdaw or a big starling? In fact feeding the birds in my garden is one of my life's great pleasures – and I've realised that you don't need a country pile for them to come and visit you either. Even if you have a balcony or a tiny roof terrace deep in the heart of the city, if you're patient and create and sustain the right environment (and if they're hungry) they will come and see you every day.

In fact even in small outside spaces there's room to experiment with things: why not try planting flowers that are well-known for attracting butterflies? Or what about arranging some colourful pots of herbs that might come in handy for your tea? If you've a garden, build a shed and give shelter to hibernating hedgehogs or set up breeding boxes for wild birds or even a beehive. Use the space to introduce your friends to a tiny slice of nature and dress it up like you would any party indoors. Add new tables, linen and lighting and trees that'll offer shade while you read. Ensure every corner is scented by thick shrubs and posies and you'll simultaneously be providing shelter to little animals.

Of course, it's most important that you get to relax in this space, so celebrate happy beginnings in the spring with snowdrops, daffodils and cherry blossom. In the summer hold garden parties scented by jasmine and roses. The summer is also a good time to lie around reading and doodling – and investigating the midgets, butterflies, wasps and ants that find their way onto my lawn.

In the autumn things slow down somewhat on the grassy patch and I harvest the lavender that grows in the beds around the lawn. Once tied in tight little bundles lavender is the perfect antidote to a smelly kitchen bin or a stuffy wardrobe.

In the winter the birds really start to rely on me for sustenance and I keep them fed as best I can with nuts and seeds. A neighbour who also feeds the birds informed me recently that I over-feed the one in my garden, but when swallows nesting under her bedroom window had two broods of chicks instead of one I was secretly pleased – they'd been eating my supplies too! It has to be said that the birds in my garden can err on the side of (er) chubbiness but their constant singing and chirping is so enjoyable you can hardly blame me for wanting them near! How could anyone ever think of putting any little wild bird in a cage?

These floral letters are by
Appley Hoare Exterieur,
30A Pimlico Road, London
(tel: +44 20 7730 7070,
www.appleyhoare.com).

187

Richard Benson,

Richard Benson's story in his book *The Farm* (Penguin Books) is a very beautiful one. I felt reading it, as I'm sure many people did, that we had walked the same dusty roads and wandered the same country fields as kids. Last summer I finally had the pleasure of meeting him and was fascinated by his knowledge of and love for wild flowers. Here is a tiny fraction of his brilliance…

I grew up, Gisèle, on a small, ramshackle farm in rural East Yorkshire, but I can't say that I was terribly interested in wild flowers when I was young. I moved onto college and then work in London, and became a fully-fledged urbanite for 10 years, but then one autumn day in the late 1990s I received a phone call from my dad. The farm, which he, my mother and younger brother had found harder and harder to keep going, was to be sold. It was the same everywhere, he said; little farms like ours were finding it harder and harder to compete in the modern age of hypermarkets and globocorps.

I spent a lot of time in Yorkshire after the sale, and I used to think a lot about the sort of old country knowledge that seemed to be being lost to us. One night in the early summer I was walking along a lane with my mum and dad, and they began talking about wild flowers.

"Birds' eyes, look," said my mum, pointing with a toe into some grasses, where there were some tiny straggles of speedwell flowers. "We used to say if you picked them, birds'd come and peck your eyes out. Same as mother-die, except with that we said, picking it killed your mum."

"What about foxgloves then?" I asked, seeing a clump of the violet and white foxgloves up ahead.

"I suppose somebody thought foxes must wear them. All these cultivated flowers you get for your garden you know, they all come from these sort. We were just looking at't flowers,"

"I used to like this one when I was a kid," said my dad, picking a stem of grass from the ground. "Cock's foot. Can tha see why they call it that? Look." He pushed the head of the grass against his palm to make the shape of a large bird's foot. "I don't know why, I just used to like t'idea that it looks like a cock's foot."

As the flowers and their names grew and intertwined in my mum and dad's conversation, I was struck by the beauty of those names, the way they seemed to capture an ancient, imaginative relationship with the natural environment.

I have collected names and grown wild flowers ever since that night, sowing a little meadow-like patch with my parents at the house they moved to after the sale, and I grew them in pots on the balcony in my flat in London. There is nothing particularly wrong or unusual about cultivating these small, tatty plants in a city; one of the pleasing things about many species is the way they grow everywhere, defiantly bringing a little bit of colour and folklore to even the most neglected urban patches. Think of the ox-eye daisies that spring up every summer alongside railway tracks, their seeds originally transported in the dust and dirt on trains. Or of Ragged Robin that sprouts in pathways, its name a link to mythological house goblin, Robin Goodfellow, who caused mischief unless he was treated nicely and given cream.

My favourite is heartsease, or Love-In-Idleness, a flower that country people like my mother have dozens of different stories about, and that Shakespeare wrote about in A Midsummer Night's Dream. These few small, yellow and purple flowers on a north London windowsill is to me a reminder of all sorts of things, not least of the fact that you don't have to compartmentalize your life according to other people's definitions of urban and rural, or old-fashioned and modern.

You can buy packets of these seeds for about a pound a throw, and get all you need to know about names in a copy of The Englishman's Flora by Geoffrey Grigson, currently out of print but easy to find for about a fiver in secondhand bookshops. In other words, for less than a round of drinks you can have a living link to the folklore of your country growing there on your windowsill. And there is not a globocorp or hypermarket on the planet that can buy it, or change it, or take it away.

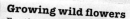

Growing wild flowers

For the Earth Goddess in everyone, nothing but wild flowers will do. Plant a whole garden-full from Naturescape (tel: +44 1949 860592, www.naturescape.co.uk), or Meadow Mania (tel: +44 1249 819 013, www.meadowmania. co.uk), and by summertime you'll have a perfect patch for running barefoot in the sun. Another shop to look out for is Landlife Wildflowers (tel: +44 151 737 1819, www. wildflower.org.uk) – a cottage lovers dream. Ox eye daisies, primroses or foxgloves anyone? Garden Organic (tel: +44 24 7630 3517, www.hdra.org.uk; online catalogue at www. organiccatalogue.com), offers everything from eco grass and veg seeds, to fertilizer.

Catherine St Germans: GROWING FLOWERS

Photograph by Poppy de Villeneuve

At the Port Eliot Lit Fest last year (see pp274), I took shelter from a torrential downpour in the Earl of St Germans's greenhouse. There I smelled the most beautiful jasmine plant I'd ever come across, nestling delicately against the glass door. I watched as Lillian, one of the Port Eliot gardeners, bent down to caress one of the tiny jasmine flowers, with a tender touch a mother might reserve for her child, and a wave of scent and then nostalgia ambushed me, salty tears scorching my cheeks. She explained to me that the Earl and Countess Catherine St Germans had carefully nurtured these plants from seeds and tiny cuttings.

The rain continued and the greenhouse began to fill with people bustling to get out of the wet and it wasn't until after the worst of it had stopped, and the crowds had dispersed, that I noticed a tiny squashed jasmine branch on the floor. I quickly wrapped it in some wet loo roll and put it in my pocket. In fact I nursed it all the way back to Dublin, placed it in a pot delicately with some rooting powder and months later planted it against my kitchen wall. It now stands proud at over five feet! Its scent always reminds me of my visit to St Germans so who better than the Countess herself, Catherine St Germans, to give me some tips on gardening and, in particular, on growing my own little, wonderfully scented, Goddess garden...

To my mind Gisèle, the only flowers and plants worth growing are those which are scented. Roses, stocks, jasmine, hyacinths, paper whites, sweet peas, lemon verbena, lavender, honeysuckle, pelargoniums, eucalyptus, Moroccan mint and trumpet lilies all grow in my garden every year. We are lucky enough to live in Cornwall, with largely mild winters, and so I can start picking in February and bring as much scent as I can into the house - just one stem of jasmine is enough to perfume a whole room for up to four days.

I am obliged to run a cutting garden as I have to fill a Stately Home for as much of the year as possible with flowers I have grown in the Walled Gardens, here at Port Eliot. With over 100 rooms to fill, I grow flowers like other people grow vegetables, in rows. If someone comes to stay, my husband and I like to drape their room with flowers, hanging them from the wardrobe tops, we have even been known to cut new beech saplings, and arrange them in a bower over a dressing table. We like to tell ourselves our guests don't mind so much if it takes them half an hour to run a bath, water pipes shaking, if they have been treated to one of Peregrine's Datura blooms from the greenhouse, or a bowl of my stocks, or paper whites.

190

My husband grows exotics in a heated greenhouse, and every spring I am allowed a corner, in which to bring on seedlings grown from seed. At first, my husband disapproved of my allotment of sweetly coloured and heavily scented blooms. He believed the grounds of a stately home should be a vista of Repton-guided green, and colourful flowers should be treated like sickly Victorian children, and be kept warm indoors in a greenhouse. He was suspicious of my seed packets which promised hardy annuals, like sweet peas – one of the easiest flowers to grow for their scent. He watched me and my friend Lillian, a local flora and fauna expert, plant out newly propagated seedlings in March in the cold earth outside, just as the frost melted. Gradually, though, he was drawn to my beds of delights as he saw their shoots take, and now spends as much time as I do out in the rain and the sunshine and the fresh air amidst the cottage garden flowers I like to grow every summer. Stocks, the most strongly scented plant I know, form banks of white, covered in flowers from late spring until mid summer. Often I find Peregrine, sitting on a low stool amidst the perfumed rows, gently tying my taller flowers up with twine helping them to hold up their heads, heavy with scent.

His favourites are my sweet peas. I grow sweet peas like others grow broad beans, in an optimistically long row, six feet tall, and as my grandfather did in his garden in Scotland when I was a child, up a trellis made of fine mesh, as sheer as fish net stockings. From June onwards every other day we pick bunches of them. The more you pick, the more they grow. Their gentle scent fills our bedroom all summer long, and if we get the timing right, we can keep them growing until just before the first frost appears again, in November.

Last year, I made a life altering discovery: that it is possible to grow roses in pots, and it is not always necessary to cut flowers. At the Chelsea Flower Show my great friend Andi came across a brilliant man called Robert Mattock, whose family have been leading rose nurserymen for six generations in Oxfordshire. Mattock uses a unique growing technique that produces show-quality blooms on mature specimen plants in easily manageable pots. Not only are they beautiful, Mattocks grow all the old and best rose.

Peregrine →

Dear Gisele, In the garden
at Port Eliot in early May,
you don't have to see my
favourite flower, to know it is
coming into bloom. You can
smell it fifty paces away,
from the other side of a 20
foot laurel hedge.
It is called the Rhododendron
'Loderi King George'.

Her favourite
Rhododendron

Gertrude Jekyll rose

To the rhododendron purist, this
plant is sometimes considered rather
too blowsy. It has a bloom half as
big again as a rugby ball comprised
of up to twelve flowering parts. All
of them twice as large as the average
flower. It is absolutely ravishing.
When it first comes into flower, it is
tinged with a flush of sherbert
pink. It has faint green markings
in its throat and blooms for up to
two weeks, or more. As it dies,
it gradually fades to white,

looking as though a dust
sheet has been thrown over
it. It is extremely difficult
to describe a scent. Suffice
to say, my rhododendron
smells as blowsy as it looks,
and is just as tarty.

Yours,

Catherine St Germans

varieties like my favourite,
the deep pink and heavily
scented, Gertrude Jekyll.
Even non gardeners can cope.
All the work has been done
for you, except, perhaps, says
Robert, 'for watering them and
casting them the occasional
adoring glance'. Mattocks
(tel: +44 1865 735382, www.
robertmattockroses.com) will
deliver orders of roses to you,
and then the game starts. You
can move your pots of rambling
roses, from garden to bedroom as
they bloom, and then downstairs to
drawing room, or even bathroom. As
you lie in the bath, you can surround
yourself with a shrubbery of live
growing roses and natural scent.'
(Catherine St Germans, 2006)

GARDEN *Kit*

Seating and lighting

The Lievore Altherr Molina chair at Arper (tel: +39 0422 7918, www.arper.it) is very stylish and has gained a cult-like status in the design world, but if space is an issue Southsea Deckchairs (tel: +44 23 9265 2865, www.deckchairs.co.uk) fold away and come in beautiful, thick, coloured fabric. To illuminate your garden try RK Alliston, 173 New Kings Road, London (tel: +44 845 130 5577, www.rkalliston.com) and Heals (tel: +44 8700 240 780, www.heals.co.uk) for tea light holders, and The Conran Shop (tel: +44 020 7589 7401, www.conran.com) for green glass jam jar candle holders which you can hang from branches. If you're expecting it to be windy opt for Moroccan lamps (see pp264).

Seeds and bulbs

Buy seasonal deluxe flower and herb seeds at The Cutting Garden (tel: + 44 845 050 4848, www.thecuttinggarden.com). Check out www.flowerbulbs.co.uk for bulb trends and inspiration, and www.gardenadvice.co.uk for hints and advice.

Garden equipment

My favourite garden tools are the Eborgnor bud trimming knife and rose pruners at Le Prince Jardinier , 37 rue de Valois, 75001 Paris (tel: +33 1 44 55 07 15, www.princejardinier.fr), and for an array of French antique enamel buckets, watering cans, plant stands and the lovely floral 'GODDESS' letters at the beginning of this chapter, visit Appley Hoare Exterieur, 30a Pimlico Road, London (tel: +44 20 7730 7070, www.appleyhoare.com). For pots and planters try Marston & Langinger, 192 Ebury Street, London (tel: +44 20 7881 5717, www.marston-and-langinger.com) and for wooden-handled spades, trowels and sweeping brushes, try Baileys (tel: +44 19 8956 1931, www.baileys-home-garden.co.uk). You can also find pocket aprons and gloves at Town and Country (tel: +44 15 3083 0990, www.townandco.com), and outdoor table clips, to stop your tablecloth from blowing away, at Cox & Cox (tel: +44 870 442 4787, www.coxandcox.co.uk).

ENJOY THE BIRDS

I'm fascinated by acrobatic blue tits, bossy starlings and greedy bullfinches and have fixed bird boxes to trees and walls to help give them shelter. I've learned that it's best to place the box 5 metres from the ground so that cats can't get at them. This is a simple way to create a safe nesting place in your garden for breeding birds. Place your box facing between North and East (no strong sun or wet winds) and line it with feathers, hair clippings wool and moss. Different birds nest in boxes with different sized hole in them. To attract blue tits have a 25mm hole; a 28mm hole attracts a wide range of garden birds; great tits and house sparrows like 32mm and starlings a 45mm hole.

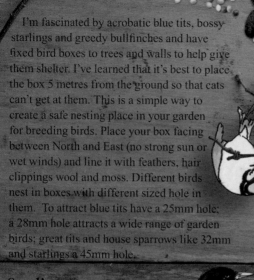

Tit *n* any of numerous small active Old World songbirds. They have a short bill and feed on insects and seeds. *Coll. n* a circus of tits. **Blue Tit** has a blue cap and yellow breast, with a dark blue line which runs through the eye. **Great Tit** has a black head and line that runs from the chin under the breast. **Coal Tit** has a black cap and chin, a white mark at the back of the head and buff coloured underparts.

Starling *n* any gregarious passerine songbird of an Old World family with a blackish iridescent plumage and a short tail. *Coll. n* a murmuring of starlings.

Blackbird *n* a common European thrush in which the male has black plumage and a yellow bill. *Coll. n* a whistle of blackbirds.

Wren *n* any small brown passerine songbird of a chiefly American family. They have a slender bill and feed on insects. *Coll. n* a herd or wrens.

Robin *n* a small Old World songbird related to the thrushes. The adult has a brown back, orange-red breast and face, and grey underparts. *Coll. n* a breast of robins.

House Sparrow *n* a small Eurasian bird with brown plumage and grey underparts. *Coll. n* a host of sparrows.

Finch *n* any of various songbirds having a short stout bill for feeding on seeds. *Coll. n* a charm of finches. **Chaffinch** has a blue head, redish underparts and a little green bit above his tail seen in flight. **Gold Finch** has a red face patch surrounding the beak, a black crown and a yellow flash on the wing. **Bull Finch** has a black head, grey above his wings, a white rump and bright red underparts.

Crow *n* any large gregarious songbird of the genus Corvus of Europe and Asia. All have a heavy bill, glossy black plumage, and rounded wings. *Coll. n* a murder of crows.

Thrush *n* any of a subfamily of songbirds, esp., those having a brown plumage with a spotted breast. *Coll. n* a mutation of thrushes.

GODDESS TIP
FOR GREAT BIRD ADVICE I TRUST RSPB (TEL:+44 1767 680551, WWW. RSPB.ORG.UK/BIRDS). THEY HAVE A GREAT RANGE OF BIRDFEEDERS AND BIRD NESTING BOXES AT WWW.SHOPPING.RSPB.ORG.UK.

Lark *n* any brown bird of a predominantly Old World family of songbirds, noted for their singing. *Coll. n* an exaltation of larks.

How can I attract birds to my garden?

6 FOOD

The Tralee Deli was jammed with soggy shoppers, jostling for cover. My Mum wheeled me in my pushchair just inside the doorway, for shelter from the rain. Peeping out I watched as sweet packets, a Tayto bag and some ice-lolly sticks were churned about in the river of water that bubbled along the gutter. Inside, when pressed for an order, people stood on tippy-toes, craning their necks to choose something small from the menu that might justify them being there. I remember the damp cold air as my mother lifted me up out of the pushchair to help her choose her order from the menu before returning me to the buggy. Ten minutes later she handed me two Styrofoam cups packed with coleslaw and potato salad, snapped shut the waterproof cover over the green frame above my head and turned me in the direction of home. Everything was grey, the scene outside obscured from view by my warm breath on the waterproof plastic, which the heat had turned opaque.

The acidic aroma of the onions clung to every corner of my tiny waterproof bubble. The movement of the buggy made me groggy but the overwhelming scent kept me awake. As the pushchair wheels bobbed over the uneven streets, my grip tightened around the quivering cups of pungent salad. Gargantuan rain drops landed above my head as if shot from an erupting volcano elsewhere in town. Between the drops I could see legs, from the knees downwards: spattered tights and soggy shoes rushing to get home for tea. Arriving back at Granny's, Mum scrubbed my hands clean with green Palmolive and handed me back my Styrofoam cup full of potato and onion and a white plastic fork. I sat on my Granny's front doorstep – warm and dry – to eat. I'll never forget that first taste experience: diced potatoes and onion mixed together with a smattering of mayo. And ever since then, potatoes, in any form, will do me – boiled, baked, chipped, roasted or mashed. I love them!

Years later, Dad let me set my own crop – late one March. Sitting on a low stool he prepared the large British Queens for planting by slicing them in half. Leaning over him I asked why he was looking for little white knobs on their jackets. "These are eyes," he said, pointing to a cream-coloured nodule with his penknife. "Each eye sprouts a new plant and each spud has as many as two or three or sometimes five eyes – so we divide them up before we plant them."

The sound of leather and metal traces dragging through the gate meant that Liam Scanlon, Dad's cousin, had arrived and un-tacked Molly, a horse, from the hay-car. She was ready to be harnessed for ploughing the haggard to prepare the ground for the new seeds. My grandfather loved chatting to Liam as they ploughed the haggard's earth together. A grating clatter would ring out around the haggard, as the plough accidentally collided with a buried rogue stone in the ground. They'd take turns at harrowing it for rocks and then open dark brown virgin drills and feed the exposed furrows with sweet, steaming horse manure. My sister, my brother and I would race between the drills to see who could sow the most scoilàns in the dung filled furrows and keep the cleanest hands. Dad gave us 50 pence for every furrow planted and like bullets we'd go about setting the halved British Queens a foot apart. Our buckets draining, we'd run through the furrows with the plough and horse, cutting through the earth and sealing them closed behind us. Upon completion we'd stick in coloured windmills with string and bunting on them to scare away crows and other night time thieves. The British Queens would be ready for harvesting in late June or early July, the Aran Banners and Kers Pink in September. Whichever we'd set, one thing was always certain, we'd need a pit full of huge spuds for making my favourite recipe, mashed potatoes with unsalted butter, Dad's home grown onions and a pinch of salt.

I loved our spuds so much that I'd eat two dinners a day just to get a double helping. One at home in Mum and Dad's house and then one in my Granda and Granny's house down the road. It was always a novelty to watch the spuds boiling away in a huge pot in the open fireplace. Granny liked to cook on an open fire and even made griddle bread and potato cakes this way. For her special mash, she'd peel the spuds, add butter, a pinch of salt and a drop of milk, to make a type of purée. She called it pandee and the last time I ate it with her we had it with chopped boiled cabbage and melt in your mouth pink spare ribs. The spuds were particularly tasty that day, because Dad had dug them fresh from the haggard's earth that morning. It was late June and these were the first spuds of the year. I'd spent the day with Dad and Granda saving hay in the meadows and all day they questioned how the spuds would taste that night. They tasted special! Later that year Granny left me; she passed away and with her went her perfect pandee recipe. I didn't taste spuds like hers again until I met Heston Blumenthal. Tears welled-up in my eyes in Marrakech when I tasted his pomme purée.

HESTON BLUMENTHAL

Entering through the courtyard, the villa rippled in the intense Moroccan heat. A bowl of quenelle of green tea and lime sat on a table poolside, next to it a small steaming bucket of liquid nitrogen and a spoon. I joined the other diners as the chef loaded the tablespoon with the white, suds-like green tea substance and plunged it quickly into the liquid nitrogen, freezing it solid into a tiny meringue. Like a parent bird feeding its young, he delicately spooned the brittle, steaming confection into our gaping mouths where it exploded to nothing, the green tea smoke running down our noses and disappearing into the air. After that came a meal of unforgettable flavours, soft purée potatoes reminiscent of mash my granny used to make, duck and a chocolate mousse cake with a brittle hazelnut base – each mouthful an uncontrollable explosion of fizziness: I had to find out more about its creator…

Excited, I ran to the kitchen to thank the chef, armed with two bottles of chilled Heineken. Offering me a genuine handshake, and with zero pretence, the genius introduced himself, "Hello, I'm Heston Blumenthal," he smiled "The popping cake you so lovingly describe as 'The Fizz Bomb' is filled with Space Dust (popping candy), if you're that blown away by it, you should come to Bray in Berkshire to my Fat Duck restaurant and learn how to make it in my lab. You can try eating it there with headphones on – it makes the popping more intense." How could I refuse? The world's number one chef, with three Michelin stars to his name, was going to show little ol' me how to bake a cake; a dessert from The Fat Duck which was voted Best Restaurant in the World in Restaurant Magazine's Top 50. Wow, I couldn't believe it! A month later, I took a flight to London, and from Paddington Station a train to Maidenhead… My knees were shaking in anticipation of the wonderful new things I was going to learn from such an inspirational man:

Heston, can you remember the first meal that arrested your five senses? *When I was sixteen, my father took us during our summer holidays to a restaurant in Provence which had become one of the great restaurants of France. I remember everything about that meal vividly; the crickets chirping, the smell of lavender in the* air. I was amazed by everything – the many waiting staff and the Sommelier and the chariot-sized cheese trolley docked at a table behind us, and the baby legs of lamb being carved at tableside. At that very moment, I realized there was quite simply no other career in the world that I wanted to pursue!

And you're self taught? *Yes, I taught myself everything from ice cream making to butchery, reading everything I could get my hands on – whether it was in English or French. In fact, I actually learned French from translating cookbooks so that I could try the recipes! In 1986, I bought the book* On Food and Cooking: The Science and Lore of the Kitchen *by Harold McGee, and it changed my life.*

The Fat Duck, in 2004 earned its third Michelin star. In your vast experience, how can we all become better cooks? *Use your senses. For instance use your ears when frying with butter, when it stops sizzling, it's ready to cook with. Any longer and it's burnt. And use your nose when preparing; have you ever chopped a delicate fruit with a knife that's been used for cutting garlic. Horrible! Right? Sniff first, cut later. Another thing to keep in mind is that to reduce bitterness (say in a soup), you add salt not sugar – seasonings are not always obvious so always keep tasting while preparing food. And when you're ready to eat it, taste with your mouth, your eyes, ears and nose and don't be afraid to touch it. Food should excite all of the five senses.*

Favourite smell? Freshly cut wet grass (wet is intrinsically British), it's the smell that Spring is coming.

Favourite sound? Summer sounds; lawnmowers in the distance, the slap of the ball against the wooden cricket bat, big bumble bees and ice cream vans – not only the jingle but the engine ticking over as you wait for your ice cream.

Favourite taste? Ice cream van ice cream, it tastes special because of the context it's eaten in.

Favourite to your sense of touch? The thrill of touching fresh produce; the firmness of vegetables, the softness of fruits and the morbidity of game and meat.

Favourite colour? Black.

Favourite bird? The Anjou pigeon.

Favourite animal? Fat Duck.

Favourite flower? Vanilla orchid.

Favourite place? Home with my wife and kids.

Favourite book? The Man Who Mistook His Wife for a Hat by Oliver Sacks, it's fascinating and I'm using it for research.

Favourite artwork? The Last Supper by Leonardo da Vinci.

Favourite possession? My new freeze drier in the kitchen.

If you could have dinner with one person who would it be and what would you ask them? Jesus, I'd like to ask him how he managed to feed so many people with so little?

Heston Blumenthal is chef/proprietor of The Fat Duck (tel: +44 1 628 580333, www. fatduck.co.uk) and The Hinds Head (tel: +44 1628 626151), both in Bray, Berkshire.

Duck *n* **1** any of a family of aquatic birds, esp. those having short legs, webbed feet, and a broad blunt bill. **2** the flesh of this bird, used as food. **3** the female of such a bird, as opposed to the male (drake). *Coll. n* a paddling of ducks on water, a flush of ducks as they leave water for air and a team of ducks as they fly in a "v" in the air.

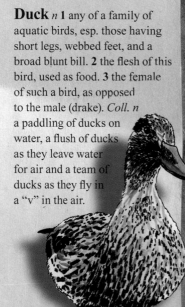

HESTON'S
Popping Chocolate Cake

I'm so thrilled that Heston offered to show me how to make the popping chocolate cake that blew my socks off in Marrakech. It's easily my favourite dish at the Fat Duck and, in my opinion, it's the best cake in the whole world.

So, Heston, whatever made you think of using popping candy and where did you get it from? *Originally Gisèle, this cake was a délice pudding from the Fat Duck Menu. I wanted to develop the dish so that it would create a "popping" sensation in... well, it's one of those areas of the body that is hard to pinpoint exactly but it's somewhere between the ears, at the back of your head. I remembered that you could get that effect from popping space dust but it wasn't available to anyone other than the big confectionery companies – that is, unless you bought a minimum order of one ton! It took several months and an awful lot of phone calls by my priceless assistant, Roisin Wesley, to finally procure these exciting little popping crystals. Nowadays, this stuff is popping up everywhere, so to speak, and there are more readily available sources: for stockist details, contact Hax Ltd (tel: +44 20 8341 1010, www.haxltd.co.uk). Once you've found this ingredient the rest is easy!*

There are three parts to this cake: the chocolate mousse, the popping candy base and the chocolate glaze. The quantities given are to fill a bottomless ring mould of 12cm in diameter and 5cm in height, so you'll need to adjust the amounts depending on the mould you want to use. Just make sure the mould has no base. For the chocolate mousse, buy the best quality chocolate you can, and under no circumstances buy any with a cocoa content of less than 55 per cent. Obviously, chocolate with a higher cocoa content than this can be used, but it will appeal more to the chocolate purist and less to the child in you. Don't balk at the addition of salt – it makes a wonderful difference. Also, please bear in mind that, although the cake can be made the day before, it is best assembled on the day you want to serve it, when the "pop" is at its strongest and the mousse is able to maintain that wonderful, silk-like texture.

Put these on to make the popping louder!

Heston's Popping Chocolate Cake Recipe

For the popping-candy base

85g whole hazelnuts
40g milk chocolate
2 tsp mixed spice
100g popping candy

For the chocolate mousse

350g dark chocolate
400ml double cream
Pinch of salt

For the chocolate glaze

10g chocolate (same brand as for the mousse)
60ml water
4 whole coffee beans
Pinch of salt
15g cocoa powder
35g golden caster sugar (unrefined)

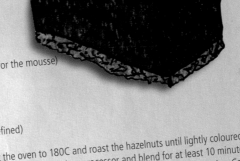

To make the base, preheat the oven to 180C and roast the hazelnuts until lightly coloured. This should take about 10 minutes. Place the nuts in a processor and blend for at least 10 minutes, until reduced to a paste, then set aside. Gently melt the chocolate and stir in the ginger spice. Carefully incorporate the popping candy, making sure all of it gets coated in chocolate. Fold in the hazelnut purée. Place the cake ring on your chosen serving dish and gently press in the popping candy mixture to a depth of about 1cm (you may find you have some left over), thereby creating a base. Set aside until you assemble the cake.

To make the mousse, chop the chocolate into very small pieces and place in a bowl. In a small saucepan, bring 150ml of double cream to the boil, then pour over the chopped chocolate, stirring to disperse the heat of the cream until the chocolate has melted. Add salt to taste. Lightly whip the remaining double cream to very soft peaks. Do not overwhisk or the mousse will become granular. Once the chocolate cream mix has cooled to room temperature, fold in the lightly whipped cream. When assembling the cake, pour the mousse mix into the cake ring on top of the popping candy base. Leave a couple of millimetres spare between the top of the mousse and the top of the ring. Place in the fridge to set for an hour or two.

To make the glaze, chop up the chocolate and set aside. In a small pan, bring the water, coffee beans, salt and cocoa powder to a boil, whisking to dissolve the cocoa. Place the sugar in a small pan and place this over medium heat. Have to hand a little cold water in a cup, as well as a pastry brush or some such. As it heats up, the sugar will begin to melt and, being unrefined, will also start to caramelize very quickly. So, if need be, dip the brush in the cold water, and brush around the inside of the pan with it - this will help to stop the sugar burning. When the melted sugar has become a golden caramel, pour in the water, coffee and cocoa mix. But be careful when doing so - stand back, because it will bubble and spit for a second or two. Beat in the chopped chocolate and, when completely melted, pass the mixture through a fine sieve. Leave to cool a little, then add salt to taste. When cool but still liquid, pour the glaze on top of the mousse and return the cake to the fridge to set. To serve, run a hot knife around the inside of the ring and slide it off; or, easier still, run the flame of a blowtorch around the outside for a few seconds, then lift off the ring. Make sure that when slicing the cake, the blade of the knife is nice and hot.

Eggs

When I was small we had Rhode Island Red chickens on our farm that laid dark brown eggs and Light Sussex chickens that laid light brown eggs. Dad explained that the breed of chicken you choose determines the colour of the eggs and that colours range from the White Leghorn chicken's pure white eggs to the Maran (see my picture of its lovely black-speckled feathers) chicken's chocolate brown ones. Black Rock chickens are the quietest around children and for chickens like the ones in nursery rhymes the Wellsummer breed is the one. They lay flowerpot-red coloured eggs and love foraging for food so you'll get delicious free range eggs if you let them scratch around a bit. Incidentally, the Wellsummer Cockerel looks like it flew straight off the Kellogg's Cornflakes box. For city dwellers the most popular bird is the Pekin Bantam; petite, colourful and cute, it lays small, cream eggs and is favoured for its manageable size and obvious beauty. If you fancy owning any of the above breeds then Richard Bett in Lincolnshire (tel: +44 1507 363 742 or +44 7946 034926, www.poultrymad.co.uk) ships chickens, or eggs ready for hatching.

Chicken *n* a domestic fowl bred for its flesh or eggs. *Coll. n* a flock/ brood of chickens.

Egg *n* the oval or round reproductive body laid by the females of birds, reptiles, fishes, insects, and some other animals, surrounded by an outer shell or membrane. *Coll. n* a clutch of eggs.

Keep your chickens safe

Even the most meagre bit of outside space is sufficient to house one of Omlet's nifty Eglus (tel: +44 845 450 2056, www.omlet. co.uk). These are badger and fox-proof chicken houses that come in many different colours and fit between two and four birds. According to Omlet, the pink-coloured Eglus encourages chickens to lay the most eggs. Omlet will install the Eglus for you as well as provide organically-reared hens. They also offer plenty of advice on caring for your little feathered friends – use only good corn or chicken pellets, please.

Spinning egg
To test whether your egg is properly
boiled, spin it on a hard flat surface. If
it's a bit wobbly, it isn't quite cooked yet.

The perfect boiled egg
Place your egg in a pot with half an
inch of cold water. Bring to the boil
and simmer for 3 minutes for soft
and 10 to 12 for hard-boiled

Heston Blumenthal's ham and eggs
Serves 4
1 sourdough pain de campagne
(available from most stores), sliced
Olive oil or melted butter, to drizzle
4 free-range eggs
Salt and cracked black pepper
A few drops of balsamic vinegar
Freshly sliced ham

Undercooked boiled egg?
Place the cap back on, wrap it up
in clingfilm, pop it back in the pot
and boil for another few minutes.

Rub the slices of bread with the melted butter
or oil and char-grill. Set aside in a warm place
while you cook the eggs. I like to cook with
super-fresh free-range eggs for this recipe using
the Bernard Loiseau method.
Preheat the oven to 220C/425FGas Mark 7.
Break the eggs and separate the whites from
the yolks, making sure the yolks are kept whole.
Add a little butter and two teaspoons of water
to a small, non-stick, ovenproof frying pan
and heat until foaming (water stops the butter
overheating and turning the whites to rubber).
Salt and pepper the pan so that the bottom of
the eggs are also seasoned.
Carefully slide the egg whites into the frying
pan, place the pan in the preheated oven and
cook for 1½ minutes. With the whites still a bit
loose, season, add the yolks and return to the
oven for 2 minutes. To serve, place the ham on
the bread and layer your perfect egg on top.
Splash a few drops of balsamic vinegar over the
egg, a bit of salt and pepper, and indulge.

Heston's egg tip
Eggs keep better in the fridge,
but should be stored at room
temperature before cooking;
the main reason for boiled eggs
cracking is the drastic change of
temperature. If you do keep your
eggs in the fridge, put them in a
bowl of hot, not boiling water, for a
couple of minutes before cooking.

Read: I love **Chicken
and Egg** by Laurence
and Gilles Laurendon
(Hachette): delicious
recipes and beautiful
photographs of exotic
looking birds.

SPUDS
according to Heston

What's the secret to good mashed potatoes, Heston?
For mash, Gisèle, I prefer using waxy potatoes; most of the red varieties make a decent purée; large Belle de Fontenay or Charlotte potatoes will also give a good result. The important thing here is the first cooking of the potatoes. This involves pre-cooking. You will need a thermometer for this recipe.

Heston Blumenthal's Pommes Purées (Great Mash) recipe:

Serves 4
1kg potatoes, peeled
220g cold butter (use up to 350g, according to taste)

Cut the potatoes into slices, about 2.5cm thick. Make sure these are exactly the same thickness, as a difference of only a few millimetres could mean you end up with a mix of cooked and uncooked potatoes. Run these slices under the cold tap to wash off any surface starch.

Put sufficient water to completely cover the potatoes into a pan and heat it to 80C/175F. Add the potatoes and keep the temperature at 70C/160F for 30 minutes. The slices will become opaque and tough. Drain them and rinse them under cold running water until they have completely cooled down.
Rinse the pan and refill it to the same level with water. Add salt and bring to the boil. Drop in the potatoes and cook them in simmering water for 10-15 minutes until soft. Be aware that, with this method, they will probably take longer than you expect, so be patient. When ready, drain the potatoes. Dry them by placing in a pan over a low heat and gently shaking the pan.
For the next stage, you ideally need a ricer, although a vegetable mill should do the job. Cut the butter into 2.5cm cubes and place in a bowl. With the potatoes still hot, push them through the ricer onto the cubed butter. You should not push the potatoes through a sieve, as this will produce a gluey mash. For the same reason, never use a food processor – unless you want to be eating savoury bubble gum. Mix well.
Once again, you can prepare the purée in advance up to this stage. It will keep in the fridge for a few days. To serve, just reheat it gently in a pan while gradually whisking in 150ml simmering milk (this takes about 3 minutes). You can add more, depending on how firm you want the mixture to be.

Heston Blumenthal's Crushed Potatoes
Potatoes carry other flavours brilliantly, so try adding chopped shallots, confit tomatoes, chopped fresh herbs (such as parsley, chives, chervil, basil or coriander), olives, capers or bacon to this. The possibilities are almost endless.

Serves 4
1kg potatoes
200g butter (up to 350g, to taste)
4 tbsp olive oil (optional)

Follow the recipe for pommes purées to the stage where the potatoes are soft and cooked. Then, using the back of a fork, crush the potatoes while adding as much of the butter as you wish and/or the olive oil, along with your choice of other ingredients. You want to end up with a rough mash that still has small morsels of potato in it, to vary the texture.
If you are not eating this immediately, refrigerate without adding the extras.
You can then just reheat the potatoes in a medium oven (170C/325F/Gas Mark 3) for 15-20 minutes before adding your choice of additional flavourings.

Guide to good potatoes
Cara (1): Use for roasting, in salads, for pommes dauphinoise and other layered potato dishes.
Charlotte (2): Try in salads and layered potato dishes.
Desiree (3): Perfect all-rounders. Use for roasting, boiling, mashing, chipping, sautéeing or baking.
Jersey Royal new potatoes (4): Good simply served boiled or in salads.
King Edward (5): All-rounders, though they do not boil well. Try baking, mashing, chipping or roasting them.
Maris Piper (6): All-rounders. Use for baking, mashing, chipping or roasting.
Pink Fir Apple (7): Perfect for salads or boiling, roasting or chipping.

STEAK *Béarnaise*

My last meal would have to be steak béarnaise; here's how they'd have to cook it to send me off in style.

Cooking your steak

Rub your steak with olive oil and lay in a very hot pan pressing gently down on it (if you can hold your hand over the pan for more than two seconds, then it ain't hot enough, baby). Now comes the important part: leave the poor beast alone, leave it to cook, this will seal it and stop it sticking. After two minutes, flip it over and let it cook for the same amount of time on the other side. Lastly, remove the steak from the heat, season with salt and pepper and keep in a warm, not hot, place for five minutes. This last step will let the steak rest after it's turmoil in the pan.

How do you like yours?

Below are approximate cooking times for a one inch thick, fillet steak. Always cook your steak to the rare stage first – if you want it cooked further, turn it over again and cook for the remaining time on a lower heat.

Rare: 1-2 minutes per side.
Medium-rare: 2-2½ minutes per side.
Medium: 2½-3 minutes per side.
Well done: 3-4 minutes per side.

Gisèle's Béarnaise Sauce:

1 tbsp chopped shallots
4 tbsp white wine vinegar
3 tbsp chopped chervil
3 tbsp chopped tarragon
1 sprig thyme
3 egg yolks
125g butter, cut into pieces

Put the shallots in a pan with 2 tbsp of tarragon, 2 tbsp of chervil, the thyme and the vinegar, then season with salt and pepper and reduce by two-thirds, over a medium heat. Mix the egg yolks with 1 tbsp of water, then add to the shallots and whisk over a low heat. Slowly add the butter as soon as the mixture starts to thicken and keep whisking. Now add the rest of the herbs. Do not reheat béarnaise once it has cooled.

DINNER *Kit*

Chopping boards

Buy two heavy wooden chopping blocks (David Mellor's are really nice), one round and one square, or at least two different sizes – so that you can always identify which one is for vegetables, which one for meat. To prevent a chopping board from slipping, wet a tea towel, wring it out and place it underneath the board. To clean a chopping board, rub it with a cut and salted lemon and then wash briskly in water and washing-up liquid. Never soak a chopping board or it will start to split.

Kitchen knives

The only knives you really need invest in are an all purpose chef's knife, a paring knife, a serrated bread knife and a carving knife. The Sabatier knife set from Divertimenti (tel: +44 870 129 5026, www.divertimenti.co.uk) has the lot – and an exquisite Bugatti espresso maker! I prefer to visit their shop at 33-34 Marylebone High Street, London, W1 (tel: +44 20 7935 0689), and hold the knife in my hand to test drive it. The experts inform me that the heavier a knife is the better, and that, whatever you end up choosing, be sure to buy a knife sharpener made in the same material. Also remember never to chuck knives into a drawer as this dulls and blunts them over time.

Cutlery

My favourite cutlery is the Continental Antik silverware available from Georg Jensen, 15 New Bond Street, London W1 (tel: +44 20 7499 6541, www.georgjensen.com), which was first designed in 1906. Pieces are simple but have a slightly beaten effect on the handle which adds character. It's expensive but really does last a lifetime so buy it bit by bit and you'll have a collection to be proud of. Alternatively, try Portobello market or Katharine Pooley Home Interiors, 160 Walton Street, London, SW3 (tel: +44 207 584 3223, www.katharinepooley-boutique.com), for eclectic pieces.

Table linen

I'm a huge fan of Irish table linen (see pp141) but I couldn't resist this 100 per cent cotton tablecloth, with printed flower plates on it, by Lisa Stickley (tel: +44 20 7764 500 751, www.lisastickleylondon.com). It's from her marigold collection and comes in two sizes: 140x140cm and 140x240cm. There are also beautiful napkins to match. (The felt steak and paper knife and fork I added myself.)

Tablewear

Most chefs are purists and prefer plain white, minimalist china. Heal's (tel: +44 870 0240 780, www.heals.co.uk) and Habitat (tel: +44 870 4115 501, www.habitat.net), and Jamie Oliver at John Lewis stores, all offer down-to-earth but stylish china. Personally though, I like something a little more exciting, and the three white china collections that I've tripped across (not literally of course) and love are the John Pawson range at Mint, 70 Wigmore Street, London W1 (tel: +44 20 7224 4406, www.mintshop.co.uk): the Platt and Young à la Carte range for Rosanthal, available at Vessel, 114 Kensington Park Road, London ,W1 (tel: +44 20 7727 8001, www.vesselgallery.com); and the Biscuit collection by designers Studio Job for the renowned Dutch company Tichelaar Makkum, also at Vessel. My favourite ceramic designer at the moment is Dutch designer Hella Jongerius, www.jongeriuslab.com, I love her fawn (seen here), for the historic German porcelain creators, Nymphenburg. For patterned china I'm a huge Wedgewood fan and for the crème de la crème, see Christiane Perrochon's work, available exclusively at The Willer, 12 Holland Street, London W8 (tel: +44 20 7937 3518, www.willer.co.uk), see also www.christianeperrochon.com.

Chocolate

Do you love chocolate? I do! Recently I found out that cocoa contains minute traces of cannabis-like compounds called endocannabinoids, though it falls well short of marijuana's level of intoxication and is broken down in the body before it reaches the brain. I've been a hopeless chocoholic since a very young age. Every Sunday morning, Dad would give my brother, sister and me one pound each to go to Lilly May's sweetshop after Mass in Listowel to buy Time bars and yummy macaroon bars, as well as the obligatory gobstoppers, Fruit Salads, cola bottles, and flying saucers with fizzy space-dust inside. Until recently I thought these tastes had been lost forever, that is until I found www.bahhumbugs.com, a website that sells all of my retro childhood faves.

GODDESS TIP

IF YOU ARE A DIE-HARD CHOCOLATE FAN YOU CAN CHECK OUT THE TOP-TEN CHOCOLATE BARS ON WWW. SEVENTYPERCENT.COM WHERE THEY ARE RATED.

Beautiful chocolatiers and chocolate shops

Bombons Blanxart, Tambor del Bruc, 13 - 08970 Sant Joan Despi, Barcelona, Spain (tel: +34 93 373 3761, www.blanxart.com). They roast and process the beans themselves and the Blanxart Chocolate Canela a la Taza bar makes beautiful hot-chocolate with its cinnamon kick.

Chocolat Chapon, 52 avenue Mozart, 75016 Paris (tel: +33 1 42 24 05 05, www. chocolat-chapon.com), also at 69 rue du Bac, 75007 Paris (tel: +33 1 42 22 95 98). Patrice Chapon, a master chocolate-maker for over twenty years, works from Paris and his Noir Mendiants (mixed nuts) and the Noir aux Éclats de Café (crushed coffee beans) bars are really special.

Godiva Chocolatier (tel: +44 20 7734 8113, www.godiva.com) makes chocolates and divine drinking cocoa. The chocolate ice cream exclusive to Godiva boutiques in the US, including New York, Times Square at 41st and Broadway (tel: +1 212 8040 6758), is wow!

Chocolat Bonnat (www.bonnat-chocolatier.com), available to order online from Mortimer and Bennett, 33 Turnham Green Terrace, London (tel: +44 20 8995 4145, www.mortimerandbennett.co.uk) or La Grande Epicerie de Paris, 38 rue de Sèvres, 75007 Paris (tel: +33 1 44 39 81 00). The Bonnat family have been making chocolate in Voiron, France since 1884. I love their bars, each made from a single 'grand cru' chocolate bean. They all have 75 per cent cocoa content.

Enric Rovira (tel: +34 93 419 25 47, www.enricrovira.com). Based in Barcelona (see pp149), his creations are art and are available in London at Brindisa, 32 Exmouth Market, London EC1R 4QE (tel: +44 20 7713 1666, www.tapas.co.uk).

Green & Black's Organic (tel: +44 20 7633 5900, www. greenandblacks.com). Available nationwide, it has rescued the Mayan Indians in the Belize rainforests from multinationals. They rely totally on shoppers buying Maya Gold, that's why I like to buy Green & Black's organic spicy, orangey Maya Gold bars.

L'Artisan du Chocolat, 89 Lower Sloane Street, London SW1W 8DA (tel: +44 20 7824 8365, www.lartisanduchocolat.co.uk). After I've been up to the Lister Hospital to see Dr Andrew Markey, my dermatologist, I can't leave Chelsea without some violet ganaches, a bag of chocolate-covered lemon peel, green cardamoms, salt toffees and drinking chocolate from my favourite chocolatier, L'Artisan du Chocolat.

La Maison du Chocolat, 45–46 Piccadilly, London (tel: +44 20 7287 8500, www.lamaisonduchocolat.com) and at Harrods, London or 225 rue du Faubourg St Honoré, Paris (tel: +33 1 42 27 39 44). Divine hand-made French chocolates in every hue and flavour by chocolatier Robert Linxe.

Michel Cluizel: Available in the UK at The Chocolate Trading Company (tel: +44 1625 592808, www.chocolatetrading.co.uk), is named the goldsmith of chocolate in Paris. The Infini (99 per cent cocoa) bar is a real treat. Yummy! Michel Cluizel is available in Paris at 201 rue St, Honore, 7500 (tel: +33 1 42 44 11 66), and in the US at ABC Carpet & Home, 1st floor, 888 Broadway (at 19th Street), New York (tel: +1 212 477 7335, www.chocolatmichelcluizel-na.com).

Rococo Chocolates, 321 Kings Road, Chelsea, London SW3 5EP (tel: +44 20 7352 5857, www.rococochocolates.com), and 45 Marylebone High Street, London W1U 5HG (tel: +44 20 7935 7780). This British Chocolatier and sweet shop is what dreams are made of. I love the organic bars of basil and lime, cardamom and chili pepper (a Mayan Indian favourite).

Scharffen Berger, 473 Amsterdam Ave. at West 83rd in Manhattan, New York, NY 10024 (tel: +1 212 362 9734, www.scharffenberger.com). Good news: this brand, available at Selfridges, does really good dark chocolate and I can eat loads of their 70 per cent Cocoa Bittersweet Pure Dark bars without feeling stuffed. Yippeeeeee!

Valrhona, at The Chocolate Society, 36 Elizabeth St, London SW1W 9NZ (tel: +44 20 7259 9222) or 32–34 Shepherd Market, London W1J 7QN (tel: +44 20 7495 0302) or The Chocolate Trading Company (tel: +44 1625 592808, www.chocolatetrading.co.uk). The Gastronomie Manjari, 64 per cent cocoa, is amazing for baking and hot chocolate and has an intense taste with notes of red berries.

Montezuma's, 51 Brushfield Street, London E1 6AA (tel: +44 20 7539 9208, www.montezumas.co.uk). Hand-made organic chocolate and drinking chocolate using only the finest organic cocoa beans from the Dominican Republic.

Prestat Ltd, 14 Princes Arcade, Piccadilly, London SW1Y 6DS (tel: +44 20 7629 4838, www.prestat.co.uk). England's oldest chocolatier, they have the best violet and rose creams.

Pierre Marcolini, 6 Lancer Square, off Kensington Church Street, Kensington, London, W8 4EH (tel: +44 20 7795 6611, www.pierremarcolini.co.uk); or 89 rue de Seine, 75006 Paris (tel: +33 1 44 07 39 07, www.marcolini.be). This alchemist creates the most breathtaking tastes from his atelier in Brussels.

Afternoon Tea

At home on the farm the kettle is always on the boil, ready and waiting to make another cup of tea. As a family we will drink tea and eat cake at any time of the day or night, and having travelled the globe, scoping out teashops, on the hunt for the perfect cuppa, I've come to realise that Mum and Dad still make the best tea - and that my Gran's Christmas Cake and Victoria Sponge are unequelled.

Brewing a great cuppa

The secret to brewing a good cuppa is to fill the kettle with fresh water that has not previously been boiled (reheating the water reduces the oxygen content and compromises the taste). Once the water has boiled swill out your teapot with it, before adding one rounded teaspoon of loose tea (or a teabag) for every two cups to be served. Add boiling water and leave to brew for a few minutes. I like my tea in a china cup, and extra milky (see pp213).

Teapots

I love my rose-print "Tea for one" teapot from Mr & Mrs House, (tel: +44 20 7639 3399, www.mrandmrshouse.co.uk). My favourite place to browse for teapots is Liberty (tel: +44 020 7734 1234, www. liberty.co.uk), where there's even a range of teapots by Squint, covered in bright and breezy Liberty prints.

Sick of office milky tea?

British designer Onkar Singh Kular's brown mugs at the Design Museum, 28 Shad Thames, London (tel: +44 207 940 8790, www.designmuseum.org), come in 128 pantone colours so whoever is brewing-up can just match your tea to the colour of your mug. Ingenious!

Good tea Stateside

Tea & Sympathy, 108 Greenwich Ave, New York (tel: +1 212 989 9735, www.teaandsympathynewyork.com) a great cuppa and scone.

My favourite tea

My favourite brand of tea is Barry's Gold Blend (www.barrystea.ie), a mixture of the finest quality teas selected from the mountain slopes of Kenya and the Assam Valley of India – and blended in Co. Cork, Ireland. I've been drinking it since I was five and won't leave Dublin without it.

Different Teas

The Tea Palace, 175 Westbourne Grove, London (tel: +44 20 7727 2600; www.teapalace.co.uk), stocks everything from jasmine tea to Yerbe Maté tea (one of the hottest teas around), which is indigenous to the Amazon and is believed to help suppress your appetite. Yippee!

Do you love dunking biscuits?

Dominic Skinner's Dunk Mug (tel: +44 208 953 8333, www.mocha.uk.com) is so clever. It has a neatly built-in little shelf to store your biscuits in and comes in right and left handed versions so you won't drop your cookies. I love it!

More tea?

For my favourite afternoon tea spots in London see pp128 for The Wolseley, Sketch and Claridges.

My favourite cakes

Cupcakes: Magnolia Bakery, 401 Bleecker St, New York (tel: +1 212 462-2572). **Vanilla sponge cake**: Melrose and Morgan, 42 Gloucester Avenue, London (tel+ 44 20 7722 0011) and Selfridges (tel: +44 870 837 7377). **Pastel coloured cupcakes**: Primrose Bakery (tel: +44 78 0227 5205, www.primrosebakery.org.uk). **Rose-water iced cupcakes**: For Goodness Cake (tel: +44 845 838 0576 www.forgoodnesscake.co.uk). **Oustanding brownies**: Seriously Good (tel: +44 870 241 7027, www.seriously-good.co.uk).

Prêt à Porter

The Berkeley Hotel, Knightsbridge, London (tel: +44 20 7235 6000, www.the-berkeley.co.uk), serves biscuits and cakes designed by fashion experts. And I love bringing them home to eat off my Patsy Hely robin print plate (see left) or Paul Smith, striped plate (see pp130).

Buy a retro mixer

Treat yourself to this classic lavender-coloured mixer from Kitchen Aid (tel: + 44 800 381 04026, http://international.kitchenaid.com/).

Don't fancy baking?

Order directly from Treacle, 160 Columbia Road, London, E2 (tel: +44 20 7729 5657, www.treacleworld.com) or take away a yummy Victoria Sponge and a cuppa on Sundays..

Put sparkle on your food

Spruce up cakes and pastries with a sprinkle of edible pearl dust available at Selfridges, London. Apparently, it's a natural aphrodisiac, don't try if you're allergic to seafood though!

Here's my Gran's Victoria Sponge recipe: (25 minutes of easypeasyness)

110g butter
110g caster sugar
110g self-raising flour
2 eggs, beaten
2 drops vanilla essence
1 tsp grated lemon rind
1 tsp baking powder
Whipped cream
Strawberry jam or fresh strawberries
1 'Let It Bleed' album by the Rolling Stones*

Firstly, take a long hard look at the album cover to 'Let It Bleed' by the Rolling Stones and take inspiration from the cake that Delia Smith baked for the shoot in 1969. Then, put on the album and preheat the oven to 190°C/375°F/Gas 5. Sift the self-raising flour and the baking powder into a bowl, holding the sieve high to get loads of air into the flour. In another large mixing bowl whisk together the butter and sugar until light and creamy. Add the beaten eggs, gradually, and then slowly fold in the sieved flour and baking powder. Lastly, add the vanilla essence and lemon rind. Lightly grease two 15cm(6 inch) x 4cm(1½ inch) sandwich tins before lining the bottom with a circle of baking parchment, also lightly greased. Divide the mixture equally between the tins and level with a palette knife. Bake in the centre of the oven for 20-25 minutes. Test with a skewer?? Turn out onto a wire rack, remove the paper and leave until cold before filling with strawberry jam and fresh whipped cream – or better still, fresh summer strawberries. Dust the top with icing sugar and slice. Mmmmm!
*Please do not put this in the oven.

Macaroons

Can't make Ladurée (see pp143), in Paris? Pick up a box at the Ladurée counter at Harrods, London, instead. For the best macaroons in New York, Payard, 1032 Lexington Avenue between 73rd and 74th New York (tel: +1 212 717 5252, www.payard.com), offer Parisian macaroons, tea, and pastries to die for.

7 HAVIN' FUN

Rice Krispie buns, ice cream, penny sweets, red lemonade and birthday cake. We'd saved our appetites all day and, starving, dove into the thick sponge slices – the pink icing sticking to our fingers and nails as we fought over the slice with the number five on it. A pink-iced "Happy Birthday Barbara" melted into the thick white icing. Everthing dripped everywhere – down our chins, dresses and all over our presents. Barbara got an orange striped teddy she immediately named Tiger, my brother Michael got a plastic sword and I got a nurse's costume and a stethoscope. We licked our fingers clean to examine our gifts and then ran back to the table to gorge ourselves on more tempting sugary treats, piled in colourful mounds on granny's best china – so plentiful they concealed the entire pattern of each plate. Sugar-fuelled singing, dancing, piano playing and ludo, followed. We had had the best birthday party ever… and the standard was set for the rest of our lives.

It wasn't only on birthdays that we had red lemonade and sponge cake. If the jobs were done, the hay and turf saved Dad was free to party. On a Sunday he and Mum would pack cushions, china and goodies into the boot of our Cherry Datsun and take us for 'a spin' to the beach. Dad would drive straight towards the coast to Ballybunion, if there wasn't a match on the radio, or take a detour to Beale strand, if there was. In Beale you could drive the car right down the middle of the sandy beach. Once there Dad would open all the doors, flick back his car seat, pull his hat down over his eyes, listen to the sports commentary and snooze. He had little need of a tan, as he spent his whole life outside on the farm, so sunbathing was the last thing on his mind.

The sound of Michael O Muircheartaigh's football commentary could be heard in stereo on most beaches in Ireland every summer. Dads all across the country relaxed in cars – windows and doors open – all listening to the same match. At half time, kids would break from building castles and Mums would serve tomato and ham sandwiches, Kimberly Mikado biscuits, Rice Krispie buns, sponge cakes, cheese and onion Taytos, red lemonade and cans of Fanta – all laid out together on red tartan rugs. My mum went one step further on our picnics and brought 'proper' cups for us kids, and real mugs for her and Dad, to drink from; 'Those plastic things affect the taste of the lemonade', she'd say. 'Hand your father over his own mug and let him sugar his tea himself, Gisèle.' It was his special ritual, putting two heaped teaspoons of sugar into the strong tea and then adding a little milk, a few dribbles at a time, until it was the correct shade of dark brown. When he was finished he'd tap the spoon three times on the side of the china - which always drove my mother mad! His mug always had to be a different colour to hers because she hated sugar and would gag if she picked up the wrong mug by mistake.

After a day at the beach, it was always the same story: sand-clogged shoes and buckets would be left outside the back door and we'd all help Mum rustle up tea – something quick and easy like fresh lettuce and scallions (from Dad's garden), hardboiled eggs and mayonnaise, slices of ham and quartered tomatoes. When we had guests this Irish salad gained coleslaw and potato salad trimmings. They'd stay late and we'd dance and sing and play music – Dad on the accordion, Mum the piano. In fact all of our happiest moments were celebrated with music, singing, dancing and food.

Of course, Christmas was always amazing! We'd have goose (never turkey) and preparations for the party would start months in advance. My Gran would hand rear the bird – or sometimes Dad would bring a full-grown one home from the mart – and, according to my parents, my first complete sentence was: 'For God's sake, will someone get that goose out of the house?" It sat in a huge hessian bag in the corner of the cottage, its long neck poking through a hole cut in the corner, swaying from side to side, staring fixedly at me the way a cobra might follow its charmer's every move. Dad explained that we must calm frightened animals and farm fowl, giving them the utmost respect, if they were going to be our dinner. He reiterated this to me a few days later when the goose was on my plate.

The sound of a bicycle being lent against the front wall of the house only meant one thing: Sunday lunchtime. Liam was one of the family (Dad's cousin), and called every Sunday after Mass without fail for over twenty years. He brought us jam tarts, bulls eyes, and great stories – and divided them up between us according to how good we'd been that week. Then my Mum would sit him down at the table and he'd be repaid for his kindness with roast chicken, ice cream, sherry trifle, apple pie and tea. He'd always look down at his dinner plate and comment on how well the spuds that we sowed together the previous April looked. We'd sit eating and talking like this for hours with the lovely Liam Scanlon. He used to say we were just like the Italians - the food was always plentiful and when it came to having fun, family and friends were key.

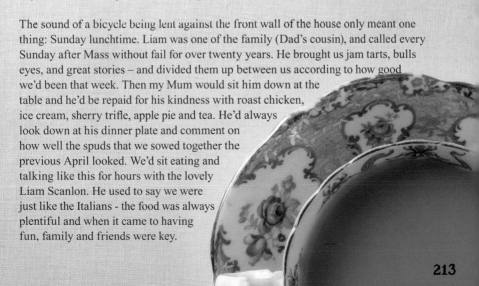

'Drinking 3a.m.', Ralph Steadman

From time to time I do enjoy a glass of wine. I prefer someone else to do the choosing for me though and preferably not one of those whiny (sorry!) wine expert types – you know the ones that go on and on about oaky this and smoky that. That's why I love Richard and Judy's wine club on Channel 4, at www.channel4.com. So big up to Richard and Judy for keeping wine tasting real on the TV.

Another truly amazing wine critic is the illustrator Ralph Steadman (www.ralphsteadman.com). I highly recommend his two wine books *The Grapes of Ralph* and *Untrodden Grapes* for which he travelled from California to Chile and Cabernet to Chardonnay, investigating wine in his own amusing way.

At the Port Eliot Literary Festival (see pp274) Ralph honoured the late Hunter S. Thompson, whose books he illustrated, with an extraordinary performance. He played two parts – himself and that of the late Thompson. It was magnificent and very, very funny. Sometime after that I got to know the enigmatic Ralph a little better and realized that he knows a million and one things about everything, including wine:

The first wine I tasted was a glass of my father's Elderberry wine. In the corner of the living room in North Wales, glooping away under a fermentation lock, my father had about a dozen demijohns of wines made from anything from carrot to raspberry to mushroom. The mushroom was a disaster of course. It does not ferment but goes bad and pongs. Though it has to be said that all wine making is really controlled putrifaction.

When I make wine these days, I never bother continually taking the stopper out to test the specific gravity or check the aroma as this stops your brew from oxidizing. I simply wait for it to clear after adding the finings which drop all solid matter to the bottom of the demijohn or carboy, which becomes the lees. You can leave the liquid on the lees there for a couple of months and then rack it off i.e. transfer it to another container which has been sterilized. You can bottle it if you want to try syphoning it off (I quite enjoy doing that because I have a spiffy 19th century corker) or you can pour it daily into a decanter and put it in the fridge. Lovely!

I have met many wine makers world wide since 1987 and everyone has a personal way of proceeding. One South African wine maker, Beyers Truter, from the Paarl region uses Pinotage grapes, their indigenous variety, which are fermented in huge concrete tanks. The wine makers push the cap back down into the juice with a flat ended spatula which seemed pretty adhoc to me. Later somebody's flip flop came off and fell into the tank and Beyers claimed it was the best vintage he had ever made, but that's his story!

What makes a good wine, Ralph? *The company you drink it with. A bottle shared with Marilyn Monroe would be so much better than one shared with Bela Lugosi. And strangely it would taste different, too.*
Do you find champagne agreeable? *I'm not a great champagne fancier myself, though I will have the odd glass.*
What are the benefits and downfalls of getting totally sloshed? *If you have gone and banged yourself up on a bender, then a beer and a brandy chaser at about 11 a.m. the day after gives you a great high if you can wait that long.*

Drinking Glasses
Riedel are the indefatigable designers of wine glasses. Their range includes a perfectly shaped glass for every wine you'll ever care to taste. Because the glass is thinner and the bowls large they expose more of the wine to the air, thus releasing more aroma and taste. The Chianti Classico glass is generally thought to be the best all-rounder in the range. Check out Wine Ware on (tel: +44 1903 723557, www.wineware.co.uk), for great advice on getting Riedel at affordable prices, and then go to Riedel for more of a selection (+44 20 8545 0830, www.riedel.com); Around Wine, 40 New Cavendish Street, Marylebone, (tel: +44 20 7935 4679, www.aroundwine. co.uk), is also great for Riedel and other accessories and Autour du Vin (www.toutautourduvin. com) is good for unusual decanters. The best wine opener I found was in Paris (see pp147)

Picnic in the Park

When my mum and dad used to take us on lakeside picnics, the rules were simple: load the contents of the kitchen and masses of cushions and rugs into the boot of the car and just go. There's still very little wrong with that concept today – at least then I know I'll have enough cutlery, condiments and cups. I wrap my antique teapot in bubble wrap just in case it gets a battering.

For a light picnic

If you're not into washing up or cutlery, then bring food you can eat with your fingers, e.g. eggs, meats, chorizo, tomatoes, fruit. Bring heads of lettuce and bread to dip in your olive oil and there'll be little washing up. Sushi is another good option.

Tea in the park

If you intend having tea, bring some flasks full of hot water to warm the pot and cups. I never, ever drink tea out of paper cups; a china cup or mug is my desert island must-have. Buy a victoria sponge or, better still, make one (see recipe on pp210) and have tea and cake, play a few rounds of backgammon, read a good book – very civilized.

I need a Rice Krispie bun just thinking about it

Rice Krispie buns
75g butter
100g golden syrup
60g milk chocolate, broken into pieces
50g Rice Krispies

Put the butter, golden syrup and chocolate into a small saucepan and melt together over a low heat. Then stir the Rice Krispies into the melted mixture. Line a bun tray with ten paper cases, fill with the mixture and place in the fridge to set. Mmmmmm!

Fresh strawberries, mascarpone and black pepper
750g fresh strawberries, sliced in half
125g mascarpone cheese
2 tbsp icing sugar
Seeds of 2 vanilla pods
Coarsely ground black pepper

Place strawberries in a bowl and dust with icing sugar. Leave for half an hour to allow juice to run out of them. Mix the mascarpone and the vanilla seeds, add a grinding of pepper and put in a sealed container for picnic. Drain off strawberries and pack in separate box. At picnic serve strawberries with a dollop of mascarpone and black pepper on top.
Serves four (or two greedy little Goddesses).

Taking your pet to the park
It is perfectly legal to drive with a dog, cat or ferret in your car. However, cats and ferrets should be kept in well-ventilated boxes and not on your lap when you're driving. Dogs should have little harnesses which attach to seat belts in the back of the car. Remaining cavalier about your canine cargo could cost you your life. In a car crash your pet will act as a canine cannonball. To prevent death by terrier torpedo or Maltese missile, download some tips on carrying your pets safely to the park from www.rospa.com. Oh and don't forget, pets can bake to death in boiling-hot cars if left unattended for long periods while you stop off to do a spot of shopping before heading for the park – your Rice Krispie buns will also die in this heat, but you knew that already didn't you? (Oops!)

Lazy days
If you can't be bothered putting a picnic together but still want the fun, order a picnic hamper from the Daylesford Organic Farmshop (tel: +44 1 608 731700, www.daylesfordorganic.com).

Checklist
Rug and cushions
Sharp knife
Corkscrew
Salt and pepper
Small screw-top bottle
of extra-virgin olive oil

Ants *n* a small social insect typically living in highly organised colonies of winged males, wingless sterile females (workers), and fertile females (queens). *Coll. n* a colony of ants.

Me and my beau
photo booth Lot 61

Clubbing

Getting in

The strictest door policy I've ever encountered was at New York's Bungalow 8 in 2003. The reason I think their door policy is so tight? Because there's a high quota of cool cats wanting to hang there and the place is absolutely tiny – the two and civilians do not mix. The owner Amy Sacco had booked a table for me and my beau through their PR firm for 11pm. After a few drinks at her other club, Lot 61 (not as strict on the door here), we pitched up at Bungalow 8's red rope at 11.05 sharp. Apparently we were too late and the burly doorman informed us that our table and entrance had been given to someone else. Had I missed something here? Did I inadvertently book an appointment for a filling? Now this is where I had to make the choice (you know the one I'm referring to). Do I scream and shout and stamp my silver sling-back stilettos or do I slope away quietly? I did neither…

How to change the doorman's mind

As I stood scuffing my toes in a modest and demure manner, a limo screeched to a halt behind me and a young girl and her bodyguard got out. He announced her name to the bouncer, to which the bouncer gave the same reply: 'Sorry, sir, your table was booked for 11pm. It's been given to somebody else' (same line, different guinea pig). The sound that came from the young girl's mouth in response was akin to that of a caged animal at the Bronx Zoo – in a Cyndi Lauper-type drawl she screamed, 'You must be jokiiiing, you stupid meathead, it's just gone eleven on my brand new Cawteay' (that's Cartier to you and me on planet earth). Our patience and consideration were finally rewarded as the doorman ushered us in to wind her up even more. Standing quietly by with dignity during a debacle can sometimes work a treat.

Try to book

Some clubs will take a reservation from you if you book for yourself and a small party (a few close friends). If not, ask if the club offers a bottle service – this means that you book a table for yourself and up to ten of your pals and you're guaranteed that table as long as you buy three or four bottles of alcohol on the night. This can be a very costly option, however.

Become a respected regular

If there's a club that you really want to socialize at on the weekend, spend time and money there midweek. Clubs take care of their regulars first and if the doorman remembers your face you're in. I always treat doormen with total respect, make a point of thanking them graciously upon gaining entry and always tip them at the end of the night. They remember this because it's rare.

Plan your attack

It's almost impossible for a large group of guys to get past a doorman. Ditto for girls if you're rowdy, but in my world everything is negotiable, so try to get in in twos or threes instead. If you're already feeling the effects of pre-nightclub cocktails, say as little as possible at the door to avoid slurring – just keep smiling and walk confidently ahead.

Keep your dignity

If the line is long, approach the doorman and lay your cards on the table with honesty. Explain that you're with two other girls, you want to visit for three hours, you realize they're very busy but what are the realistic chances of gaining entry. Leave your bullshit at home – you're not rich, successful or somebody important – and bouncers' bullshitometers are finely tuned. Never, ever, ever under any circumstances plead or beg for entrance. It makes you look desperate and it really pisses bouncers off.

Chill out

You can't get into that exclusive nightclub? Big deal! It's not where you are, it's who you're with that's important. I was refused entry last year to a nightclub in Milan – apparently we were dressed too casually. We cut our losses, gathered our posse and headed for home. Once there, we pulled the rum from the frigo, cranked up our iPods and partied hard!

Bungalow 8

bar/lounge
515 West 27th Street (10th & 11th)
Mon - Sun from 10 pm to 4 am
Private Line: 212 629 3333
concierge@bungalow8.com

Party chez toi

Okay so an impromptu bash at chez toi is what we all hope to organize – one where we fall in the door with our friends in our glad rags, rustle up some Mojitos, put on the hippest music or leave the tunes to a DJ friend who just happens to turn up with his decks in his van. A party so mental that you've even put the police on the guest list because of course they'll be calling. To make a party like this a success it's best to do a little forward planning.

Ask experts for advice

Your local butcher is much more likely to know how many cocktail sausages it takes to feed a ravenous rowdy crowd then some 19 year old down the supermarket. A good cheese monger will also plan a good smorgasbord for you.

Booze Bath

Wash bath and fill half with water, half with ice, and drop two cases of champagne bottles in it. If you've two bathrooms, use one bath of ice for chilling champagne bottles (usually where the girls can be found) and one bath for chilling beer (boys love this). Pop a bottle opener in the little boys' room and a tiny container marked bottle caps (yeah right) and you're all set.

Vacuuming

Leave the vacuuming of the living room and hall carpets until two hours before your party, being just an olive store's throw from the kitchen, it's likely that bits of canapé will find their way there on your heels.

Clean up in a hurry

Books, letters, coats – take all of this clutter and toss it into one closet which you can lock. This way, everything will be easy to find the following day. The bed in the spare room can be used for guests to leave their coats.

220

Chairs and tiny tables
Make sure you've loads of cosy little corners with chairs for guests to chat and flirt in. Also, tiny tables are handy dotted about the house so that guests can put their drinks and nibbles down and not ruin the floor.

Removing wax from tables
Remove as much as you can with a blunt knife, then place brown paper over the wax and place a towel around the paper to protect the table from the heat. Iron over the brown paper in short bursts and watch the wax melt off.

Vomit stains
Wherever you have too much booze you'll definitely have one vomiter. Attack vomit stains as soon as they happen (yeuch!) with a clean cloth soaked in cold water. Then wash the patch with lukewarm water and washing-up liquid or shampoo. If odour continues the next day, sprinkle with baking soda, leave for twenty minutes and vacuum.

To jump the loo queue
Stagger towards the bathroom door making retching noises, rolling your eyes and clutching your chest. This works particularly well if you're the hostess – seeing as it's your house, who's going to argue?

To bag a shy guy
Sympathize with him by saying, 'God, I didn't know this many people would turn up. It's very crowded, isn't it?' His confidence gained, pour on a few more shyness stories and round it off with the one about you just being upstairs in your own house but being too shy to ask to use the loo.

Red wine stains
For red wine stains, soak the stain with club soda, then sprinkle table salt or baking soda on it, let it sit for fifteeen minutes, and vacuum clean. The result? Impressive! These tips also work well on your pet's stained bed.

Gate-crashers
Irvine Welsh's wedding party (best man and pals) crashed a party at my house in Dublin last year. It should have become a drug fuelled scene from Trainspotting, but no, we ended up drinking tea till 10a.m. You never know what to expect with gatecrashers, sometimes you can be pleasantly surprised.

Say thank you
If you've been invited to a particularly good party bike round a box of chocolates from L'Artisan du Chocolat, (see pp209) and a handwritten thank you card (see pp243).

Read The Great Gatsby
Jay Gatsby's party on that summer night with its ethereal music and green beacon at the end of the pier is how to do it, baby!

My fave party playlist
Saliva
by Viktor Vaughn AKA MF Doom
Murder She Wrote
by Chaka Demus & Pliers
Nan You're a Window Shopper
by Lily Allen
It's Yours
by Lazy Dog
Dare
by Gorillaz
King Without A Crown
by Matisyahu
The Big Jump
by The Chemical Brothers
Where's Your Head At
by Basement Jaxx
Your Mrs is a Nutter
by Goldie Lookin Chain
Love Is Energy
by Joe Roberts

CHRISTMAS

Buying the tree

I love shopping for the Christmas tree with my Dad, because he has the best Christmas tree buying tips ever – the closer to Christmas you buy it, he says, the better and breeds he favours include Scots pine, Lodgepole pine and Nordmann fir. He doesn't ever buy Norway spruce, as they drop their needles too quickly. He runs his fingers along the branches to test for freshness and if needles come off, he won't buy it. He also bounces the tree up and down on its trunk to see how fresh the tree is – if needles don't fall off, then it is. For other tree buying tips see www.christmastreeland.co.uk. If you don't fancy lugging a tree home then the kilted guys at Pines and Needles (tel: +44 845 458 2788, www.pinesandneedles.com), will deliver one to your door and collect it and recycle it for you when you've finished with it.

Grow a tree

If you don't want a cut tree, order a potted one at your local garden centre and plant it outdoors after Christmas.

Decorating the tree

The highlight of putting up my own tree is placing the angel I grew up with on the top. My mum gave it to me last summer and even though it's a bit battered and worn I love it for what it reminds me of. Peter's angel is also really cute – he made it when he was just a boy from crêpe paper and doilies. We all have different baubles which contain personal childhood memories; new ones are like little sponges, waiting to soak up the essence of our joy.

GODDESS TIP

FILL YOUR TREE STAND WITH 7UP (ABOUT TWO SMALL BOTTLES) AS THE SUGAR HELPS THE TREE RETAIN ITS NEEDLES.

Mistletoe

The ancient Druids believed that kissing under the mistletoe brought friendship, goodwill and (ahem) fertility in the run-up to springtime. These ancient observers also noticed that mistletoe only sprung up on twigs in trees where the Storm Cock and Mistle Thrush had left their droppings. Mistletoe is parasitic and lives high up on the branches of oak and apple trees.

GODDESS TIP

I HANG MISTLETOE OVER THE FRONT DOOR WITH A HUGE RIBBON AT CHRISTMAS... AND THEN CONVENIENTLY SEND SOMEONE ELSE TO GREET THE POSTMAN!

Lovely baubles

With your tree in mind, visit gift, museum and gallery shops when you're travelling and pick up one new decoration per trip. Keep it simple though and choose something that'll fit with what you already have. Otherwise Mojzeszek (tel: +44 20 7275 9904, www.mojzeszek.co.uk) have gorgeous glass decorations including birds handmade by happy people in Poland. The US website www.bronners.net also has a huge range. Decorate your own baubles with a decorating-set from Cox & Cox (tel: +44 870 442 4787, www.coxandcox.co.uk). I found this deer in Lapland for our tree – isn't he beautiful?

The crib

My grandparents always made a huge deal out of putting up the crib, and it took pride of place in the hallway of their cottage greeting visitors just inside the door. Baby Jesus was added on Christmas morning. I remember the donkey the most.

Donkey *n* a long-eared member of the horse family *Coll. n* a drove/herd of donkeys

Visit Santa

Fish out a picture of yourself with Santa when you were small and then find a Santa in your area and go and have your pic taken with him again. It might make an amusing Christmas card… Cheeeeeeese!

Chocolate stocking

I love the Christmas stocking-shaped chocolate box filled with dark, milk and praline truffles from Prestat Ltd, 14 Princes Arcade, Piccadilly, London (tel: +44 20 7629 4838, www.prestat.co.uk).

GIFT BUYING

Weddings, birthdays and Christmas – what to get a Goddess? Easy peasy – choose a personal gift that she can enjoy as part of her daily life. If she likes cooking buy her something that she can display, like a cookbook stand or some beautiful glasses or plates (note this does not mean that she'll be ecstatic if you give her a deep-fat fryer or a toaster for her birthday, mind).

Wedding gifts for her

If she's a reader buy her a first edition of her favourite book (see pp245); if she's a writer get her a fountain pen from Yard-O-Lead Pencil Company at Harrods. Buy some sealing wax, a personalised wax seal with a glass handle, all at Papyrus, 48 Fulham Road, South Kensington (tel: +44 20 7584 8022, www.papyrus.uk.com); some cards from the V&A museum shop at the V&A Museum, Cromwell Road, South Kensington (tel: +44 20 7942 2000, www. vandashop.com); hand-made tissue-lined envelopes from Wren Press, 1 Chelsea Wharf, 15 Lots Road (tel: +44 20 7351 5887, www.wrenpress.com – also available at Brown Thomas, Dublin); and coloured ink and paper from The Italian Corner (see pp243).

GODDESS TIP

IF YOU'RE VISITING ANY GODDESS WITH KIDS THEN CHECK OUT WWW.FOUNDAT.COM FOR WOODEN TOYS, OR BRING A POPCORN POPPER FROM WWW. CUCINADIRECT.CO.UK

Stocking fillers

Harriet Vine and Rosie Wolfenden of Tatty Devine, 57b Brewer Street, London (tel: +44 20 7434 2257, www.tattydivine.com) – these trusty purveyors of cute oddities produce name necklaces in a million different colours, decked-out with either a heart or star charm, perfect for an Urban Goddess. If you buy someone lingerie, also buy a Gerbe mesh hosiery washbag at www.mytights.com for machine-washing more than one delicate item at a time without fear of tangles.

Girly gifts

For a beauty treat buy Ormande Jayne Osmanthus Essential Bathing Oil (see pp240) or try a facial, massage or pampering session from an expert. A vintage mirror from Butler & Wilson (see pp70) or an antique picture frame, which you can have made into a mirror, makes a great wedding gift. Also, Austique, 330 Kings Road, London, SW3 5UR (tel: +44 207 376 4555, www. austique.co.uk) is great for girly finds, including Gal Pal – a little sponge that removes white deodorant or food stains from your favourite dress – perfect as a stocking filler if you've bought your best friend a great top and you intend to party hard with her.

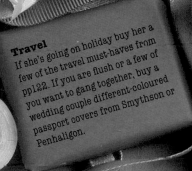

Travel

If she's going on holiday buy her a few of the travel must-haves from pp122. If you are flush or a few of you want to gang together, buy a wedding couple different-coloured passport covers from Smythson or Penhaligon.

Home

Why not get her a fridge magnet for her to store her note-making, recipe-taking pens in, from Divertimenti (tel: +44 20 7935 0689, www.divertimenti.co.uk)? Or a book for her to write her recipes, or keep her favourite kitchen-related clippings in, is a sweet, thoughtful idea. Combine with a wine-tasting or cookery class, also from Divertimenti, and you have a wonderful gift. The Divertimenti team will also try their best to source any other product that you think might suit her in the line of kitchen gifts. Homewear gifts such as monogrammed linen (see pp238), china (see pp204), a beautiful decanter or tray, or a Nigella Lawson parmesan grater at Harrods are also super gifts for your very own Home Goddess.

Make a Christmas stocking

Stitcher (tel: +44 1380 738 072, www.stitcher.co.uk) sells cross-stitch tapestry and felt applique Christmas stockings. Do the tapestry (it'll take a few months), or you could order the stocking itself and give it to a Goddess in your life around August so she can do the tapestry herself – otherwise order the felt version, which she can make quickly. Trust me, if she's into making things she'll love this idea.

GODDESS TIP

NO MATTER WHAT TYPE OF GODDESS SHE IS, YOU CAN'T DO BETTER THEN A SIBERIAN GOOSE DOWN DUVET FROM JOHN LEWIS (SEE PP238) AS A WEDDING GIFT – SHE'LL REMEMBER YOU FOREVER FOR IT!

Anniversary gift

For an anniversary wedding present why not commission a portrait of the couple? Many portrait painters are happy to work from a photograph, and prices range from £600 to £3,500 at the Royal Society of Portrait Painters, 17 Carlton House Terrace, London SW1Y 5BD (tel: +44 20 7930 6844, www.therp.co.uk) or the Fine Art Commissions, 79 Walton Street, London SW3 2HP (tel: +44 20 7589 4111, www.fineartcommissions.com). See pp259 to see what the more customary buy is for each anniversary.

WRAPPING

Can you tell what it is yet?
The most memorable present I ever received – apart from my Lilliput 2000
typewriter from Santa – was a beautiful burgundy bike. Glowing under the tree,
it had pink ribbons attached to the handlebars as wrapping. Santa even had the
organizational skills to have the stabilizers attached. The fact that it wasn't swathed
in paper made no difference to how special it was. For the past few Christmases,
however, Peter has been doing as good a job as the elves.

The chair

A few Christmases ago Peter bought me a chair. Yes,
a chair! He asked me to close my eyes and surprised
me with it by lifting it into the kitchen. (He couldn't
roll it because he'd even wrapped the wheels and
the pedal.) It had taken him over an hour to wrap it
completely in brown paper earlier that day and even
though I knew immediately that it was a chair, the
way it was so lovingly wrapped in brown paper and
the fact that he had found something to improve my
back ache made it the sweetest and most thoughtful
gift in the world.

The pillow

Another Christmas after returning from the
Benjamin Hotel in New York where I'd tested
practically every pillow on their pillow menu
to help cure my jetlag (see pp126), Peter
ordered my favourite one (the NASA memory
foam) when we got home. No, this gift was not
expensive, but it cost him and arm and a leg
to have it shipped. He made it extra special by
wrapping it beautifully and drawing this little
pillow card to go with it – that's what proper
pressie giving is all about, thoughtfulness.

Jewellery

If you want to surprise someone with a
piece of jewellery, cut the centre out of an
old hardback book using a Stanley knife,
fill it with tissue paper and pop your
brooch or earrings into it. Smile secret
smiles as your unsuspecting friend
broods silently at the boring hardback.

Happy
Christma
Ba

HER MAJESTICAL THRONE
TO DREAM ON

Use brown bags

Forget wrapping paper and go for plain paper bags instead. With a few ribbons and tags they can look really stylish and it's quick and easy.

Use newspaper

I like to wrap Christmas pressies with black gross-grain ribbon and the Financial Times; not only is the paper a lovely colour but the Weekend section is addictive reading.

Use recycled paper

Yes, you can buy recycled wrapping paper from Natural Collection on (tel: +44 870 331 3333, www.naturalcollection.com) at £3.95 for four sheets.

Wrapping books or boxes?

Cut pieces of felt into the shape of big diamonds and fold over books in an envelope shape. Forget the Sellotape and secure with black or orange gross-grain ribbon instead. Peter Jones, Sloane Square, London (tel: +44 20 7730 3434, www.peterjones.co.uk) stocks the lot. For boys add masking tape to some pinstripe paper to make a book look masculine. Pile kid's pressies into cardboard suitcases from the Letterbox mail-order catalogue (tel: +44 870 600 7878, www.letterbox.co.uk).

The art of surprise

If you really want to surprise that special someone (and it doesn't have to be a child), buy a huge stocking, fill it full of pressies and hide it somewhere in the house. While your child or partner is asleep tie a ribbon from the end of the bed to the place where the gift is hidden. You could even dot the route with little pressies along the way.

Self gift

A survey last year found that 48 per cent of women buy gifts for themselves while shopping for pressies. In the US they call it 'self-gifting' so treat yourself – repeat after me: 'Um, don't bother wrapping that big one, I'll do it myself at home …'.

Colour-code

Choose a different coloured tissue paper for each family member. Paperchase, 213-215 Tottenham Court Road, London (+44 20 7467 6200, www.paperchase.co.uk) does the best range of colours. Add ribbons, sequins, feathers, tassels, beads and braids from Temptation Alley, The Old Haberdashery at 359 Portobello Road, W11 (tel: +44 20 89642004).

Small gift

If you feel your gift looks a bit small, bulk it up by buying a set of beautiful boxes and tying a ribbon around each one. Then store one inside the other Russian doll-style.

8
JOIE de VIVRE

For the first three years of my life there was nothing – no "Joie de Vivre", no shapes, no understanding, no colour, no reference – a blank canvas. Those first few years still remain elusive and I certainly have no recollection of being born a premature, sickly baby who wouldn't drink or eat. My mother told me that at the age of one I actually stopped breathing in her arms for a few minutes – a reaction to penicillin she thought. She remembers vividly the race to the hospital in the car with my father. Upon arrival the doctors resuscitated me. I remember nothing of this! As a child growing up I never really appreciated how close I had come to death that day. I suppose, because of this, my parents were extra attentive to all three of us children, packing only good things into our tummies and brains. They'd stretch each day out longer than the one before it, giving us ample time to sponge up facts about animals, insects and hedgerows. I grew to love the world around me very quickly and have only good memories of the innocent little life that we led. Sheltered in our tiny world of beauty, I was blissfully unaware, like all children, that if something stopped breathing, it stopped living – and flew away to a place that wasn't to be found on any map.

I did not really comprehend the idea of death until I took life one summer. Aged four, my memory of the wildlife around us stretches back as far as that, I tried to tame any animal, bird or insect that I came into contact with – or that accidentally wandered onto my father's fields or vegetable garden. One day I spotted a Painted Lady butterfly flitting among some thistles. Dad had shown me pictures of one in a nature book which explained that they were a migratory breed – its red eye at the top of each wing was very distinctive. "It arrives at the same time as the swallows, from North Africa", he quoted. The book he was reading from also explained that Painted Ladies can travel up to 10 miles per hour. Ecstatic at having found one for him, I followed it to the corner of the haggard and coaxed it off one of his lettuce heads. Cupping it softly in my hands and screaming in his direction, I headed towards the yard to show him. But I tripped on a stone and, to my horror, squashed the butterfly's life in my tightly cupped palms. It struggled for a moment, its wings torn, and then lay dull and lifeless. My tiny quivering fingers, stained brown and red, poked at it but it wouldn't move. I slumped down and cried with frustration as the realization hit me that the butterfly was broken, just like several of my old, battered toys.

With the knowledge of death comes a certain urgency to enjoy things. To breathe in everything and enjoy as much as you possibly can before you too have to go. My first real "Joie de Vivre" moment came a few days later as my sense of smell awoke early one morning to my mother's neck, her loose face powder and floral perfume, and to my father's arms around us both – tanned, strong, musky – guarding us both under freshly washed linen sheets. A sense of safety and peace greeted us as we welcomed in a new morning. To this day I take that journey most mornings as I stretch towards the future, fearing little as the warm sun on my pillow nudges me gently awake. Rested and peaceful, it doesn't matter what country I'm in – I'm alive and healthy and just feel total happiness! This is what I describe as pure joie de vivre! Through the window I see the outside world waking; white clouds and beyond them snatches of the dreams I've dreamed the night before. The stories slip away with the changing sky and I begin, loosely, to plan my day, trying to put aside tiny chunks of time to savour more moments of joie de vivre.

What I love most in the world are these tiny moments in which I can really indulge in a little honest happiness; it could be enjoying a cool glass of water in the shade of a tree in the summer or spending an hour emptying my mind in the bath on a cold winter's night; it could be sitting down with a new pile of magazines that have that special newly printed smell from them or an un-put-down-able old book that smells of a different age – flicking through the first few pages and then beginning to read as I sip a hot cup of tea; or inhaling great big gulps of the lush green grass world around me and watching butterflies and birds flit, full of life, from tree to tree. I also love drawing simple little pictures of my favourite birds or animals in my sketchbook. I doodle flowers, bees, trees, dogs, cats, mice... speaking of mice, what are baby ones called? Is it babies... or pups... or is it mini micees...? And ponder such questions as who decides these important things! Time is suspended as I seek answers to these conundrums – big or small they are what make up the fabric of my life (as well as a thousand stored smells which instantly give me back my childhood). Certain smells bring with them the deepest level of nostalgia – I'm suddenly transported to somewhere else if I accidentally brush by someone wearing strong scent on the street. This is particularly true if I'm visiting Paris and even more so if I'm there sniffing about for a new perfume.

When travelling, joie de vivre rides along with me. Walking an empty country road at home on a warm evening or seeing the glow of a taxi light when you need one in a city in the rain – every single one of these things gives me that special feeling; like finding a pathway back to that first moment of overwhelming glee you felt as a child. No one can ever take that sensation away from you – it's yours, yours alone, and yours to celebrate in whatever way you see fit. Here are some of my suggestions on where to get joie de vivre supplies...

PERFUME

Fragrance families

Most fragrances are categorized as belonging to one of six different fragrance families: Oriental, Chypre, Fougère, Floral, Citrus and Ozonic. Here is how I have been touched by scent from each of the six.

Orientals

Oriental fragrances are so called because their ingredients are synonymous with the Orient. The Oriental family is broken down further into three different "groups" namely musks, smoky leathers and incense – these "groups" evoke strong childhood memories for me and a perfume from any is my all-time favourite treat.

Musks

The smells of my very first al fresco tea party are still with me (see pp216): mossy stones and black earth, foxgloves, grass, honeysuckle and sun parched cow dung; familiar, powerful and deeply comforting as I dozed in the soothing sun. Only recently I learned that the greatest perfumers in the world (the French) used to dissolve children's faeces in their millefleurs (essence of a thousand flowers) to give it depth and warm character! Similarly, animal ingredients like civet (from the anal glands of the civet cat), musk from deer, castoreum (from the scent gland of beavers) and ambergris (a by-product that the whale spits up from its digestive tract to help it eject indigestible squid beaks, and which is more expensive then gold) were all used to add depth when making perfume. Nowadays these mammal molecules are mainly produced synthetically in labs to great effect. For me a mere hint of any type of furry musk molecule, whether natural or synthetic sends me straight back to that childhood field, with the puppies' fluffy bodies nestled against my face, my arms wrapped around Dinky and a loud pheasant's call waking us to the smell of horse and cow dung permeating the air.

My favourite musk scents contain large, deep, complicated musky molecules like the depraved Musc Ravageur created by nose Maurice Roucel for Editions de Parfums Frédéric Malle in Paris (see pp237), or Caron's Narcisse Noir (see pp237). I go to Paris if I run out of either (any excuse), but they are also available from Les Senteurs in London (see pp236). It's also hard to resist Bal à Versailles by Jean Desprez, created in 1962 with over 300 essences – it's my secret dark symphony in a bottle (also at Les Senteurs). Overall though, the one that sits best on my skin daily is Narciso Rodriguez Musc for Her in oil formula (see pp56).

Smoky leathers

Another element associated with the Oriental perfume family, and one that I find equally comforting, is the smell of old leather armchairs, rich wood and cigars. Dad and Mum used to take me to furniture auctions when I was tiny, and more often than not I'd end up falling asleep on an old leather library chair. Permeated with the smell of tobacco and cigar smoke, a bottle of Shiseido's Féminité du Bois exclusive to Harrods (tel; +44 20 7730 1234), brings me straight back there. But I don't ever buy it in Harrods, instead I schlep off to Paris to wallow in the Shiseido store at the Salons du Palais Royal (see pp237). This store stocks both Shiseido and Serge Lutens fragrance (also at Harrods and Liberty) and I can never visit Paris without popping in. As well as buying a bottle of Shiseido Féminité du Bois, I get my next favourite leather perfume here, Serge Lutens Bois de Violette (very similar to Féminité du Bois). Then it's onto Chanel (see pp237) for a bottle of Chanel's Cuir de Russie, which holds the scent of leather and birch tar with a hint of iris (try also Chanel boutiques) and then on to Caron, (see pp237) to buy my fourth favourite Parisian leather scent, a bottle of Tabac Blond eau de parfum decanted from a huge fountain on the wall into a beautiful little bottle. Leathery with a hint of sweetness, it was created in 1919 and is based on sweet golden tobacco with tuberose, vanilla and hint of musk (I pop a bottle of Caron's Narcisse Noir from the musks types opposite also into my basket here). Heaven!

Pheasant *n* any of various long-tailed gallinaceous birds, having a brightly coloured plumage in the male. *Coll. n* a nye of pheasants. Twitchers don't consider them wild birds, as they were bred in captivity and released for shooting. Most end up stuffed, because they're a bit slow.

Perfume and gloves in Paris

Of course, a weekend in Paris is never complete without visiting Maître Parfumeur et Gantier on rue de Grenelle (see pp237) for bottles of Centaure, Ambre Précieux, (Orientals) and Grain de Plaisir (Chypre). After putting a little of either on my arm, I catch hints of amber, precious woods, musk and leather as I explore the stationery shops and bookstores and streets of Paris in the cold winter air. Incidentally, Gantier are also master glove-makers and should you be on the lookout for a beautiful pair you can pick the softest and largest array of leather colours here.

Some more leather scents from the Oriental family

Creed's Angelique Encens – made specifically for Marlene Dietrich – is another great leather-inspired scent. It's available at Les Senteurs in London (see pp236) as are Habanita by Parfum Molinard (www.molinard-boutique.com), which smells like Cuban cigars, and Knize Ten – created in the 1930s by a Viennese tailor who used to accommodate Kaiser Wilhelm II and make Marlene Dietrich's trousers. Speaking of which, if you find yourself at a loose end in Vienna and you're stuffed to bursting with Sacre Torte visit the men's tailoring Knize Ten shop at Knize & Co, 1st district Graben 13 (tel: +43 1 51 22 11 90) to buy a bottle of Knize Ten fragrance – a much less calorific and longer lasting bring home treat (also available at Les Senteurs in London). This and Santa Maria Novella's Nostalgia (see pp236) always nail for me the smell of the expensive leather seats in Dad's black car as we'd sit back, breathe in and watch the world go by.

Incense

Ah incense, the third sister in the Oriental family and one of the strongest characters – how could I be Irish and not have experienced church incense? Funerals, Easter, sitting quietly as the pungent aroma ripped through the church pews; a spritz of Bois d'Encens from the Armani Privé collection (available from department stores) and I'm back with my grandmother sitting in Mass. It's the nearest thing to church I've ever smelled with two types of incense in it – it's easily the best of all of the incenses that I've ever had.

My favourites

So, that's the Oriental family, with its exotic spices, rich musks, amber, sandalwood, leather and incense; although clawing and heavy, they're dear to me, I love them all and in the winter their reassuring presence helps to keep out the cold. I defy anyone to try Serge Luten's Ambre Sultan (see pp231), and not feel sexy as hell. You'll never catch me without a bottle of dark musky scent, in fact any of those previously mentioned, hidden secretly away somewhere in a corner of my handbag between September and March.

Chypre

If I want to take a break from Oriental, I turn to Chypre (pronounced 'sheep-ra'): the smell of fresh-cut grass, walks in woods, earth, peat bogs, heather and mosses without an animal molecule in sight. This smell reminds me of when my grandfather and father would take me to the bog to save turf for the winter fireplace. To get to the turf we'd have to trudge through heathers, moss and gorse. The turf would be cut off a bank by hand, dried in stooks and then collected in the summer and stored for burning. These rich dark bog memories are always sparked in perfume boutiques by vetiver – an essential oil extracted from the roots of a grass found in India. I choose men's vetivers as they capture these memories best. Guerlain's and Annick Goutal's men's vetiver scents (see pp237), spicy with a touch of salt in the case of the latter, and Dominique Ropion's Vetiver Extraordinaire for Editions de Parfums Frédéric Malle (see pp237), all evoke these special days. And of course Ormonde Woman by Linda Pilkington at Ormonde Jayne (see pp236) with its cardamom, coriander, grass oil, black hemlock, violet, jasmine absolute and vetivert, cedarwood, amber and sandalwood are my bog days captured perfectly in a bottle. One of my all time favourites, it's one of the most intoxicating mysteries of the fragrance world.

Fougère

Next up on my list are the Fougère family of scents (pronounced 'foo-gare', this is the French word for "fern"). Quite close to Chypre, they are made up of the scent of moss, herbs, lavender and spicy citrus fruits. The Fougère fragrance that sends shivers down my spine is the man's fragrance Racine from Maître Parfumeur et Gantier (see opposite and pp237). Sisley's Eau de Campagne, with its herby, grassy basil scent, is also a lovely choice, grassy, green and fresh it's a great spring/summer scent.

Florals

There are a huge variety of florals that either contain loads of different floral notes or one, single, strong note. I shied away from them for years thinking them too flowery, girly and sweet. Then Christian Louboutin suggested I try Lys Méditerranée and he introduced me to his friend Frédéric Malle's fragrance gallery on rue de Grenelle in Paris (see pp237). After one sniff I was hooked. Fashioned from ginger lilies, orange-blossom and a hint of sea air, Lys Méditerranée was created by one of the greatest white-flower perfume noses on earth: Edouard Fléchier. As well as Fléchier, the owner Frédéric Malle (the grandson of Serge Heftler, who created Dior's classic fragrances) asked eight of the world's greatest noses to create fragrances without constraints for his shop come gallery. The results are stunning and my second favourite fragrance here is created by world renowned nose Dominique Ropion, and is called Carnal Flower; Tuberose intensified with musk, it's seductive and erotic. These two scents are also available in London from Les Senteurs and in Barneys in the US.

Citrus

If you love the smell of lemon, orange, bergamot, grapefruit and lime, these scents are for you. For ages I found them a bit, well, sickly (lemony scents from big scent manufacturers always smelled of fruity petrol to me). Then I sampled Luxe by Mona Di Orio, at Les Senteurs, London and realized that lemon didn't have to smell sharp. Fizzy and fresh, like lemon sherbet and home-made lemonade and lemony ice pops from my granny's shop, Mona's scent explodes out of the bottle like champagne – quite fitting then that the bottle is tied at the top with a wire muselee just like on a champagne bottle. For the best citrus orange smell I turn to Hermès Eau d'Orange Vert – so beautiful and fresh that it instantly lifts me, and for a citrus mix with a hint of jasmine, Eau d'Été by Parfums de Nicolaï in Paris is unequalled (see pp237). Also, if you're planning a visit to Barcelona, stock up on the huge plastic bottles of baby bath cologne for sale in the Spanish supermarkets, for just a few euros. A splash of this in your bath water is really divine! Acqua di Genova Stefano Frecceri, at Les Senteurs, with lemon bergamot and sweet orange with neroli, is an expensive and more refined version of these. For summer holidays I can't resist Bahiana by Maître Parfumeur et Gantier (see pp237 and also at Les Senteurs). For me it's the smell of Rio de Janeiro in a bottle which makes sense I suppose as Bahiana are the fruit-selling girls in the markets in Brazil and their skin and hair always smells of the beautiful fruits.

Ozonic

Ozonic scents smell of those days at the seaside: fresh air, sea water and salty breeze. I have only found one fragrance from this family that is worth mentioning – Ecume de Rose de Rosine by Bernard and Marie-Helen Rogeon from their Parisian boutique, Les Parfums de Rosine (see pp237). Every single fragrance they create is based on roses and this one has an added saltiness and was created in homage to the birth of Aphrodite (if you remember from school she was born out of the sea). It's also available from Harvey Nichols, Harrods and Les Senteurs in London.

Want to impress a Goddess, boys?

There are four scents that'll instantly earn any man a definite second date with a Goddess. Linda Pilkington's Isfarkand, available from Ormonde Jayne in London (see pp236) is the best hands down. Linda, a self-taught nose, travelled far and wide in the Middle East to source the ingredients: pink pepper, mandarin, lime, bergamot, cedar, vetiver and moss. I'm told that the men at Wallpaper magazine can't get enough of it and a little left on a shirt collar is utterly irresistible. Serge Lutens Ambre Sultan, (see pp237) available at Harrods and Liberty, is another sophisticated Oriental and at Les Senteurs why not try either Caron Pour Homme Cologne by Caron (see pp237 for Paris store) a rich citrus cologne – especially great for daywear or Impact by Creed. The sileage (like the stream a jet leaves in its wake on the skyline) is so gently effective from Creed's Impact that I've seen Goddesses literally fall at men's feet.

GODDESS *Fragrance Tips*

Shop around

It's worth spending time shopping around for the right scent; once you find the one you like, much like a man, you could end up being together for many years. So persevere. Firstly, you should test no more then three perfumes in any one day. Bring a little muslin bag of coffee beans with you and when your nose starts to experience scent-overload, take a good long sniff of the coffee beans – they'll help to neutralize your sense of smell.

Testing scent

Spray a paper spill lightly and get the shop assistant to write the name of the fragrance on it. Remember that citrus notes (lemons, orange etc.) are used worldwide and are the first thing that you'll smell when a fragrance is sprayed. Let the perfume dry out on the spill for a bit, in your bag or pocket, to allow the true smell to develop. Keep smelling it throughout the day and if there is something about it that continues to attract you, go back to the shop, have it spritzed on your skin, and ask for a little sample. Then take the sample home and live with it; if it's still working for you over a period of time, buy it and enjoy!

Applying scent

Scent works best when applied to slightly damp skin. Resist the temptation to rub the wrists together after spraying on as this crushes all of the fragrance's notes. Let them unfold naturally, instead. Apply eau de toilette by spritzing it onto your hands and rubbing it gently up your arms and all over your legs and tummy. If you're going on a date apply scent to the inside of your elbows and wrists, the hollow of your collarbones, and along the hair line – especially if you suspect someone will be whispering into your ear... Try not to apply fragrance behind the ear, however, as the sebaceous glands here may change the scent, for the worse. I also apply scent to my ankles, the backs of my knees and in my bellybutton (a great little place to conceal perfume), as as the day wears on the warmth of your body causes the scent to diffuse.

Storing it

Over the years I've realized that it's not extreme temperatures that have ruined my perfumes but strong sunlight – in as little as three short weeks... nooo! To guard against this, keep all scents in the box that they arrived in, out of direct sunlight (unless they come in opaque bottles, like the black Narciso's Musk For Her Bottle).

PERFUME SHOPS

LONDON

Angela Flanders perfumery, 96 Columbia Road, E2 (tel: +44 20 7739 7555, www.angelaflanders-perfumer.com) – bespoke scent-creating service.

Floris, 89 Jermyn Street, SW1Y 6JH (tel: +44 20 7930 2885). Buy online at www.florislondon.co.uk or for mail order call +44 845 702 3239. You'll also find it available in Harrods, House of Fraser, John Lewis, Liberty, Fortnum & Mason and Peter Jones.

Guerlain, in Chester, Glasgow and Wolverhampton (tel: +44 20 7563 7563 for store details, also see www.guerlain.com for the companies vast perfume history). Worth the trip to experience the specially trained staff who use visual prompts to help you find your perfect scent. The process is very enlightening but limits you to fragrances from within this house's range.

Haute Parfumerie, Fifth Floor Urban Retreat, Harrods, SW1 (tel: +44 20 7893 8333 or for mail order + 44 20 7893 8797, www.urbanretreat-harrods.co.uk). Set up by Roja Dove, this boutique offers a range of carefully selected scents (including exclusive 're-launches' of long-gone classics by Creed and Guerlain). The unique 'olfactory fingerprinting' will help guide you through the confusion of scent selection. It's pure, luxurious Goddess!

Jo Malone, 150 Sloane Street, SW1X (tel: +44 20 7730 2100, www.jomalone.co.uk). Her lime, basil & mandarin range is universally coveted. Also available as mail order online.

L'Artisan Parfumeur, 17 Cale Street, SW3 (tel: +44 20 7352 4196, www.artisanparfumeur.com) sells a great range of fragrances, which it creates itself. Buy from the store or online at www.mkn.co.uk/perfume. They offer a scent sample service and also have concessions at Harvey Nichols, Liberty, Fenwick, House of Fraser and Harrods.

Les Senteurs, 71 Elizabeth Street, SW1 (tel: +44 20 7730 2322, www.lessenteurs.com). An old-style perfumery and a gem of a shop, it mainly stocks classics such as Caron and Creed plus several of my favourite new names, including Frédéric Malle and Mona di Orio. Staff are very knowledgeable about scent, and if you request their mail-order catalogue it explains each scent and demystifies the whole perfume industry. Better still, if you fancy the look of something they'll decant it into a tiny little scent phial and send it to you to try. How good is that?

Miller Harris, 21 Bruton Street, W1J (tel: +44 20 7629 7750, www.millerharris.com). They also offer a bespoke service. The most beautiful citrus orange fragrances and candle, ever.

Ormonde Jayne, The Royal Arcade, 28 Old Bond Street, W1S (tel: +44 20 7499 1100, www.ormondejayne.com). Owner Linda Pilkington's signature perfume, called Ormonde Woman, is a luxurious treat containing black hemlock – it'll transport you to another world! This is one of my favourite perfumes and a beautiful store to visit in London. Linda is a real talent!

Penhaligon's (tel: +44 800 716108 in the UK or call from overseas on +44 20 7590 6111, www.penhaligons.com). The violet and bluebell are popular but a little too girly for my tastes.

Santa Maria Novella, 117 Walton St, SW3 (tel: +44 20 7460 6600). Beautiful soaps, the best pot pourri on the planet, my favourite moisturizer and Nostalgia – one of the best leather scents on the market in my opinion. Made by Dominican monks since the sixteenth century, the packaging is so vintage it's even used in period films.

Scent Systems, 11 Newburgh Street, W1 (tel: +44 20 7434 1166, www.scent-systems.com). Great choice, exclusive and elusive modern fragrances.

Annick Goutal, 14 rue de Castiglione (tel: +33 1 42 60 52 82). Also at Liberty in London.

Boutique Chanel, 31 rue Cambon (tel: +33 1 42 86 26 00, www.chanel.com).

Caron, 90 rue du Faubourg Saint Honoré (tel: +33 1 42 68 25 68, www.parfumscaron.com), or my favourite store at 34 Avenue Montaigne (tel: +33 1 47 23 40 82). Fill a gorgeous bottle at Caron's superb Baccarat fountain in Paris or buy bottled Caron from Les Senteurs in London (see below). Caron is also available in New York at 675 Madison Avenue (tel: +1 212 319 4888).

Editions de Parfum Frédéric Malle, 37 rue de Grenelle (tel: +33 1 42 22 77 22, www. editionsdeparfums.com). Two of my favourite florals are from the Frédéric Malle range. His fragrances can also be bought at Les Senteurs in London and Barneys across the United States.

Guerlain, 68 avenue des Champs-Elysees (tel: +33 1 45 62 52 57, www.guerlain.com) – revel in old favourites such as Mitsouko, L'Heure Bleu and Samsara.

L'Artisan Parfumeur, 24 boulevard Raspail (tel: +33 1 42 22 23 32, www. artisanparfumeur.com), The Mûre et Musc has been a best-selling vanilla scent in Paris for over 20 years. Also available in London at 17 Cale Street, SW3 (tel: +44 20 7352 4196).

Maître Parfumeur et Gantier, 5 rue des Capucines (tel: +33 1 42 96 35 13) or 34 bis rue de Grenelle (tel: +33 1 45 44 61 57, www.maitre-parfumeur-et-gantier.com). Not only will you find beautiful scent here, they also sell fabulous gloves.

Parfums de Nicolaï, 80 rue de Grenelle (tel: +33 1 45 44 59 59, www.pnicolai.com). This is the granddaughter of famous nose Pierre Guerlain, and she's also based in London at 101a Fulham Road, SW3 6RH (tel: +44 20 7581 0922). Her fragrances are also available from Les Senteurs. Eau de lisque is divine.

Les Parfums de Rosine, 43 Galerie de Montpensier (tel: +33 1 42 60 47 58).

(Serge Lutens) Salons du Palais Royal Shiseido, 142 Galerie de Valois, Jardins du Palais-Royal (tel: +33 1 49 27 09 09, www.salons-shiseido.com). This violet-coloured boutique is enchanting and sells Serge Lutens' exclusive perfumes (20 different scents, €95 each). For an extra fee they'll even etch your initials into the bottle. Also available at Les Senteurs, London.

NEW YORK

Bond No. 9, 680 Madison Ave, 61st Street (tel: +1 212 838 2780, www.bondno9fragrances. com). This perfume company owned by Laurice Rahme (Annick Goutal's business partner for seven years) is a celebration of New York city, where she's lived for 25 years. Different fragrances represent different New York post codes. Also available at Harvey Nichols in London.

Slatkin & Co (tel: +1 212 759 3600, www.slatkin.com) – available to buy in London from Harrods or online at www.hqhair.com. In the US buy online from www.neimanmarcus.com or visit the Fred Segal store. This is one of the most avant-garde companies around. Although they do provide scent, I turn to them for their beautiful black fig & absinthe shampoo (attracts guys like flies) and their home fragrances instead. Madonna hooked up with them to create the Kabbalah range and The New York Times rated their candle the number-one burning candle in today's marketplace. Elton Rocks, four pot pourri fragrances created in conjunction with the star Elton John, are like nothing you've ever seen before – little aqua-coloured scented rocks, they're designed to be displayed in any room in the house, in any container of your choosing. My favourite is No. 3, the essence of iced pineapple, peony, dianthus and white musk. Stunning!

ALL BUNDLED UP

When I was young, if I missed a day of school due to illness, my mum would tell me that I'd have to get out of my bed and retire to the couch downstairs with a pillow and blanket to have my toast and tea. 'Bedbugs love munching breadcrumbs too,' she'd reason. We'd do nice things like read books and draw pictures and I'd get to watch telly snuggled up on the couch. Some days I like to take a day off and relive this Utopia, just lounging around in bed, reading, writing in my diary and watching great movies – utter bliss!

Get togged up

Any day's lounging is not complete without an ultra-fluffy duvet: the best is the 10.5-tog Siberian goose-down king-size duvet at John Lewis, (see www.johnlewis.com). Don't dry clean it (the chemicals ruin the filling) just wash it in your machine at home and it'll last up to 20 years. Never be tempted to lie, or sit on top of your duvet, on a day's lounging, (it squashes the stuffing), instead pull it over you on the couch, snuggle up and enjoy! Oooh!

The kit

Buy yourself a new nightie by Little Joe at www.net-a-porter.com or a vintage one at Miss Lala's Boudoir, 144 Gloucester Avenue, Primrose Hill, London (tel: +44 20 7483 1888). A bathrobe at the Monogrammed Linen Shop (tel: +44 20 7589 4033, www.monogrammedlinenshop.com) and a pair of Cashca cashmere slippers and a cashmere hoodie and bottoms from Biondi, 55B Old Church Street, London (tel: +44 20 7349 1111) are also snuggly treats. The store also sells Holistic Silk eye – masks and lavender neck cushions (see www.holisticsilk.co.uk). Keep a little movie box hidden in your wardrobe and now and then, when you're online or out shopping, buy a good movie and squirrel it away safely until your lounging day arrives.

My favourite lounging movies

I love My Favourite Year because it makes me laugh out load and I'm Not Rappaport because Walter Matthau looked and behaved like my grandfather. Otherwise I'll watch anything by Tim Burton, David Lynch or Jean Cocteau – they have an ethereal, magical quality.

In Jaws I always wondered how the Brodies moved three times and the shark always found them?

Squirrel *n* any of various arboreal rodents having a bushy tail and feeding on nuts and seeds. *Coll n* A dray of squirrels.

Classic must-sees

Magnolia – The Wizard of Oz – Days of Heaven – Portrait of a Lady – Goodfellas – Jaws – Psycho – Schindler's List – Blade Runner – Gladiator – It's a Wonderful Life – Some Like It Hot – Pulp Fiction – The Godfather II – Rebecca – North by Northwest – Notorious – Paris/Texas

COZY BY THE FIRE

Keep a diary

The biggest excuse for not keeping a diary is having no time for yourself, so I'd warmly recommend that you make some. When filling it in, remember it's the tiniest little things that'll really count many years from now. For the past six years Peter and I have recorded in photos, doodles and smudged ballpoint everything we experience and feel while we explore. Recently I realized that distinctive constants become glaringly clear, momentous events sandwiched between promises to stop nail-biting. Even Winston Churchill fought World War II and kept a diary, many of his entries cataloguing normal daily routine.

Ever wondered where diary writing started? The Greeks wrote on tablets of stone in 450 BC, and the diary was in use around 400 BC. You can see one of these Greek versions which was unearthed in Constantinople in 1422 by making an appointment with the Special Funds Department at the British Museum.

The most amazing diary I've ever read is *The Journey Is the Destination: The Journals of Dan Eldon.* In 1992, Dan and a friend set out from Kenya for the Somali town of Baidoa to investigate African famine. On 12 July 1993, UN troops bombed a house believed to be the headquarters of the warlord known as General Mohammed Farah Aidid. Eldon, retained as a freelancer by Reuters, went to photograph the damage and, along with three other journalists, was stoned to death by an angry crowd. At www.daneldon.org/journals you can see his journals and the days leading up to his sudden and tragic death.

Bono's little green jumper

Bono works so hard to right injustices in the world that it's difficult to ever imagine him switched off and just lounging. He once to.d me that when he returns home to Dublin from travelling, he puts on his favourite green jumper and just relaxes around his house. It's got holes in it but that doesn't matter; it's soft, cosy and warm, and it offers comfort when he's ill or feels exhausted. Do you have a favourite jumper that you wear around your home?

After dragging my frostbitten cheeks and frozen face home from the city, there's nothing as karmic as a warm, scented bath. At home, the bathroom is the one room in the house where I don't take phone calls; I can be silent and alone there and think clear and calm thoughts. There's something very sensual and therapeutic about soaking for hours in bath water perfumed with aromatic salts and oils and I keep my bathroom shelves stocked with the very best that I can possibly find. No amount of money in the world can replace that lovely in-the-bath feeling – it's one of my little indulgences.

Luxurious oil

For a truly luxurious soak and a scent that will transport you to a place of dreams Ormonde Jayne Osmanthus Essential Bathing Oil created by expert nose Linda Pilkington at Ormonde Jayne, Royal Arcade, 28 Old Bond Street, London (tel: +44 20 7499 1100, www.ormondejayne.com) is divine. The ancient Romans soaked in huge communal baths for hours daily and used exotic oils to cleanse and seduce. This is what they must have smelled like.

Aromatherapy bath oils

I love the Aromatherapy Associates range of bath oils, available by mail order (tel: +44 20 8569 7030; www.aromatherapyassociates.com). Once in the bath a tiny capful of one of their scented oils will travel through the air in waves and perfume the whole house. Their Deep Relax Oil really does induce deep relaxation and their Revive Morning Bath and Shower Oil offers a great wake-up call. And I'm not alone in my love of this fine aromatherapy range; Kathy Phillips (see pp117), International Beauty Director for Condé Nast Asia, told me that she loved one of these bath oils so much that she used it for twenty years before getting together with its creators, Sue Beechey and Geraldine Howard, to create her own range, This Works, 18 Cale Street, London SW3 (tel: +44 20 7584 1887, mail order +44 8452 300499, www.thisworks.com), also available at Harvey Nichols. Preservative-free and blended using 30 per cent concentration (most other blends are less than 1 per cent essential oil), the This Works range is flawless. I particularly love the In the Zone Bath and Shower Oil packed full of Somalian frankincense and Portuguese eucalyptus for morning, and Deep Calm Bath and Shower Oil which contains vetiver, lavender and camomile for relaxing evening soaks – the scent really engulfs me. Ahhhhhh!

Wallpaper: Dorset Flock by Cole & Son, www.cole-and-son.com.

BATHING

I want to stay in the bath long after my fingers have shrivelled up.

240

Bespoke soak

Aromatherapist Sam Cowan (tel: +44 20 7244 7300) will create a custom-made bath blend, experimenting with both the therapeutic properties and beautiful scents of different essential oils.

Flower power

Ren's Moroccan Rose Otto Bath Oil at Space NK or www.renskincare.com is steam distilled from Moroccan rose petals harvested at dawn when they're at their best and turns bath water a milky white with the scent of pure roses. Known as the queen of flower oils, Moroccan rose oil is one of the most expensive and revered essential oils in the world. This bath oil is scrummy!

My favourite Japanese bathing ritual

Mineral bath soaks had never been something that I thought I needed in my life, that is until I came upon Japan Hinoki Mint Mineral Bath Soak from Red Flower. I purchased my first tall, sleek canister labelled 'mineral bath soak' from their beautiful store on 13 Prince Street, New York (tel: +1 212 966 1994, www.redflower.com; also available in the UK from Harvey Nichols), while I was staying at Soho House Hotel in the Meatpacking District. The bath in my room there was so beautiful that I decided to make the most of it and searched New York for some quality bath soak. Not only do these aromatic crystals turn your bath water an intense green but the blend of hinoki wood, mint oil, chlorophyll and minerals soothes and relaxes. Now I use the seven products that make up the seven-step Red Flower Japanese bathing ritual at home as a special treat. After the bath soak, I wash with the Sea Algae Wash and then exfoliate with the Gingergrass Bamboo Scrub; this is rinsed off with the Rice Buff Cloth Bag steeped in water. After a spray of Rose Camellia Plum Soft Water Mist, I then apply some Kinmoxei Wild Lime Silk Oil. I finish off by moisturizing with Plum Blossom Silk Cream and my skin goes from lack to lustre in no time. This range is so beautiful I can't stop smelling my own arms all day. This ritual is perfect for when you have a whole evening to spend just by yourself. Gorgeous!

Remove your jewellery

Soap and body washes cause a build-up on gold rings which can easily dull them, therefore it's best to remove all your gold jewellery before you have a bath. Likewise if you get your ring stuck on your finger, don't use soap and water to get it off, try a squirt of Windolene instead.

GODDESS TIP
BECAUSE FRAGRANCE RISES, SPRAY OR SMOOTH PERFUME OR CREAM ONTO SKIN FROM THE FEET TO THE SHOULDERS, OTHERWISE IT WILL EVENTUALLY RISE FROM YOUR NECK AND CHEST AND DISAPPEAR.

GODDESS TIP
WARM YOUR TOWELS IN THE TUMBLE DRYER OR ON THE RADIATOR BEFORE YOUR BATH FOR A SNUGGLY AFTER-BATH TREAT.

Letter writing.

We all remember writing letters to Santa don't we? But with email being so nifty, when is the last time you got to really enjoy the perfect weight of a piece of paper so smooth your pen just glided over it, like silk? I discussed this at length with Isabella Blow at a Paul Smith show in London. She explained to me that she chooses not to use a computer, preferring to do all of her correspondence by pen and paper – writing lovely thought-out letters instead. How wonderful and romantic, and how stylish!

Choosing Paper

The first thing you need to do is find some good paper (it will make writing, sending and receiving the letters so much more enjoyable), and you'll need a very good stationer for that. Alastair Lockhart, 97 Walton Street, London SW3 (tel: +44 20 7581 8289) offers the most salubrious service, and everything from paper and envelopes to bespoke invitations and cards. Alastair Lockhart maintains that the most beautiful way of individualising your letter-writing paper is to have your name printed onto it in coloured ink. The three most popular processes are flat, thermo-graphic (raised) and engraved (a matt finish). Have your details printed onto cream, white, pale blue or grey, woven, inlaid or matt paper, and choose envelopes with tissue paper linings that match the colour of your ink.

Writing your letter

There's something very temporary about emails so we tend not to care so much what we tap in but I think we all worry about appearing witty and stylish in print, don't we? Don't feel you have to agonise about what to put though, you'll write a far more touching letter, if you just try to be yourself. A special letter should always be written by hand on letterheaded paper with, if you get your letterhead done in the UK, your address, telephone number and email, centred at the top. In the US the name usually appears alone, top centre, and the address printed on the back flap of the envelope. Place the date on the right hand side of your page and your greeting on the left usually, 'Dear'.

Thank You

If it's the sheer vastness of space confronting you in a letter that scares you, why not send a smaller card instead? Just a few lines on one of these, to family, colleagues and friends, will always be appreciated; in fact as long as you say thank you from the heart for dinner, lunch, tea or after receiving a birthday or Christmas present, you can use any form of card you like. So why not get yourself a couple of blue boxes of plain correspondence cards from Smythson, 40 New Bond Street, London W1 (tel: +44 20 7318 1515, www.smythson.co.uk), or some bespoke correspondence cards from Alastair Lockhart (as before), and always hand-write your note. These correspondence cards are by far the most useful and best value stationery. Leave out the words 'Dear' and 'Yours Sincerely' but do pop on the date. These postcard sized cards originated as a method of correspondence between a lady of the house and her staff – almost like an early version of the email!

Surprise

I believe there's nothing as personal as writing a letter or note to somebody. And receiving one, well it's always an honour and a treat, especially if it's unexpected. You can imagine my excitement then, in the course of putting *The Goddess Guide* together, at finding letters on the mat in my hallway from Tracey Emin, Geordie Grieg, Marvin Scott Jarrett… and my Gran. All on different stationery, in different handwriting, and all reflecting individuality and genius. There is no way email or text messaging will ever replace that.

Personally, I always use handmade writing paper from Pineider (www.pineidershop.com) in Florence. It's also available in London from The Italian Corner, 16 Royal Arcade, Old Bond Street, London W1 (tel: +44 20 7499 9469).

Other Stationers you should try:
The Wren Press, 1 Chelsea Wharf, 15 Lots Road, London SW10 (tel: +44 20 7351 5887, www.wrenpress.com).
The Jasmine Factory (tel: +44 20 7585 19118, www.thejasminefactory.co.uk).
Anzu (www.anzu.co.uk).
Green & Stone (tel: +44 20 7352 0837).
For an online stationer go to www.heritage-stationery.com or www.caxtonlondon.com.

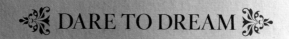

It was in Geneva that Mary Shelley wrote Frankenstein, conceiving the idea during one of the most famous house parties in literary history in the summer of 1816. She wrote it to settle a wager between her husband, the poet Percy Bysshe Shelley, and the poet Lord Byron –she was only nineteen at the time. If she were around now, Vanity Fair would be singing her praises and I'd be an avid fan. It was in Geneva, while looking up at the Italian Alps that inspired her, when this thought struck me: I hadn't finished reading a full book in almost ten years. I'd dip into one, read it, then leave it, fearful of disappointment for the hero or heroine at the end.

On the flight back from Geneva to Heathrow, I wondered whether Mary Shelley was a looker as well as being clever (an honest-enough query you'll agree). Passing the National Portrait Gallery, I decided to pop in and investigate. There she was in all of her modest glory on the first floor – what clever eyes she had.

I stayed in the gallery all day, soaking up the portraits, and dreamt of having them all come to my house for tea and home-baked sponge cake. For variety, I even added names to the guest list whose pictures weren't there at all. It being my tea party, of course, I got to choose. I'd have Charles Darwin seated right next to Jesus (they'd be chatting for hours). I'd put William Morris with Roy Strong, Jane Austen and Aldous Huxley, Tracey Emin and Oscar Wilde. Of course, you couldn't leave out Percy Bysshe and Mary Shelley, seeing as the couple quotient is really quite low, and then the naughty and mischievous Emily and Charlotte Brontë (they'd probably be passing tiny written notes to each other about the state of the food). Samuel Beckett would put manners on David Sedaris, who'd probably love F. Scott Fitzgerald. And no mad tea-party would be complete without Charles Dickens and Louis de Bernières, and Irish poets Brendan Kennelly and Patrick Kavanagh – they'd be well up for chatting up all the girls. Finally, I'd have myself and Peter (well, with that crowd you'd have to have at least two people to pour). This happy little thought coerced me into buying books by many of these poets and authors. The one I completed first was? (see p132).

Read a poem

Nourished on a diet of Irish poetry from a very early age, I loved it almost as much as my mother's Sherry trifle. Both had one thing in common: rationing! To this day Mum still likes to save her favourite verses to recite to her pupils at school but she can often be heard singing out her cherished poems while doing the cooking or the dishes in the kitchen. As a child my mind scratched at the bunched up words to extract pictures.

Seamus Heaney's 'Death of a Naturalist' brought with it the greatest imagery and a comforting familiarity too, as I had also bred frogs from frogspawn on a National school window-ledge. Similarly, I had enough green-stained dresses in the cupboard, from falling into heaps of hot cow shit on the farm, to know that special, acrid fragrance. At the time, I thought that apart from my Dad and me, Seamus Heaney was the only other person in the world who really understood cow shit!

Several years later I found another brilliant poem. Irish poet Brendan Kennelly (I knew him from home), recited it to me one summer's evening, outside the gates of Trinity College in Dublin; it was called 'Poem from a Three Year Old' and it made me weep on the public pavement. The next morning I went straight to Eason's to buy every single poem he'd ever penned. When I discovered I was too broke to buy it all I rang home for some money – but Mum instead posted all of his books to me in a parcel.

I keep a copy of Kennelly's book *Familiar Strangers* by my bed – his poems leave a special taste in my mouth and in fact when I heard this poem by Irish poet Maggie O'Dwyer, it sparked off that same sensation. This really nails the abuse of the English language, and I can't think of robins or hedgehogs without smiling and thinking of Maggie's great words.

I hate how you use me

Call the sky paranoid, skulking
behind the clouds, the grass mad
with rain, the wisteria neurotic.
Call the robin a loser, waiting
for someone else to turn up
a worm, the fox a cretin,
for standing on the train tracks
Call the hedgehog a fuck-wit
in the glare of a car, the sunflower
a slut, the peacock a poofter,
Call the evening light a cunt
for fading, Artemis a bimbo,
the moon a big fat moron
the fallen apple, a failure.

In 2004, the editor of British *Tatler*, Geordie Greig, held a fantastic auction at Sotheby's to raise money for a charity called the 999 Club. Far from being a typical charity fundraiser Geordie asked various artists, politicians and dignitaries to create tiny little books – with whatever they wanted inside – that were then auctioned off for the cause. Little books were created by Bill Clinton (who rewrote Martin Luther King's speech), Tracey Emin, Muhammad Ali, Seamus Heaney, David Hockney, J.K. Rowling and Madonna. (The latter two can be seen here.)

Why did you choose little books as the subject for your charity auction, Geordie? *Books are universal and I thought little books had a big appeal.*

So you like books then? *I have always been addicted to reading – a holiday without a book always seems a little lonely.*

Do you remember your first book? *The Jungle Book by Rudyard Kipling.*

What are your favourite books? *Ones with great stories.*

So you like fiction and poetry? *Very much, especially Trollope, William Trevor, Kazuo Ishiguro and Ted Hughes.*

Do you have favourite writers? *I am always hungry for young new writers.*

What advice would you give to someone who is just starting to discover the beauty of reading? *Ask people for recommendations. It was how I discovered William Trevor, the greatest living short-story writer.*

Do you have any hotspots where one should look for good books? *I am drawn like a magnet to second-hand bookshops.*

Favourite smell? Tobacco leaves on the plant in a field in India.
Favourite sound? My children's voices.
Favourite taste? Fig.
Favourite to your sense of touch? Ice.
Favourite colour? Blue.
Favourite bird/animal? Elephant, octopus and jaguar.
Favourite flower? Lily of the valley.
Favourite place? India.
Favourite book? The Way We Live Now by Anthony Trollope.
Favourite piece of art? Bellini madonnas.
Favourite possession? My cufflinks.
If you could have dinner with anybody, who would it be and what would you ask them? J.D. Salinger. Can I have an interview with you?

Gisèle's Favourite book shops
Magma, 8 Earlham Street, Covent Garden (tel: +44 20 7240 8498, www.magmabooks.com).
Stanford's (Travel), 12-14, Long Acre, (tel: +44 20 7836 1321, www.stanfords.co.uk).
Bookartbookshop, 17 Pitfield Street, (tel: +44 20 7608 1333, www.bookartbookshop.com).
Biblion, Grays Antique Market (see pp70).
Simon Finch Rare Books, 53 Maddox Street, W1 (tel: +44 20 7499 0974, www.simonfinch.com).
John Sandoe Books, 10 Blacklands Terrace, SW3 (tel: +44 20 7589 9473, www.johnsandoe.com).
Daunt Books, 83-84 Marylebone High Street, W1 (tel: +44 20 7224 2295, www.dauntbooks.co.uk).
Ian Shipley Specialist Art Booksellers, 70 & 72 Charing Cross Road, WC2 (tel+44 20 7836 4872, www.artbook.co.uk).
Secret Book and Record Store, Wicklow Street, Dublin 2, (tel: +353 1 679 7272).

March 2006

Dear Gisele,
The first book that I remember catching my imagination was The Jungle Book by Rudyard Kipling. My copy had a beautiful blue cover with a gold engraving on the front. I was hooked on its exotic stories of adventure and derring-do all centred around a little boy who I longed to be. How could I become friends with wild animals in the jungle and actually talk to them? I was taken into another world that was vivid, exciting and very real. It was a parallel universe to my own and made me realise that books opened up the world. They continue to change my life.

Geordie Greig

Books by JK Rowling (left) and Madonna (right).

HOGWARTS
SCHOOL OF
WITCHCRAFT
AND
WIZARDRY

Hanover Square, London W1S 1JU
62 F (Promotions) 020 7499 8745 www.condenast.co.uk

Madonna
♡ Sept. 2004

MAKE & DO

I'm completely besotted with making things and become so engrossed in cutting and gluing that recently someone at a perfume counter in Dublin told me that I had what looked like a tube of Prittstick dangling from my hair. I knew it was getting serious when I opened the front door to the postman once only to realize that I'd super-glued my fingers to my face. Regardless, I love creating things! We live in a boring, beige world so creating something bespoke sets us apart. If you hand-make something yourself no one will ever have the exact same thing as you – no matter how much money they have – it's unique!

Embroidery
If you're into creating with stitches then Jenny Hart at www.sublimestitching.com will sell you little embroidery patterns to get started.

G-Spot
The Design Museum, Shad Thames, London SE1 2YD (tel +44 870 909 9009, www.designmuseum.org) is stuffed full of professional designers. Check out Tord Boontje's papercuts, www.tordboontje.com, Timorous Beasties' printed textiles, www.timorousbeasties.com, and Committee's 'Kebab' lamp, www.gallop.co.uk. The latter is made from skewering several junk shop finds and the one on the left is called Mountain Rescue, cool eh? Speaking of skewering, People Will Always Need Plates (www.peoplewill alwaysneedplates.co.uk), 'skewer' old dinner service plates together and turn them into three tier cake stands. So what are you waiting for? Get creating now!

Customize some socks and pumps
Buy some new Falke ankle socks at Selfridges and customize by sewing satin ribbon around the top of each. Find the most delicious ribbon nearby at MacCulloch & Wallis Ltd, 25-26 Dering Street, London W1S (tel: +44 20 7629 0311, www.macculloch-wallis.co.uk). Do the same with a pair of ballet pumps (see pp131)

Make a pin cushion
Pick up fabric and trimmings at Temptation Alley, 359 Portobello Road, London W11 (tel: +44 20 89642004, www.temptationalley.com) and make a pincushion for your needles and pins. This old haberdashery sells ribbons, sequins, feathers, tassels, beads and braids.

Stitch
Make a stitched bird like Claire Coles' (tel: +44 20 7371 7303, www.clairecolesdesign.co.uk) on pp186.

Knit a scarf
Gain inspiration from the best and try and meet up with the Cast Off Crew at www.castoff.info who knit all over the country.

GODDESS TIP
PLACE A PIECE OF WHITE PAPER BEHIND YOUR NEEDLE WHEN YOU'RE THREADING IT TO HELP YOU SEE THE EYE MORE CLEARLY.

Add a trim to your cashmere sweater
You'll find some great gold trims at Barrett & Lawson, 16-17 Little Portland Street, London W1 (tel: +44 207 636 8592, www.bltrimmings.com) to stitch onto your sleeves.

Tunes to make stuff to
You Are My Sister by Antony and the Johnsons
Time Is My Everything by Ian Brown
The Girl from Ipanema by Stan Getz
Rapp Snitch Knishes by MF Doom
Now and Then by Silje Nergaard
Karmacoma by Massive Attack
On the Radio by The Concretes
Intwenjani? by Ma Willies
Rose Rouge by St. Germain
Tender by Blur

Read
Readymade magazine,
www.readymademag.com,
for a million ideas about
what stuff to make.

Flamingo *n* a large wading bird having a
pink and red plumage and downward bent bill
and inhabiting brackish lakes. *Coll. n* a stand
of flamingos when standing and a skein when
flying. Now go paint your favourite bird.

Giraffe *n* a large ruminant mammal
inhabiting savannas of tropical Africa,
the tallest mammal with very long legs
and neck. *Coll. n* a tower of giraffes. I
love drawing them.

249

9
PILLOW TALK

It was after lunch on a warm summer's day in the beginning of June, 1980. My classmates had clattered and crunched their way across the gravel and back into the classroom for the afternoon. "Shhhhhhhh! Shhhhhhhh!" coaxed Mrs Baker. "Take out your books and stop talking." Stillness, save for the rustle of pages and the creaking of wooden desk joints. For one brief moment there was that special silence. And then: Crash! Chak chak chak! Lagging behind as ever, my hand on the handle of the classroom door, ready to enter, I stepped back, intrigued. Chak chack chak. The sound was coming from deep inside a clump of trees across the road near the grotto. I couldn't resist it and tiptoed out the door, along the school wall and across the main road.

I approached the shaking foliage and peered through the knotted branches: a magpie lay on the ground, its mate dancing about it, calling, it seemed, for help. Lying in a pool of its own blood and brutally hurt down its right side, the bird's head craned awkwardly backwards revealing a gaping wound in its neck. I knew from seeing a goose look like this a few Christmases previously that his prospects were not looking good. I reached down to offer the little fella some warm school milk from the carton that I was still clutching (Dad had explained to me some years before that you always knew when a cowboy was about to die in a movie because as he lay on the ground bleeding he'd ask for water to replace his lost fluids) but as I inched closer to the little casualty, his partner, her green and blue tail feathers iridescent in the sun, flew violently at me. I backed away. There was nothing I could do to save him – and within a few minutes the ailing magpie had died.

That evening Dad explained that magpies live their lives as one half of a monogamous pairing. They spend their whole lives as a pair – foraging for food, having babies and taking naps together in trees. Even that old superstitious rhyme

("One, for sorrow. Two, for joy..."), aludes to the loss of one through tragedy or accident. That day Dad seized the opportunity to explain that no matter how difficult things became for the birds they always managed to stay together: "A bit like your mother and myself," he chuckled. "And communication is vital – chak chak chak!" I promised myself that one day I'd find a magpie partner like my father; someone who would be there to chat when something extraordinary happened to me – good or bad.

Of course to attract a magpie partner as an adult I'd need a certain amount of, well, know-how. The parents of my friends fell into two camps: the ones who had dog-eared editions of *The Kama Sutra* or *The Joy of Sex* and left them casually around for their kids to sneak a peak at, so they wouldn't have to discuss sex; and the ones who explained procreation by using examples of different animals having little babies every springtime on the farm. And wouldn't you know it, my parents had to be the King and Queen of the latter camp!

A friend at school once told me that her parents' Kama Sutra had pages and pages of intricate drawings of men and women, draped in gold jewellery, and twisted into positions that would make a contortionist's eyes water. At the time I remember agreeing and laughing along whole heartily despite, even at 15, not having a clue what she meant. What if I grew old without ever finding my Prince Charming? What if no frog would kiss me at all? For years I watched the just-moved-in-togethers dress their nest boxes with matching his 'n' hers mugs, bathrobes and slippers. Yeuch! Their relationships were comfy and convenient and they'd sit ignoring each other over brunch – reading the Sunday supplements and not even bothering to check each others' horoscopes. Okay, so relationships everywhere go through good and bad bits… crushes on workmates, periods of work-aholism, low libido(s), financial pressures, sickness, alongside birthdays, Christmases and kids. But to be left with nothing to talk about over a meal out (or in)? How lonely must that be? And that's when you really know it's time to pull the plug.

As my Dad said to me all those years ago, the most important thing of all in a relationship is proper communication – that, and the question you must keep asking yourself: Is he really that into you? Well, is he? Take Kermit the Frog for instance; for years I watched him on the telly trying to rebuff the advances of Miss Piggy, the ultimate diva. But did she ever get the message? No! Interviewing them I soon realized that he's definitely not that into her. So Miss Piggy, and all the other Miss Piggy's out there, please take note: a frog hopping fast in the opposite direction is not teasing you; no, he's actually trying to escape!

Okay, so I'm not a sophisticated, lip-licking, hair-flicking man-eater. I spent several years on the bench working out my own stuff and prioritising me. I was happy and single for years, until one day Dad asked if I was waiting to make and cut a man from my own paper pattern so that he'd be perfect. I went on a few dates just to skirt feebly around the minefield before crossing – trust me, since then I've either been blown up, maimed or smooched by frogs! Well, until fairly recently.

Is there a Mr Right? Yes, when everything is effortless
Is there a Mr Wrong? Yes, when everything is a worry and a fight

Attract Mr Right with your eyes, hair and scent

'Glances are the heavy artillery of the flirt', wrote French novelist Stendhal in his epic *Love*. Everything can be conveyed in a look. Enhance it by adding Shu Uemura eyelashes from their fantasy range. Check out www.shuuemura-usa.com (see pp87) or Tokyo Lash Bar, Harvey Nichols (tel: +44 20 7235 5000, www.harveynichols. com). Smoky Parisian eyes with dark mascara and smoky eye pencil (see pp142) are also very alluring. Wash your hair with the Slatkin Black Fig & Absinth range (see pp237), wear it messy or loosely 'up' to expose the scent. When in flirt mode, use a darker, heavier scent as an aphrodisiac in the winter (see pp230), and a smoother smell like Edouard Fléchier's Lys Méditerranée dry oil in the summer, from Editions de Parfums Frédéric Malle at Les Senteurs (see pp233).

My number one Goddess rule

Flirtation is tantalising, teasing and sometimes dark and dangerous. One too many cocktails and it (hopefully) leads to some red-hot action. However, in modern life adultery lurks constantly, waiting in the shadows to destroy you. Have respect for every other Goddess on the planet, and if her weak partner approaches you, unbeknownst to her, never ever give in. These men are all wrong!

Nail him

If he suits all of your requirements and is easily the best man for the job, he'll need to prove it, so sit back and let him try. My golden rule is never go back to his place, well not until you're satisfied he's not a psycho, and set out your ground rules – he'll respect you more for it in the end. So, unless your flat looks like a battlefield or your carpet like a swamp, invite him back to yours – remembering to resist the temptation to create Hollywood low-lighting and to stay well away from Chris de Burgh and Celine Dion. Act casual and in control and offer him a glass of good wine… Relax and enjoy… and always use protection.

Smoochin'

The smooch, when it eventually happens, must be long, lingering and memorable. The rest is a minefield littered with casualties and is dictated by your own personal tastes. A wise woman once told me that seduction should be conducted at two-thirds the speed of normal interaction. I tried this advice and made the mistake of even slowing down my speech. My lover dropped me on the secluded beach and ran screaming towards the sand dunes for a doctor: he thought I was having a stroke.

Pucker up

Two-thirds of us instinctively tilt to the right when we kiss – reflecting our tendency to turn our heads to the right in the womb and for six months after birth. And did you know that if you can kiss your elbow, your gender will change. Go on, try it.

Need a little help?

To wow the socks (or stilettos) off your luuuurved one, check out Buy a Gift (tel: +44 870 444 2524, www.buyagift.co.uk), a one-stop shop for romantic pressies. From naming a rose or a star (in the galaxy) after your boyfriend/girlfriend, to proposing with a banner attached to a plane high in the sky, they've got it covered. If you're just starting out on the path to luuuurve with someone new, why not go on a chocolate-making course together and make each other Easter eggs, or give him/her a sterling silver last Rolo, or a silver Love Heart.

Make sparks fly

Treat your loved one to some fireworks (in the sky) from Kimbolton fireworks (tel: +44 870 076 2538, www.kimboltonfireworks.co.uk or try www.firework-review.org. uk). Fireworks are my most favourite thing in the whole wide world. Wow!

Frog *n* an insectivorous amphibian, having a short squat tailless body with a moist smooth skin and very long hind legs specialized for hopping. *Coll. n* a colony of frogs. In breeding season, when a male frog finds a female he grabs her from behind with the help of special pads on his fore limbs and holds on as tight as he can. As soon as the female releases her eggs into the water they are fertilised by the male. What no jollies?

The amazing iced cakes on the following pages were created especially by Debbie's Sweet Art (tel: +44 1932 240274, www.debbiebone.co.uk). She's the industry's best kept secret, until now. Damn!

Miss Piggy et Moi

I had a real blast with vous at London Fashion Week – is your schedule totally packed? Packed? Are vous kidding? Moi invented multi-tasking. For instance, while doing this lovely little interview with vous, I'm simultaneously downloading cuts for my new album onto my iPod, re-entering celebrity addresses into my Blackberry (in descending order of box office clout), uplinking to the satellite for the semi-annual World Divas video conference call, getting my nails done, shopping online for minor cosmetic surgery, and penning an unauthorized tell-almost-all autobiography. Uh-oh, I think I just downloaded a diva into my iPod.

As someone who attends so many fashionable engagements, where do you look for a dress? I look for dresses wherever wealthy people are. You see, people who make dresses are smart. They know that wealthy people will give them money for their dresses. And while the designer is busy kissing up to the rich folks, I'm busy going through their trunk looking for stuff that fits. Everyone benefits, especially moi.

Hair and make-up seem to travel with you everywhere – is staying beautiful a constant job? Of course it is. Naturellement, moi has the advantage of being quintessentially beautiful, but that doesn't mean I don't have to be fussed over constantly. And it is true that my hair and make-up travel with me everywhere; although on occasion, my hair flies ahead of me, in which case I wear a hat.

I understand you have to be beautiful for the cameras but do you ever just lounge around your dressing trailer on movie sets? I notice you hide chips and snacks in your wardrobe in your trailer on www.muppets.com. I love chocolate, but do you have a salty or a sweet tooth? I have a sweet tooth. I've made no secret of my love affair with chocolate. (Of course, Kermie is my first love, but chocolate, jewellery and real estate all tie for second.) As for salty foods, I don't crave those quite as much. Moi is salty enough already, n'est-ce pas?

Kermit is really dishy, isn't he? Why is he the perfect escort? Kermie is adorable, isn't he? Here, let me take out a picture of him and study it. Hmm, that is one stud frog, non? Let's face it, he and moi are perfect for each other. He's handsome, witty, talented and green goes with everything. As for moi, what's not to love?

How long have you and Kermit been friends now? With your busy schedules, is it difficult when you're apart? Friends? Pardon?! Kermie and moi are not just friends, which implies a certain emotional and physical distance; we are soul mates, one-true-loves, co-dependents, joint-custody-of-our-hearts holders. We're the real thing, sweetie. As for being apart, it is much easier these days than in the past. Thanks to global positioning systems and those très fashionable ankle bracelets, I always know where my dear sweet frog is … and he knows it.

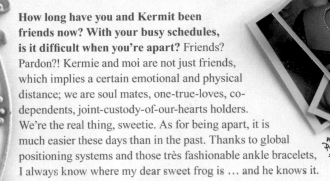

Me and Miss Piggy at London Fashion week. (The Divas!)

You wore a Prada dress to die for in Colette in Paris. What's your perfect dress? First of all, it must be little, showing a lot of leg and drawing everyone's attention to your glorious gams and those ridiculously expensive shoes you're wearing. Second, it must be black, so that it provides a dark palette against which one can accessorize with wild abandon and someone else's credit card. And third, you've got to fill it with the perfect body, which for moi is a fait accompli. (Actually, I think I drove here in a Fait Accompli. Do you have any idea where I parked?)

As one of the most photographed icons on the planet, what are your secrets for posing for shots? What do you most want to be remembered for? Looking sensational in a photograph is simply a matter of looking sensational and transferring that to film or digital media. If you don't have the goods to begin with, no amount of pouting, posing or industrial-strength airbrushing is going to help. I simply let the camera discover my beauty and the rest is magic. As for what I want to be most remembered for – being there for others to enjoy.

You are without a doubt one of the twenty-first century's blonde screen Goddesses. Having played several different witches in *The Wizard of Oz* and experimented with different hair colours, do you think blondes have the most fun? And you are one of the greatest interviewers of all time. Do you really think that moi is 'one of the twenty-first century's blonde screen Goddesses'? Oh, you are so astute and smart and whoever is paying you should double it this instant. It's true, though: I am breathtaking as a blonde, which is why it was such an acting and career challenge for moi to experiment with different hair colours. And yet, somehow, I pulled it off, didn't I? It is my belief that one's hair colour does not determine how much fun you can have. That's up to you, and your frog.

What's your secret to being so cute, Kermit? Me? Cute? Gee, thanks. I was actually going for the ruggedly handsome action hero type, but if it comes across as 'cute', that works too. Mostly I think it comes from being short and green. Try it, and I'll bet folks will call you cute, too.

.

What part does Miss Piggy play in your life? She plays the part of the pig. It's a big part, and one that stays with you for a long, long time. We're colleagues, co-workers, co-stars and dear friends, but we're NOT romantically involved. Believe me, even though she doesn't.

256

Is she hard work? Piggy hard work? It's like the myth of Sisyphus meets the Labours of Hercules with the invasion of Normandy thrown in for good measure. But otherwise, no.

She's a real diva sometimes, isn't she? Yes, Piggy is a diva. In fact, she recently won the World Diva Lifetime Achievement Award for her many years of service being difficult, demanding, dissatisfied and unreasonable in any and all circumstances, while simultaneously waving and smiling to her adoring admirers. Boy, did she deserve that one. I presented the award to her, but she sent it back for a bigger one with more gold.

Like all modern guys, are you a stickler for time? Do you and Miss Piggy ever row when it takes her hours to do her hair and make-up before you appear in public together? I've never figured out how long Piggy takes to get ready, but I know you have to use a calendar to keep track of the time. We only fought about this once. I know better now.

You went on a huge tour, even to NASA. Does Miss Piggy get jealous easily when you meet other girls? Jealous? Never. Ballistic? Yes. In fact, NASA wants to study the propulsion system that powers her karate chop. It packs a punch, and I oughta know.

What are her most endearing qualities? Miss Piggy believes in herself. She's relentless. She's a force of nature. You've got to love that about her. I know I do.

Is it easy being green, Kermit? It gets easier. For instance, as it says in the song: being green means I blend in with so many ordinary things. This makes it easier to hide, and heaven knows I need to do a lot of that.

I've heard you're left-handed (I always remember you having your microphone in your left hand on Sesame Street) – is this true, Kermit? The reason I ask is that I know of a shop that specializes in everything for left-handed people here in London. I could give you the address of it, if you like. I'd love to visit that shop, but actually, like most frogs, I'm amphibidextrous.

GODDESS TIP
PICK UP LEFT-HANDED SCISSORS, KITCHEN IMPLEMENTS, TOOLS AND THE BEST GIFTS IN THE WORLD FOR THE LEFTIE IN YOU LIFE FROM: ANYTHING LEFT-HANDED, 57 BREWER, STREET (TEL: +44 20 8770 3722 WWW.ANYTHINGLEFT-HANDED.CO.UK

Surviving O.P.N's

OPN's (Other People's Nuptials)

My stomach is heaving with the taste of profiteroles. I'd be fine if it were all just 'Ooh, look at Sarah, doesn't she look gorgeous?' or 'Ah, look at the way she looks at Bob?' But the questions, and expectations, fuelled by booze then turn in your direction. 'God, you're thirty-two and still single, darling. Do you think it's because you've piled on the pounds?' Give yourself a break and side-step the beady-eyed interrogators. Use a couple of these tips and have a ball.

Time your arrival

If you arrive early, you'll get noticed – but only by the interrogators. Come bang on time and your toes will get trodden on and your unique beauty lost in the stampede of relations rushing for the drink and the food. Really, the only option is to be half an hour or more behind the main wedding party. So, arrive late, locate the bar and quickly down a stiff drink. This will give you time and courage to compose yourself, check out the facilities and see if there are any male cuties on the prowl.

Drink

Proceed with caution, as this could be your first and last stumbling block. Have a few glasses of champers and then leave it at that for a while. Most cocktails contain several different spirits so suddenly you're holding your third booze grenade in your hand and trouble is lurking like paparazzi in the twitching bushes. Pace yourself, there's a long road ahead. Sip water between drinks and smile.

Who to bring

I've been to so many weddings where friends turn up with a last-minute break-the-glass-in-case-of-emergency female or male escort. Obviously they've trawled clubs with this single mission in mind a mere week before. Unfortunately, it's too late to turn back once your freeloader's downed his sixth cocktail and decided that now would be the perfect time to negotiate the dance floor on all fours. I know people who've had to endure selfish arm-candy like this, canoodling in the corner with someone else, half naked. If you're stuck (and desperate), you're best

"Damn! Always the brides maid... chak, chak, chak"

off bringing a (boy) friend of the same sexual persuasion; you never know, there might be great scope to find you both a date at the actual event.

Alternatively…

Your goal is simple, you're an Urban Goddess and it's all about having an unforgettable party. 'Fuck the couple' (not literally of course), it's a party and you're here to get drunk. Everyone is well dressed, high on champers, well fed, and far from home and inhibition. Surrounded by attractive strangers, it's easy to get carried away… On second thoughts, deciding to sneak upstairs with the bride's brother at four o'clock in the morning may have been a wonderful idea in champagne land but fielding his fiancée's interrogations over a full English breakfast the next morning…? You decide.

Think it's about time your man popped the question…

Befriend the butcher, baker and candlestick maker if they're in a serious relationship and bring them into your group of friends. In turn, graciously accept invitations to their nuptials – and bring your commitment-phobic boyfriend along with you. Surround yourself with these happily married couples and their equally happily married friends, while sidelining crazy, sex-mad singles; it's a great way to market marriage to your scared-stiff man.

"Will you marry me? Chak! chak"

Buying suitable wedding gifts

Assuming they stay together, this is what you'll have to buy them for the rest of your life (see also pp224):

1st: Cotton	14th: Ivory
2nd: Paper	15th: Crystal
3rd: Leather	20th: China
4th: Fruit, flowers	25th: Silver
5th: Wood	30th: Pearl
6th: Sugar	35th: Coral
7th: Wool, copper	40th: Ruby
8th: Bronze, pottery	45th: Sapphire
9th: Pottery, willow	50th: Gold
10th: Tin	55th: Emerald
11th: Steel	60th: Diamond
12th: Silk, linen	70th: Platinum
13th: Lace	75th: Diamond

Magpie *n* a bird having a black-and-white plumage, long tail, and a chattering call. *Coll. n* a tiding of magpies. Yes, magpies do like shiney things, like wedding rings. Ahem!

"1 Mississippi 2 Mississippi 3 Mississippi"

Gisele Scanlon

10 G-SPOTS

The most exhilarating discovery of my childhood was my set of World Book Encyclopaedias. My parents bought them for me and I loved them so much that if they wanted to punish me they would confiscate one of the set. I'd pick my way though the gold embossed letters and it was like going on a safari – the letters "A" to "Z" inviting me to search between the covers. Inside were bolded definitions, dressed with brackets and punctuation and offering alluring new prospects and recipes for dreams. I must have known that they were more special than all of the other books in my parents' library because I never attacked them with my crayons.

I couldn't read a word of these books for the first few years of us having them but Mum broke down the information for me until it was bite-sized. All of this information rattled around in my little head for ages: ice caps and igloos, deserts and hammams. The world, it seemed to me, was one big playground scattered with a million new things to smell, touch, taste and enjoy.

Growing up, my education was simple. We were taught to appreciate the smaller things in life above anything else – like having a toasty hot water bottle when you went to bed in the winter or turning over your pillow in the heat of a balmy summer's night to rest your cheek on the cooler side. We'd discuss all this, in great detail at breakfast next morning, and the day we woke up to snow one winter, we didn't stop talking about it for weeks! I was particularly reminded of this as I lay on a bed made of ice at the Ice Hotel, above the Arctic Circle (see pp265). We talked so much as children about snow, when and if it was ever going to arrive, and so lying there it felt like all of my childhood dreams had been fulfilled.

But as well as loving snow and cold dark winters, I loved warm, scented summers too. As a little girl my idea of heaven was roaming off down the fields on my own, with our sheepdog Dinky in tow. One evening I carted all my dolls, about twenty teddies (all my sister's) and three of Dinky's new born puppies down the field (it took three trips with my pram) to a spot behind the stables and the hayshed. The puppies, their eyes barely open, snuggled into their mother's tummy and and dosed in the evening heat.

I propped all of my toyshop tea guests up against the ditch and the trunk of the plum tree and made them daisy chains, mud-cakes and tea with sugar lumps made from small stones. We talked for hours about all sorts of subjects, then with Dinky on look-out, we all went for a long snooze. This was my first ever G-spot, a piece of flat grass behind a patch of foxgloves; a dark and intoxicating spell of a place made heady by the scent of foxgloves, puppies' necks and heated cow shit scattered around the lush green field. Thirty years later this picture flashed in my head vividly as I drove through the streets of Marrakech (see pp262). Its musky souks, sun baked orange-blossoms, trips of goats and flocks of camels created the same olfactory effect.

And Iceland (see pp272), why did I choose that as a G-Spot? For years I'd wanted to venture to the top of its Snaefellsjökull glacier and also to get a look at its special breed of pony – which has a five step gate. My Dad came from a long line of horse lovers and, true to his word, a few weeks after I turned six, a black little Shetland called Dandy arrived in the yard. His feet were so small that Dad had to make special shoes for him and I still remember the acrid smell of scorched hoofs and fireworks of metal sparks flying around the yard as he hammered heavily the shoes into shape at the anvil, doused them in water and then tacked them onto the hooves. He also had to hand-make a complete set of harness for the little fella as we couldn't find harness anywhere to fit a pony this small. Evening after evening, I'd bundle up and join him in the comfort of his workshop, our conversations under spotlight from a moth infested Anglepoise lamp, were always ponies and their breeds. As I handed him the tacks one by one he'd hammer them carefully into the fragrant brown leather. We were hoping for a rosette at The County Fair in early summer, so the more I knew about my pony when the judges asked the better chance we had of winning a prize. "We'll have a bit of a do if we win," said Dad "and even if we don't win, we'll have a bit of a do anyway." We won first prize, a cup and a rosette and all of the questions the judges asked me and the answers I gave that day suddenly seemed so appropriate twenty years later standing in front of this pure, rare little Icelandic breed.

Moving to Dublin over ten years ago, I left the ploughed fields, the foxgloves and the home cured bacon of my childhood for busy streets, noisy buses and street lights. I've learned that the darkness of a city night is always illuminated by artificial tungsten and to get real dark you have to stand in a deep black country night – a treat every Christmas when I get home. The Blind Cow however (see pp270), pulled me into an even deeper level of darkness, into a black hole for two hours in Zurich – lost without colour, shape or form I didn't know what to do. However, it still gave me something special, that G-Spot feeling, that indescribable electricity, that crackles in the air when your mind searches for comfort and familiarity. It reminded me of the day I got lost on Grafton Street in a sea of Christmas shoppers as a child, bright lights everywhere, my parents faces nowhere to be seen…

marrakech

First Impressions

The pungent smell of goats and camels; the scent of jasmine and
orange-blossom tumbling out over the walls of the locals' riads; the
clock striking five and the square igniting—a heady mix of sound and
colour; jugglers, water-boys and snake charmers perform for those
exiting the souks, suddenly blinded by the sun and laden down with
leathers, rare spices, lamps and slippers.

As we rolled on towards Marrakech, the scent of orange-blossom
filled our vehicle. We approached Morocco's 'red oasis' and I
closed my eyes, breathing in the floral-scented air.
Suddenly the car came to an abrupt standstill,
hemmed in by a sea of pungent, hairy goats.
Their goatherd, an old woman, shook the red dust
out of her long black skirt and slapped the trunk of
the Argan tree to get them moving. Ignoring
her, they scampered up the tree, feasting on its
green berries, nibbling their way down the
spindly brown branches which bended
and bounced under their weight. Our
driver explained that once the goats
had digested the Argan seeds, the outer
casing of the berries would be expelled

in their droppings. Then the droppings would be collected by Berber women and ground between large stones to extract an oil which forms the base for most of Morocco's beauty treatments. In fact before my trip I'd heard the term Argan oil bandied about in beauty press releases and knew that the Parisian skincare range, AR457, available at Space NK and Sephora, in France (tel: +33 1 05 56 43 56 43, www.ar457.com), used it in their exclusive Silky Body Oil. Argan oil was clearly making huge waves in the Western beauty world – however messy the collection process – in the Eastern world it's the Berber woman's answer to Crème de la Mer.

The hunt was on to find the purest Argan oil and Argan oil treatment in the city. That evening I found my answer in the hammam at Marrakech's Palais Rhoul, Route de Fes – Dar tounsi (tel: +212 24 32 9494, www.palais-rhoul.com), in the posh Palmeraie district. After several hours sipping sweet mint tea poolside, I was ready for my Moroccan hammam treatment. I pitched up at the spa and lay down on a hot tiled floor (in a bathing suit), as the hammam master exfoliated my body with a brush and lashings of sudsy black soap (savon noir). In the past, Moroccan women exfoliated their bodies in this way, with the savon noir and a goat-hair mitten. Then my hair was packed with a mud mask and I was given a muscle-tweaking, twenty minute massage before being dipped into a pool of cold water and moisturized, from head to toe, with the famous Argan oil. My body smooth, glistening and spritzed down with orange-blossom water, I sloped back to my room in a floral haze.

Later that evening we took a taxi to Al-Fassia, 232 boulevard Mohammad V (tel: +212 44 43 40 60) for dinner. This restaurant is run completely by women and the food is really excellent. I devoured my artichoke starter and lamb tangine and, a few hours later, back at Palais Rhoul, nodded off like a baby – the orange-blossom scent from my warm body, lulling me to sleep.

Next day we were primed for adventure so we called Hilali Ahmed (tel: + 212 61 14 98 28) to help us negotiate the city. He drove us into the Atlas mountains to buy heavy handmade woolen bales from the local Berbers and then back to the city later that day where he led us through the North Medina, pointing out doorways where carpenters hammered in silence, and tailors and bag-makers sat at sewing machines, barefoot, stitching together slices of camel leather that lay in piles on the floor. (The leather smelled particularly pungent and Hilali suggested I wash it gently with lemon juice, salt and water to get rid of the strong aroma.)

Then Hilali took us to Twizra, 361 rue Bab Agnaou (tel: +212 44 37 66 65) to get a feel for the best; with three floors of jewellery, furniture and no pressure-selling, there's no need to haggle here. But I love bargaining so we headed deep into the souk to find good value kaftans, spices and textiles. We learned quickly that when negotiating over the cost of a pair of embroidered slippers, you start by offering a quarter of the asking price, raise your bids slowly and don't ever pay more than 50 per cent of what the seller originally asks. They expect you to haggle and it's brilliant!

As 5 o'clock approached, the Jemaa el Fna Square was preparing for action. Up ahead we could hear the sound of snake charmers, drummers, acrobats and dancers as we emerged from the bowels of souk. Monkeys shrieked, fortune-tellers wailed, and water-carriers, in their bright red robes, searched the crowd for thirsty customers. As night fell the square emptied and the show was replaced by food carts – their steamy smells wafting up to the Moroccan sky. We sampled sheep's brain and eyes, and goats' testicles (a bit chewy!). After all the excitement we climbed up to the rooftop terrace of the Café de France, took a seat, and watched the square's theatre unfold. I woke next morning feeling very sad to be leaving this magical place; I keep longing to return - five visits are clearly not enough!

Pack
A bathing suit, if you intend on having spa treatments, a kaftan (www.sexykaftans.com) and trousers, for when you're scouring the souks and medina (bare arms and legs don't go down well here). If you've forgotten these last few items, buy beautiful embroidered kaftans and pointy slippers at Beldi, 9-11 Sovikat Laksour, Medina, Marrakech. A bottle of Tangerine Vert Eau De Parfum by Miller Harris or Serge Luten's Fleurs de Citronnier at Les Senteurs (seep237) prepares you scent wise. For colour try Guerlain's Terracotta Secret Gold Sublime All-Over Powder (tel: + 44 19 3223 3909, www.guerlain.com), which comes in a little tagine pot, how Moroccan is that?

Didn't get there?
If you want to test Argan Oil before you get here buy it mail order from Marrakech's Palais Rhoul (as before) or from London-based specialist, Elisabeth Dancey (tel: +44 20 7821 8257). Likewise, you can find black soap, in the La Sultane de Saba range from the Moroccan-inspired Momo Boutique, The Tea Room, 25 Heddon Street, London (tel: +44 20 7434 2200), along with an array of other covetable Moroccan items. Talisman Trading (tel: +44 20 8896 1717, www.talisman-trading.co.uk) and Maroque (tel: +44 14 4972 3133, www.maroque.co.uk) also sell Moroccan lanterns and decorted tagines.

Goat *n* any sure-footed, agile ruminant mammal with hollow horns, naturally inhabiting rough, stony ground in Europe, Asia and North Africa. *Coll. n* a tribe or trip of goats.

Camel *n* a cud-chewing, humped mammal that is adapted for surviving long periods without food or water in desert regions. *Coll. n* a flock of camels. There are two distinct species of camel, namely the Bactrian, a camel with two humps, and the Arabian camel or dromedary which has but one. Each can live three weeks without water... but did you know that a rat can last longer than that?

First Impressions

The sound of muffled voices cushioned by the snow; the sensation of everything crunching and crackling underfoot; fresh coldness, pink light and the tart aftertaste of lingenberries.

As a child, for me winter was the most mysterious time of the year. Every Christmas we would ask Santa for a surprise and some snow so that we could build snowmen. Then it came, and, at the same time, a parcel from my aunt in Canada with the perfect apparel for sloshing around in the snow. Kitted out, we headed off to wallow in the cold white magic.

Snow is wonderful stuff. The first walk I took in it was with my Dad and our dog Dinky to look for animal tracks. Our Wellington boots (his big, mine small) and Dinky's paws made clear footsteps in the virgin snow, and we poked and sniffed through sparkling snow-dusted trees for wildlife. We saw fox tracks, rabbits and hares, and I wondered where each unique snowflake had come from, and what secrets lay beneath the snow's iridescent glow. Ever since then I've been fascinated by it.

The huskies' barking, as they strained with the sleigh in front, brought me back to my surroundings, 200 kilometres above the Artic circle. The dogs sprinted and then stopped for quick mouthfuls of snow to cool their loud panting – at minus fifteen they were overheating fast! Day one and we were an hour and a half from Jukkasjärvi's Ice Hotel (www.icehotel.com). I was traveling with Peter and my friends – British street artists D*Face, Mysterious Al, E*Face and Irish street artist Asbestos – they had arranged to carve huge ice blocks into ice sculptures outside the Ice Hotel. We were also hoping to see what it would feel like to sleep on a bed made entirely of the same clear ice blocks.

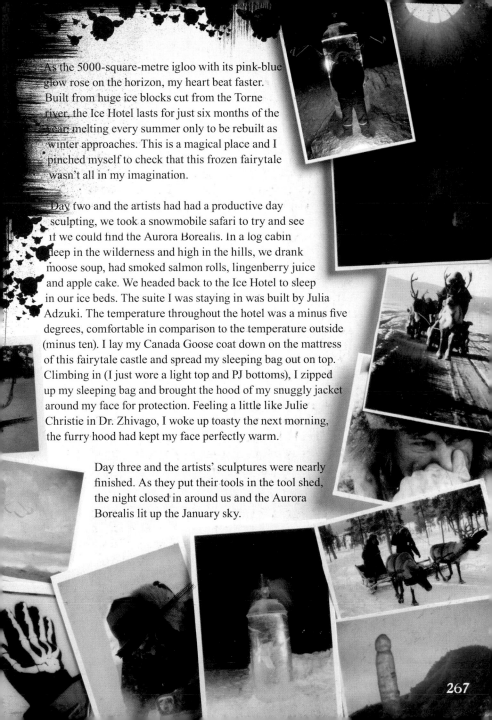

As the 5000-square-metre igloo with its pink-blue glow rose on the horizon, my heart beat faster. Built from huge ice blocks cut from the Torne river, the Ice Hotel lasts for just six months of the year, melting every summer only to be rebuilt as winter approaches. This is a magical place and I pinched myself to check that this frozen fairytale wasn't all in my imagination.

Day two and the artists had had a productive day sculpting, we took a snowmobile safari to try and see if we could find the Aurora Borealis. In a log cabin deep in the wilderness and high in the hills, we drank moose soup, had smoked salmon rolls, lingenberry juice and apple cake. We headed back to the Ice Hotel to sleep in our ice beds. The suite I was staying in was built by Julia Adzuki. The temperature throughout the hotel was a minus five degrees, comfortable in comparison to the temperature outside (minus ten). I lay my Canada Goose coat down on the mattress of this fairytale castle and spread my sleeping bag out on top. Climbing in (I just wore a light top and PJ bottoms), I zipped up my sleeping bag and brought the hood of my snuggly jacket around my face for protection. Feeling a little like Julie Christie in Dr. Zhivago, I woke up toasty the next morning, the furry hood had kept my face perfectly warm.

Day three and the artists' sculptures were nearly finished. As they put their tools in the tool shed, the night closed in around us and the Aurora Borealis lit up the January sky.

267

I lay on my back in the snow looking up at it as it danced about, curling its way round the sculptures. It was the most beautiful sight in the world. E*Face and I toasted Mama Nature with huge glasses of vodka. The next day we would see the sculptures in daylight. I couldn't wait.

Day four and the sculptures looked brilliant. D*Face's can with wings was magnificent, and Asbestos's two-headed reindeer was beautiful – it even had snice (that's snow and ice mixed with water) as horns. Mysterious Al's skull reflected his love of all things boney – he was even wearing skeleton gloves on the trip! Job well done, we needed a break and went to meet up with the local Sami, the oldest indigenous people in Europe, and spent the rest of the day learning how they'd lived there for over two thousand years. Nils – a Sami himself – let us drive reindeer sleds and then prepared us his favourite dish, pan fried reindeer, around an open fire in his tent. The Sami use reindeer for everything and the shoes that he was wearing were even made from reindeer skin.

Back at base camp we said our goodbyes to the sculptures. It was hard to believe that three days before they had been huge blocks of ice, so humungous that they had to be placed on the site by an earth mover. As we left for the airport our snowmobiles wizzed past the beautiful ice sculptures, standing proud as they battled the elements. Like all street art they would be left there to disintegrate, we couldn't save them: come April they would melt and return with the Ice Hotel to the River Torne.

GODDESS TIP

IF YOU'RE PLANNING TO VISIT THE ICE
HOTEL, FIRST CONTACT THE SWEDISH
TRAVEL & TOURISM COUNCIL (TEL: +44
20 7108 6168, WWW.VISITSWEDEN.COM) IN
LONDON; OR IF YOU'RE IN THE US THEN THE
SWEDISH TRAVEL & TOURISM COUNCIL, PO
BOX 4649, GRAND CENTRAL STATION, NEW
YORK, NY 10163-4649 (TEL: +1 212 885 9700)
GIVES THE BEST ADVICE.

What to pack

The best coat you can buy for the trip is by
Canada Goose (www.canada-goose.com or
www.sub-zeroboots.com).
Elizabeth Arden's Eight Hour cream.
Clinique CX Moisturising SPF 15.
Light socks, layered they provide more
warmth than thick ones.
Skinceuticals (see pp95).
Good sunglasses are imperative.
The Hotel offers, boots, suits,
gloves and hats.

järvi

269

the blind co the blind cow

How would I know if something was black, red or blue in the pitch dark? Would I know from touching something what colour it was? I've always imagined red as a hot colour, but is this because fire engines and cooker rings have a red-hot glow? And blue would surely be icy-cool to the touch…

We were dining at The Blind Cow (named after the Swiss equivalent of blind man's buff) in Zurich, and the blackness had hit me like a bus as I was led through the heavy black velvet curtains, my right hand placed firmly on the shoulder of a blind waitress in front of me. Entering the room, I couldn't even see my own gardenia-scented fingers as I pressed them tightly to my cheek. How large was the room? What colour was it? My eyes leeched at the air to see something, anything, as we were led to our table and asked to stand behind our chairs before sitting. I was facing an Italian businessman and another man, and next to Peter but if you asked me to this day what either of these men, or our waitress, or indeed the entire meal, looked like, I couldn't tell you. As the waitress helped us pull out our seats I closed my eyes, exhausted from searching the black void.

A tiny flash on my right startled me as a woman opened a sachet of sugar: the static across the top of the sachet flashed a fluorescent green. I tried hard to pretend to everyone around me that I wasn't petrified, but breathing became slowly more difficult, each breath deeper and longer than the last, causing me to have pins and needles in my fingers and, seemingly, in my brain. Time was at a standstill. I cocked my head to the right as Peter asked if I fancied a glass of vino.

Who were the two men sitting opposite me? Was the Italian wearing an Armani suit, and hand-made Italian leather shoes? Did he have dark hair, dark eyes and olive skin? In fact was he really Italian at all? What age was he? I couldn't tell. The waitress cam back to the table with two glasses of water (the water levels in a glass can only be determined on a weighing scale, where the needle can be felt). Disorientated, I asked her to bring a bottle.

I lost track of time, and as the cutlery clattered around me and Mr Italian droned on and on (in Italian) about politics, I put my head on the table and began to snooze (like the doormouse at the Mad Hatter's tea party). I know it sounds strange but it was as if my whole body was somehow defeated by the blackness. The conversation continued perfectly normally without me, stipped of my sight and unable to look Mr Italian in the eye, I found myself unable to participate. Half groggy, I asked myself, 'What colour is your water bottle, Gisèle? Is it clear glass, brown glass, or magenta? That's it, it's magenta, isn't it?' Politics…religion… As they talked on, oblivious, I dropped in and out of my snooze. I sensed a sudden, awkward silence: Mr Italian had apparently asked me a question. Elbowed from my sleep by Peter, the moment passed and the others seamlessly moved on to a new topic of discussion.

Eating was a messy affair – in fact it was a nightmare. The waitress encouraged me to pour my own water, so I used the index finger of my left hand to check how full the glass was. But after that I cheated and started drinking out of the bottle instead. I had a salad to start – I know this because I recognized I was eating lettuce. The tomatoes baffled me, however; tasteless, cold and rubbery I couldn't figure out what they were and at one point mistook them for slabs of cheese. Next, and only when I'd located my knife and fork, I had beef, green beans and potatoes. But to begin with I spent a full five minutes eating just beef and gravy. I couldn't find the potatoes or the green beans as they kept slipping away, off my plate and onto the table.

Mr Italian and his companion, let's call him Mr Swiss, excused themselves and we finally parted company – not that I'd contributed much to the polite dinner party chit-chat. Cheques – in both Braille and type – were paid in the lighted lobby after the meal. Mr Swiss had already settled our bill and left his business card and a complimentary note which read, 'You are delightful and charming company, look forward to seeing you both later in Zurich. Call me!' I stared down at the empty water bottle I had taken with me from the dining room as a souvenir, hoping it was magenta. It was dark green!

Blind Cow Restaurant (Blindekuh), Mühlebachstrasse 14B, 8008 ZürichúSeefeld, Switzerland (tel: +11 44 421 50 55, www.blindekuh.ch).

Guide Dogs

Most Guide Dogs are female – they're easier to train than the more excitable males. You can look after a puppy from The Guide Dogs for the Blind Association until they are twelve months old. The job entails getting the puppy used to public transport and things about the house. For information on becoming a puppy walker, call +44 807 600 2323, or visit www.guidedogs.org.uk .

ICELAND

First Impressions: the Blue Lagoon from the plane approaching Keflavik, different-coloured earth every few miles, geysers, 23 hours of daily sunshine and the special Icelandic pony.

We arrived in Keflavik airport (very hip) and hired a car immediately for our mission. We would be scaling the heights of the shimmering Snaefellsjökull glacier – the one which the fictional Professor Lidenbrock and his nephew Axel descended into to explore the underworld in Jules Verne's *Journey to the Centre of the Earth*.

Staying in the capital our first night we booked into 101 Hotel, 10 Hverfisgata, 101 Reykjavik, Iceland (tel: +354 511 6999, www.101hotel.is) and started exploring. A stroll through the main square and we met the famous French photographer Yann Arthus-Bertrand; in Reykjavik for his 'Earth from the Air' exhibition (www.earthfromtheair.com), we asked him how he captured all of those breathtaking global images. He explained that he uses a helicopter and a special pilot who gets him close to his subject, and that he balances on the edge of the huge, gaping door, camera in hand. He was visiting Ireland later that summer and asked if we'd like to help him with locations for a horse shoot. We agreed immediately: his photography is spectacular and the idea of working with him, as we later did, a dream.

The next morning we set out along the west-coast scenic route, with the scenery along the roadside changing every few miles from red to green to black. We arrived at Hotel Budir (tel: +354 435 6700, www.budir.is), in the evening, and after dinner walked, at 1 a.m., along the beach, in near daylight! Black guillemots, fulmars and Arctic terns chattered and screeched, and seals splashed and played in the water. This small hotel, with its distinctive black wooden church set just off a beach, lies in the path of the 4743-foot Snaefellsjökull – the active volcano, capped with ice (a glacier) that has built up over the last 70,000 years.

The following morning we drove up the brow of the volcano, and about an hour from the summit the road came to an abrupt end. Switching to a snowmobile, our guide warned of huge crevasses – a wrong turn could send us over the edge of the volcano. Our ascent was a steep, straight, upward climb. We approached the top through the clouds (yes, clouds), and there it was, suddenly: the magical icy peak. Just ahead. Leaving the snowmobiles, we struggled the remaining ten minutes to the top of the glacier on foot a drop of thousands of feet lay over the peak ahead of us. The Snaefellsjökull conquered, we turned, lay down and skidded on our backs all the way back to the guide. Magic!

The Icelandic Pony *n*

Coll n – a string of ponies. The Icelandic horse (note horse, not pony) is a unique breed directly descended from the horses brought over from Norway by the first settlers. No other breed of horse has ever been taken into Iceland since those first settlers landed, so the breed has remained pure and distinctive: they have a unique gait, the tölt – a smooth, fast trot, to which the rider sits rather than rises in the saddle. Peter and I helped Yann Arthus-Bertrand with his book, *Horses*, when he came to Ireland. He's an absolute genius with a camera.

The Blue Lagoon

Situated only a few miles from the airport, leave The Blue Lagoon (tel: +354 420 8832) until last. I sat in this lava field of geothermal milky-coloured seawater, letting it purify my skin and soaking up the surroundings. My skin glowed as we drove to catch our plane. Bring a plastic bag to pack your wet swimsuit in so it won't ruin the rest of your luggage. Read **Earth from the Air** by Yann Arthus-Bertrand and keep his beautiful photograph of the Blue Lagoon in your mind as you approach Iceland from the air.

Port Eliot Lit Fest

First Impressions

The scent of stephanotis and jasmine provide a canvas to the sound of poetry, prose and laughter. The smell of a summer field mixes with my Barry's tea (I take it with me everywhere and drink it out of my favourite china mug, wherever I am in the world), the buzzing of bees – nature's alarm clock – and the sight of children, free and happy, chasing each other round the huge oak tree.

Arrest all your senses outdoors in the summer

What's so special about Port Eliot?

The Port Eliot Lit Fest (www.porteliotlitfest.com) is a living thing. For 3 days in July the Earl of St Germans beautiful estate in south Cornwall is transformed into a tiny fairyland where a festival-going population of 1,500, including writers, poets, artists and musicians, perform and party hard. Refreshingly, speakers are asked to do something other than just read from their work. Last year Louis de Bernières played his mandolin; Richard Benson did a little talk on one of his passions, wildflowers; Martin Parr gave a cracking lecture on photography-book collecting; Ralph Steadman pretended to be Hunter S. Thompson and Michael Eavis wowed the crowd with a behind-the-scenes talk on Glastonbury, past and present. This is a magical place – get there now before the bowling green and the walled garden overflow.

Pitching my tipi under the stars

Ever since I watched cowboys and Indians with my dad I wanted to live in a tipi. So, with the summer well and truly in full swing (or so I thought) I decided that Port Eliot would be the perfect place to live out my childhood dreams. Hearthworks (tel: +44 17 4986 0708, www.hearthworks.co.uk)

will assemble, furnish, dismantle and collect your tipi for you for a fee of £500. As luck would have it, it rained cats and dogs at Port Eliot last summer and though the 'rain catcher' on the tipi did its best, the open smoke hole was a little leaky. We did have some amazing parties around the fire in it, though.

Could you imagine the damage these two would do if they got into your tent?

When you go down to the woods today...

The British Bear Centre says you're more likely to be killed by literature overload than by a bear at Port Eliot and, while they're probably right about that, I had a bit of a sneaky suspicion that my teddies came to life in this magical place when I wasn't looking. To avoid teddy-ambush make sure you party hard and make as much noise as possible before entering any thickets where a teddy might be lurking with another teddy, dancing, or, you know, making little teddies – and remember, teddies can ambush you at any time of the day or night!

I ♡ Teddies

What to pack (See pp161)

Bear *n* a plantigrade mammal typically having a large head, a long shaggy coat, and strong claws. *Coll. n* a sleuth of bears. If a camper leaves food lying about a bear will smell it three miles away. A bear's sense of smell is seven times greater than any Bloodhound. The most vicious bears are thought to be black bears but pregnant or nursing female bears of all species are also scarily territorial. Weighing on average 450lbs a grizzly female can run as fast as a horse when in chase. Yikes!

Teddy bear a stuffed toy bear. *Coll n* a cuddle of teddies. The Teddy Bear was invented almost simultaneously in the United States and in Germany, in 1902. It is named after Theodore 'Teddy' Roosevelt, 26th President of the United States, because he refused to kill a tethered bear while out hunting in Mississippi with the words, "Spare the bear!" The Washington Post ran a "Spare The Bear" cartoon of the incident and Brooklyn shop keepers Morris and Rose Michtom made a soft bear toy, which they named 'Teddy's Bear' in his honour. They displayed it in their window with a copy of the cartoon and the 'Teddy' was born.

Spiced Indian redbush **CHAI** TEA ONLY £1·50

INSIDE STORY

INSIDE STORY

I'm the only z

THE END
100 per cent organic and made in Ireland
especially for you by Gisèle Scanlon
using 40 Prittsticks, 60 pens, 10 tubes of
watercolour, 2 spools of thread, 4000
sheets of paper, 4 scissors and 1 brain.